CLASS ACTIONS

AND OTHER MULTI-PARTY LITIGATION

IN A NUTSHELL

Third Edition

By

ROBERT H. KLONOFF
Douglas Stripp/Missouri Professor of Law
University of Missouri/Kansas City School of Law
Of Counsel, Jones Day
(Washington, D.C.)

Dean Designate, Lewis & Clark Law School

THOMSON

WEST

Mat #40528660

© West, a Thomson business, 1999, 2004

© 2007 Thomson/West

       610 Opperman Drive

       P.O. Box 64526

       St. Paul, MN 55164–0526

       1–800–328–9352

Printed in the United States of America

ISBN–13: 978–0–314–17224–2

TEXT IS PRINTED ON 10% POST
CONSUMER RECYCLED PAPER

To my parents

*

PREFACE

This text addresses class actions and other devices for litigating multi-party cases. It is intended for students taking courses in civil procedure, complex litigation, class actions, and mass torts. It is also designed for use by practicing lawyers who are involved in litigating multi-party cases. This edition follows the same approach and structure as the first edition, published in 1999, and the second edition, published in 2004. There have been numerous significant developments since 1999, including substantial revisions to Federal Rule of Civil Procedure 23, several important court decisions, and the publication of the *Manual for Complex Litigation (4th)* in 2004. Moreover, after the publication of the second edition in 2004, Congress enacted the Class Action Fairness Act of 2005, and the Supreme Court and other federal courts decided a number of important cases. This edition covers all of these developments.

In addition to teaching class actions and serving as Associate Reporter for the American Law Institute's project, "Principles of the Law of Aggregate Litigation," I have prosecuted and defended numerous class actions and other multi-party cases. I or others at my law firm served as co-defense counsel in several of the cases cited in this Nutshell: *Allapattah Barnes, In re Bridgestone/Firestone,*

Castano, In re Domestic Air Transportation Antitrust Litigation and Duffy.

In addition to those whom I acknowledged in the first and second editions, I wish to acknowledge the contributions of my research assistants, Zhijun Gong, Rory Kane, Andrew Lonard, Uzo Nwonwu, and Jeremy Wikler. In addition, several people reviewed drafts of this third edition and provided excellent comments, including Sean Costello, Mark Herrman, David Horan, Charles Morse, and Professor Patrick Woolley. The statements and conclusions in this text are mine alone, however, and do not necessarily represent the views of my law firm, any other attorney affiliated with that firm, or anyone who had input into this text.

ROBERT H. KLONOFF

Kansas City, Missouri
February, 2007

OUTLINE

Page

OUTLINE

OUTLINE

Page

*

TABLE OF CASES

References are to Pages

TABLE OF CASES

TABLE OF CASES

*

CLASS ACTIONS

AND OTHER MULTI-PARTY LITIGATION

IN A NUTSHELL

Third Edition

*

Text of
Federal Rule of Civil
Procedure 23. Class Actions

(a) Prerequisites to a Class Action. One or more members of a class may sue or be sued as representative parties on behalf of all only if (1) the class is so numerous that joinder of all members is impracticable, (2) there are questions of law or fact common to the class, (3) the claims or defenses of the representative parties are typical of the claims or defenses of the class, and (4) the representative parties will fairly and adequately protect the interests of the class.

(b) Class Actions Maintainable. An action may be maintained as a class action if the prerequisites of subdivision (a) are satisfied, and in addition:

(1) the prosecution of separate actions by or against individual members of the class would create a risk of

(A) inconsistent or varying adjudications with respect to individual members of the class which would establish incompatible standards of conduct for the party opposing the class, or

(B) adjudications with respect to individual members of the class which would as a practical matter be dispositive of the interests of the other members not parties to the adjudications

1

or substantially impair or impede their ability to protect their interests; or

(2) the party opposing the class has acted or refused to act on grounds generally applicable to the class, thereby making appropriate final injunctive relief or corresponding declaratory relief with respect to the class as a whole; or

(3) the court finds that the questions of law or fact common to the members of the class predominate over any questions affecting only individual members, and that a class action is superior to other available methods for the fair and efficient adjudication of the controversy. The matters pertinent to the findings include: (A) the interest of members of the class in individually controlling the prosecution or defense of separate actions; (B) the extent and nature of any litigation concerning the controversy already commenced by or against members of the class; (C) the desirability or undesirability of concentrating the litigation of the claims in the particular forum; (D) the difficulties likely to be encountered in the management of a class action.

(c) Determining by Order Whether to Certify a Class Action; Appointing Class Counsel; Notice and Membership in Class; Judgment; Multiple Classes and Subclasses.

(1)(A) When a person sues or is sued as a representative of a class, the court must—at an early practicable time—determine by order whether to certify the action as a class action.

(B) An order certifying a class action must define the class and the class claims, issues, or defenses, and must appoint class counsel under Rule 23(g).

(C) An order under Rule 23(c)(1) may be altered or amended before final judgment.

(2)(A) For any class certified under Rule 23(b)(1) or (2), the court may direct appropriate notice to the class.

(B) For any class certified under Rule 23(b)(3), the court must direct to class members the best notice practicable under the circumstances, including individual notice to all members who can be identified through reasonable effort. The notice must concisely and clearly state in plain, easily understood language:

- the nature of the action,

- the definition of the class certified,

- the class claims, issues, or defenses,

- that a class member may enter an appearance through counsel if the member so desires,

- that the court will exclude from the class any member who requests exclusion, stating when and how members may elect to be excluded, and

- the binding effect of a class judgment on class members under Rule 23(c)(3).

(3) The judgment in an action maintained as a class action under subdivision (b)(1) or (b)(2),

whether or not favorable to the class, shall include and describe those whom the court finds to be members of the class. The judgment in an action maintained as a class action under subdivision (b)(3), whether or not favorable to the class, shall include and specify or describe those to whom the notice provided in subdivision (c)(2) was directed, and who have not requested exclusion, and whom the court finds to be members of the class.

(4) When appropriate (A) an action may be brought or maintained as a class action with respect to particular issues, or (B) a class may be divided into subclasses and each subclass treated as a class, and the provisions of this rule shall then be construed and applied accordingly.

(d) Orders in Conduct of Actions. In the conduct of actions to which this rule applies, the court may make appropriate orders: (1) determining the course of proceedings or prescribing measures to prevent undue repetition or complication in the presentation of evidence or argument; (2) requiring, for the protection of the members of the class or otherwise for the fair conduct of the action, that notice be given in such manner as the court may direct to some or all of the members of any step in the action, or of the proposed extent of the judgment, or of the opportunity of members to signify whether they consider the representation fair and adequate, to intervene and present claims or defenses, or otherwise to come into the action; (3) imposing conditions on the representative parties or on intervenors; (4) requiring that the pleadings be amended to eliminate therefrom allegations as to representation of absent persons, and that the action proceed accordingly; (5) dealing with similar procedural matters. The orders may be combined with an order under Rule 16, and may be altered or amended as may be desirable from time to time.

(e) Settlement, Voluntary Dismissal, or Compromise.

(1)(A) The court must approve any settlement, voluntary dismissal, or compromise of the claims, issues, or defenses of a certified class.

(B) The court must direct notice in a reasonable manner to all class members who would be bound by a proposed settlement, voluntary dismissal, or compromise.

(C) The court may approve a settlement, voluntary dismissal, or compromise that would bind class members only after a hearing and on finding that the settlement, voluntary dismissal, or compromise is fair, reasonable, and adequate.

(2) The parties seeking approval of a settlement, voluntary dismissal, or compromise under Rule 23(e)(1) must file a statement identifying any agreement made in connection with the proposed settlement, voluntary dismissal, or compromise.

(3) In an action previously certified as a class action under Rule 23(b)(3), the court may refuse

to approve a settlement unless it affords a new opportunity to request exclusion to individual class members who had an earlier opportunity to request exclusion but did not do so.

(4)(A) Any class member may object to a proposed settlement, voluntary dismissal, or compromise that requires court approval under Rule 23(e)(1)(A).

(B) An objection made under Rule 23(e)(4)(A) may be withdrawn only with the court's approval.

(f) Appeals. A court of appeals may in its discretion permit an appeal from an order of a district court granting or denying class action certification under this rule if application is made to it within ten days after entry of the order. An appeal does not stay proceedings in the district court unless the district judge or the court of appeals so orders.

(g) Class Counsel.

(1) Appointing Class Counsel.

(A) Unless a statute provides otherwise, a court that certifies a class must appoint class counsel.

(B) An attorney appointed to serve as class counsel must fairly and adequately represent the interests of the class.

(C) In appointing class counsel, the court

(i) must consider:

- the work counsel has done in identifying or investigating potential claims in the action,

- counsel's experience in handling class actions, other complex litigation, and claims of the type asserted in the action,

- counsel's knowledge of the applicable law, and

- the resources counsel will commit to representing the class;

(ii) may consider any other matter pertinent to counsel's ability to fairly and adequately represent the interests of the class;

(iii) may direct potential class counsel to provide information on any subject pertinent to the appointment and to propose terms for attorney fees and nontaxable costs; and

(iv) may make further orders in connection with the appointment.

(2) Appointment Procedure.

(A) The court may designate interim counsel to act on behalf of the putative class before determining whether to certify the action as a class action.

(B) When there is one applicant for appointment as class counsel, the court may appoint that applicant only if the applicant is adequate under Rule 23(g)(1)(B) and (C). If more than one adequate applicant seeks appointment as class counsel, the court must appoint the applicant best able to represent the interests of the class.

(C) The order appointing class counsel may include provisions about the award of attorney fees or nontaxable costs under Rule 23(h).

(h) Attorney Fees Award. In an action certified as a class action, the court may award reasonable attorney fees and nontaxable costs authorized by law or by agreement of the parties as follows:

(1) Motion for Award of Attorney Fees. A claim for an award of attorney fees and nontaxable costs must be made by motion under Rule 54(d)(2), subject to the provisions of this subdivision, at a time set by the court. Notice of the motion must be served on all parties and, for motions by class counsel, directed to class members in a reasonable manner.

(2) Objections to Motion. A class member, or a party from whom payment is sought, may object to the motion.

(3) Hearing and Findings. The court may hold a hearing and must find the facts and state its conclusions of law on the motion under Rule 52(a).

(4) Reference to Special Master or Magistrate Judge. The court may refer issues related to the amount of the award to a special master or to a magistrate judge as provided in Rule 54(d)(2)(D).

CHAPTER 1

INTRODUCTION

The first edition of this nutshell, published in 1999, noted that the subject of class actions had received more attention by courts, legislators, scholars, and practitioners than any other area of civil procedure. This is even more true today. Class actions involving such subjects as asbestos, airplane crashes, securities fraud, antitrust, employment discrimination, breast implants, Agent Orange, blood transfusions, tobacco, human rights abuses, employee benefits, and dozens of other high-profile issues touch all of our lives. Moreover, no area of civil procedure has been as controversial. On one side are those who claim that class actions should be used with greater frequency—to effect major social change and to provide recourse for those who otherwise would find it economically infeasible to litigate their grievances. On the other side are those who claim that class actions have done nothing but force corporations into bankruptcy, enrich attorneys, and clog the courts. Those in the latter camp have been working for years to convince Congress to overhaul the rules governing class actions. In 2005, they were partially successful: Congress enacted the Class Action Fairness Act ("CAFA"), which (1) permits defendants to remove most multi-state class actions from state court to federal court and (2) imposes restrictions on certain kinds of class-action settlements.

In the past several years, courts have rendered numerous pathbreaking class action decisions. Furthermore, scholars have written literally hundreds of articles on various class action topics. In addition to the enactment of CAFA, many other important developments have occurred in recent years, including long-awaited changes to Federal Rule of Civil Procedure 23 and the release of numerous significant decisions by the Supreme Court and federal circuit courts.

The purpose of this text is to survey this important and controversial area of law—to consider where it has been, where it is today, and where it is likely to go in the years ahead. The field of class actions covers a wide variety of topics and builds upon a host of basic civil procedure concepts. This text endeavors to address all of the major topics of class action law and practice, including commencement of a class action, class action discovery, the class certification process, notice to class members, "opt-out" rights, communications with class members, constitutional issues, class settlements, jurisdictional issues, class trials, appellate review, and issue and claim preclusion. It also focuses in greater detail on three of the most important areas of class action litigation: mass torts, securities fraud, and employment discrimination cases. In addition, it addresses three kinds of less traditional representative actions: defendant class actions, shareholder derivative suits, and suits involving unincorporated associations. Finally, the class action discussion concludes with a survey of ethical and policy issues.

Although most of the attention and debate has centered on class actions, several other devices exist for resolving multi-party claims. These devices are important as well, and they are a topic in most courses on federal civil procedure and complex litigation. Accordingly, the final two chapters of this text address these various devices. Many of them—including joinder, impleader, interpleader, intervention, and consolidation—are set forth in the Federal Rules of Civil Procedure. Others discussed in this text are set forth in federal statutes, including transfers pursuant to the multidistrict litigation statute; transfers for the convenience of the parties and witnesses and in the interests of justice; and aggregation of parties pursuant to the Bankruptcy Code. One device—informal cooperation between multiple courts—is entirely voluntary and has no statutory foundation.

All of these devices for litigating multi-party claims share a common goal: increasing the efficiency of judicial decision making, thereby reducing the time and expense for the courts and the parties. In addition, these devices all seek to reduce the likelihood of inconsistent adjudications. Some of these devices also enable participation in litigation by nonparties whose interests may be affected, and other devices enable participation by individuals who would not find it cost-effective to litigate if they had to do so individually.

Nonetheless, while each device has its advantages, each has the potential for yielding unfair results for particular parties involved. And, depending on the kind of case, each device has the potential for making matters *more* complicated rather than less complicated. For these reasons, each device (with the exception of informal cooperation among courts) has specific, detailed requirements that must be satisfied. Furthermore, virtually all of these devices give the district court substantial discretion in light of the facts and circumstances involved.

While this text refers at times to procedures under state law, and even includes a separate discussion of state court class actions, the main focus is on federal practice and procedure. In many of the areas addressed in this text, the approaches of various states differ substantially from the federal approach. It is essential, therefore, that the student or litigator focusing on a particular state's procedures review the rules and case law on multi-party actions applicable to that specific state. Even with respect to federal practice, the governing principles often differ from one federal circuit to another, and this text identifies several issues that have sharply divided the federal circuit courts. As a result, when there is no controlling Supreme Court case, the circuit law applicable in a particular case must be scrutinized in connection with any issue involving multi-party litigation.

This text refers in several places to two important secondary sources: the Advisory Committee Notes and the *Manual for Complex Litigation*. The Advisory Committee Notes were written by the Advisory Committee on Civil Rules. That committee, under the direction of the Standing Committee on Rules of Practice and Procedure, is responsible for drafting proposed changes to the Federal Rules of Civil Procedure. The Advisory Committee Notes are cited frequently by courts in construing the Federal Rules, although the Notes do not control over the language of the rules. The *Manual*, published by the Federal Judicial Center, is relied upon heavily by federal judges in managing complex cases. The fourth edition of the *Manual* was published in 2004. In addition to these sources (and applicable case law), the student or litigator should also consult the local rules of the particular court at issue.

CHAPTER 2

EVOLUTION AND OVERVIEW OF FEDERAL COURT CLASS ACTIONS

Although the principal focus of this text is on class actions, many other devices exist for adjudicating, in one proceeding, the claims of multiple parties. For example, joinder under Fed.R.Civ.P. 20 allows multiple plaintiffs to sue, or allows multiple defendants to be sued, in one proceeding when common legal or factual questions are present and the claims arise out of the same transaction or occurrence. Impleader under Fed.R.Civ.P. 14 allows a defendant to bring in third parties who may be liable to defendant for all or part of any claim that the plaintiff has against the defendant. Intervention under Fed.R.Civ.P. 24 allows a nonparty in certain circumstances to join a lawsuit to protect its interests. Interpleader under Fed.R.Civ.P. 22 allows multiple parties claiming entitlement to a particular fund or piece of real or personal property to have all issues of entitlement adjudicated in a single proceeding. Consolidation under Fed.R.Civ.P. 42(a) allows a court to order a joint hearing or trial with respect to separate actions involving one or more common questions of law or fact. These devices, all of which are discussed in detail on pp. 367–410,

14

infra, share a common feature: All of the players are actually parties to the proceeding and are present before the court.

Class actions are different. Unnamed members of a class action are not parties in the traditional sense and do not participate in—or usually even attend—the classwide proceedings. Indeed, the reason a class action exists is that, because of the number of class members and other factors, it is not practical to join all of the class members and try their claims individually. If the claims of class members share common issues, great efficiencies can be secured through aggregate pretrial and trial proceedings. In a class action proceeding, the named plaintiffs (also known as class representatives) and class counsel adjudicate the claims on behalf of the unnamed or "absent" class members. Assuming that the representatives and counsel are adequate for the task, and assuming that various other requirements are met (such as notice to the class members in certain circumstances), the absent class members are bound by the adjudication of all common issues on behalf of the class. This is true whether the result of the classwide trial is favorable or unfavorable. In some circumstances, class members can "opt out" (remove themselves from the case) before the judgment and pursue their claims individually. In other circumstances, however, the rules, by their terms, do not allow class members to exclude themselves.

Before a court will allow a class action to go forward, it must first determine that various criteria are satisfied. Ultimately, these criteria (which are discussed in detail in later chapters) serve two overarching purposes: (i) to ensure that the representative class members and class counsel will effectively represent the absent class members' interests; and (ii) to ensure that a class action will be more efficient and manageable than alternative methods for adjudicating the claims.

Although the basic model of a class action—a representative suit on behalf of large numbers of people—has always been the same, the ground rules have changed substantially over time. In fact, at the federal level, multiple revisions of the class action rules were necessary to establish that unnamed class members were in fact bound by a judgment in favor of or against the class.

The modern class action has its roots in English chancery practice. According to the Supreme Court, "class actions as we recognize them today developed as an exception to the formal rigidity of the necessary parties rule in equity, as well as from the bill of peace, an equitable device for combining multiple suits.... " *Ortiz v. Fibreboard Corp.*, 527 U.S. 815, 832 (1999). Although a broad historical focus is beyond the scope of this text, this chapter provides a brief overview of class action procedures in United States federal courts. In particular, it summarizes the various federal class action rules enacted in 1842, 1912, 1938, and 1966, as well as Rule 23 amendments in 1998 and 2003. It also provides a brief summary of the Class Action Fairness Act of 2005.

§ 2.1   Equity Rule 48

The first codification of a federal class action rule in the United States occurred in 1842, and applied only in equitable proceedings. That rule, Equity Rule 48, provided that a case involving numerous parties could proceed on a representative basis without the need for each individual to appear personally. The rule made clear, however, that "in such cases, the decree shall be without prejudice to the rights and claims of all the absent parties." Thus, under the language of Equity Rule 48, and under the practice of most courts, a class action judgment had no binding effect upon those not actually before the court, who could choose not to be bound if they did not like the result.

§ 2.2   Equity Rule 38

In 1912, Equity Rule 38 supplanted Equity Rule 48. Like its predecessor, Equity Rule 38 applied only in equitable proceedings. The main difference between Equity Rule 38 and the prior Equity Rule 48 was that the new rule specifically eliminated the reference to the non-binding effect of a judgment on absent class members. Under Equity Rule 38, which remained in effect until 1938, judgments in class actions could bind the absent parties in limited circumstances. Nonetheless, courts continued to display confusion over when a judgment could bind an absent class member.

§ 2.3   The 1938 Version of Rule 23

The original version of Rule 23 was adopted in 1938. One of its major purposes was to make class actions available in both legal and equitable proceedings. (Indeed, a major purpose of the 1938 Federal Rules of Civil Procedure was to provide unified rules for both suits in equity and actions at law.) In addition, the rule sought to provide more guidance than the prior equity rules by attempting to fit class actions into one of three categories: (1) "true," (2) "hybrid," or (3) "spurious." These three categories, however, proved difficult to define, let alone to apply with precision.

The "true" category described the purest type of class action, where the "unity of interest" was "joint or common" to all members of the class. It included the situation in which a class member other than the owner of a primary right was entitled to enforce that right because the owner refused to do so. Examples of "true" classes included claims for breach of fiduciary duty resulting in the depletion of trust assets brought by trust beneficiaries against the trustee, and claims for conspiracy and interference with contract brought by labor union members against another labor union.

The "hybrid" category recognized interests that were "several" rather than "joint" but involved the same property or fund. Examples of "hybrid" classes included claimants to insurance policy proceeds, trust accounts, bank accounts, and other types of funds.

The last category of original Rule 23, the "spurious" class action, again described the interests of the class members as "several," but recognized that aggregation was appropriate when "a common question of law or fact affected the several rights and common relief [was] sought." Spurious classes included securities fraud claims by stockholders in which there was no common fund available for recovery.

Under the law that developed under the 1938 rule, true and hybrid classes were binding on un-named class members, but spurious classes were not. This problem—that not all class actions were binding on unnamed class members—was compounded by the fact that courts had great difficulty distinguishing one category of class actions from another.

§ 2.4   The 1966 Version of Rule 23

The 1966 version of Rule 23 represented a substantial change from the 1938 version. The Advisory Committee Notes discuss in detail the purposes behind the changes to Rule 23. As the Notes explain, the 1938 version of Rule 23 was abandoned because differentiating among true, hybrid, and spurious classes "proved obscure and uncertain." Moreover, the spurious class action proved to be of only limited utility because it did not "adjudicate the rights or liabilities of any person not a party." Finally, the 1938 rule, according to the Notes, "did not squarely address itself to the question of the measures that might be taken during the course of the action to assure procedural fairness, particularly giving notice to members of the class, which may in turn be related in some instances to the extension of the judgment to the class."

To correct these concerns, the 1966 amendments to Rule 23 eliminated the true, hybrid, and spurious categories and instead adopted a practical, functional approach to representative litigation, with an emphasis on fair and adequate representation. Moreover, as the Advisory Committee Notes indicate, the 1966 rule "provides that all class actions maintained to the end as such will result in judgments including those whom the court finds to be members of the class, whether or not the judgment is favorable to the class. . . . " In addition to making clear that class action judgments were intended to be binding on all class members, the 1966 rule also sets forth a variety of measures that trial court judges can use to assure the fairness of class actions. A brief overview of the 1966 rule (as amended through 2003) follows. Subsequent chapters describe in detail the many issues that have arisen under the current Rule 23.

§ 2.5   Overview of Current Rule 23

The current version of Rule 23 is, in many respects, the same as the 1966 version, although (as discussed below) some important changes were made in 1998 and 2003. Rule 23 contains numerous requirements that must be satisfied to maintain a class action. The burden is on the proponent of the class to show that each requirement is met. Some courts, however, have stated that doubts should be resolved in favor of certification because the class can always be "decertified" later should that remedy prove necessary.

Before analyzing the explicit requirements of Rule 23, the court must determine that certain implicit threshold requirements are met. Specifically, the court must find that: (1) a class exists that is capable of ascertainment; (2) the class representatives are members of the class; and (3) the claim is live, not moot. The explicit requirements of Rule 23(a) that must be met are (1) a class so numerous that joinder of all members is impracticable; (2) the existence of common questions of law or fact; (3) the presence of class representatives whose claims are typical of those of the class; and (4) the existence of class representatives and class counsel who will adequately represent the interests of the absent or unnamed class members. These requirements are fundamental, and the failure to satisfy any of them will preclude class certification.

In addition to satisfying the threshold requirements and those under Rule 23(a), the proponent must also establish that a class is maintainable under one of the Rule 23(b) categories. The first category is (b)(1)(A), which applies when numerous individual actions would result in inconsistent standards of conduct for the party opposing the class. The second part of (b)(1), subdivision (b)(1)(B), applies in "limited fund" and other class actions in which numerous separate actions would substantially impair or impede the interests of individual class members.

Subdivision (b)(2) is limited to cases seeking primarily declaratory or injunctive relief and does not extend to situations in which money damages are the exclusive or predominant relief sought. Civil rights cases are a common example of class actions maintained under (b)(2).

A Rule 23(b)(3) class action is appropriate when questions of law or fact common to the members of the class predominate over individual issues and a class action is superior to other methods of relief. Unlike classes under Rule 23(b)(1) and (b)(2), which are mandatory classes (unless the court orders otherwise), class members in Rule 23(b)(3) class actions have the right to "opt out" of the action.

Rule 23(c) provides courts with managerial authority over class actions. Subdivision (c)(1) addresses the timing of the certification decision, stating that the court must determine whether to certify the case as a class action "at an early practicable time." Subdivision (c)(2) addresses issues of notice to absent class members of class certification decisions. It requires notice and opt-out rights for absent class members in class actions maintained under (b)(3), and also provides that the court "may direct appropriate notice to the class" in suits under (b)(1) and (b)(2). Rule 23(c)(3) requires the judgment to set forth and describe the members of the class. Rule 23(c)(4) permits the court to create subclasses or to certify particular issues.

Rule 23(d) enables the court to enter appropriate orders dealing with procedural matters, such as requiring notice to absent class members of important developments and imposing conditions on class representatives or intervenors.

Rule 23(e) requires court approval for settlement, dismissal, or compromise of a class action, after a hearing and a finding that the settlement, dismissal, or compromise is fair, reasonable, and adequate. It also requires notice to class members of the settlement, dismissal, or compromise in such manner as the court directs. Any class member is entitled to object to any proposed settlement or voluntary dismissal that requires approval under Rule 23(e). As amended in 2003, Rule 23(e) gives courts authority to permit class members in cases certified under Rule 23(b)(3) a second opportunity to opt out of the class if they do not wish to be bound by a proposed settlement. That same amendment also requires parties seeking approval of a settlement, voluntary dismissal, or compromise under Rule 23(e) to "file a statement identifying any agreement made in connection with the proposed settlement, voluntary dismissal, or compromise."

Rule 23(f), which became effective in 1998, permits immediate appeal, at the discretion of the court of appeals, of orders granting or denying class certification.

Rule 23(g), added in 2003, provides that the court shall appoint class counsel, and it contains a list of criteria that the court must consider in making such appointment. It addresses situations in which multiple counsel have applied to be class counsel, as

well as situations in which there is only one applicant.

Rule 23(h), also added in 2003, authorizes reasonable attorneys' fees upon the filing of a motion for
attorneys' fees. It allows class members or the party
from whom payment is sought to object to such
motion. The court must accompany its decision on
fees with findings of fact and conclusions of law.

These requirements of Rule 23 are examined in
detail in the following chapters. Because many
states have adopted class-action rules that are pat-
terned after Federal Rule 23, *see* pp. 195–196, *infra*,
federal authority interpreting Rule 23 may have
significance even in state courts.

§ 2.6   Class Action Fairness Act of 2005

On February 18, 2005, President George W. Bush
signed into law the Class Action Fairness Act of
2005 ("CAFA"). CAFA affects two important areas:
(1) the jurisdiction of federal courts over multi-state
class actions involving state-law claims, and (2)
various types of class-action settlements in federal
court.

A.   JURISDICTIONAL PROVISIONS

As described in detail below, *see* pp. 214–227,
infra, CAFA significantly expands the original jurisdiction of federal district courts over class actions
involving state-law claims. Under CAFA, federal
courts have jurisdiction over state-law class actions
if (1) the case involves 100 or more class members,

(2) there is "minimal diversity" between the parties, and (3) the aggregate amount in controversy for the class exceeds $5 million.

There are several exceptions to this expanded jurisdiction, discussed on pp. 218–221, *infra*. One group of exceptions is designed to keep truly local controversies in state court. Another exception is for class actions in which the primary defendants are government entities or officials. CAFA also does not apply to actions involving securities or internal corporate affairs. (As discussed on pp. 320–334, *infra*, other federal legislation specifically addresses securities claims.)

In addition to expanding original federal jurisdiction to cover many more state-law class actions, CAFA also authorizes liberal removal from state to federal court of cases covered by the Act. *See* pp. 221–222, *infra*.

As a result of CAFA, most major multi-state class actions involving state-law claims will be adjudicated in federal court.

B. SETTLEMENT PROVISIONS

CAFA also addresses class-action settlements in federal court. In particular, it imposes significant restrictions on how class counsel can be compensated for so-called "coupon" settlements (in which class members receive, for example, coupons good for discounts on future purchases of the defendant's product). *See* pp. 266–267, *infra*. CAFA also imposes restrictions on "net loss settlements" (*i.e.,* settlements resulting in a monetary loss to class members); prohibits settlements in which some class members receive more merely because of their closer proximity to the court house; and requires the parties to a federal class settlement to notify appropriate federal and state officials regarding the terms of the settlement. The settlement provisions of CAFA do not apply to state court class actions, even if those class actions could have been removed to federal court.

CHAPTER 3

CLASS CERTIFICATION REQUIREMENTS: THRESHOLD REQUIREMENTS AND RULE 23(a)

Before a case is "certified" or allowed to go forward as a class action, it is often referred to as a "putative" or "potential" class action. Likewise, the members of the proposed class are often referred to as "putative" or "potential" class members. To obtain certification of a putative class, the proposed class representatives (or named plaintiffs) must satisfy the explicit requirements of Rule 23(a)—numerosity, commonality, typicality, and adequacy of representation—as well as the requirements of one of the subdivisions of Rule 23(b)—(b)(1)(A), (b)(1)(B), (b)(2), or (b)(3). Most courts hold that the plaintiffs have the burden of proof to satisfy those standards. A few courts, however, require the defendant to identify any failure to comply with Rule 23, and will hold each element of Rule 23(a) and (b) satisfied unless the defendant contests it. In addition to the Rule 23(a) and (b) requirements, courts generally require the class representatives to satisfy a number of threshold requirements not directly set forth in Rule 23(a). This chapter addresses the threshold requirements and those under Rule 23(a). The following chapter addresses Rule 23(b).

I. THRESHOLD REQUIREMENTS

Most courts and commentators agree that three threshold requirements must be satisfied even though they do not appear as separate requirements under Rule 23(a) or (b) (1) the existence of a definable class; (2) the presence of at least one representative who is a member of the class; and (3) a claim that is live, not moot.

§ 3.1 A Definable Class

A clear, precise definition of the class is critical to the proper functioning of the class action device. The class definition determines who is entitled to favorable relief obtained in the suit and who is bound by an adverse ruling. It also determines who will receive notice in circumstances where notice is required. Surprisingly, despite the importance of the class definition, Rule 23 says nothing about how to define a class. To be sure, Rule 23(c)(1)(B), which became effective in 2003, does state that "[a]n order certifying a class action must define the class," a provision cited by the Third Circuit in holding that a certification order must define the claims, issues, or defenses subject to class treatment. *Wachtel v. Guardian Life Ins. Co. of America,* 453 F.3d 179 (3d Cir. 2006). But the rule does not provide any criteria for defining a class.

Nonetheless, guidance can be found in the case law and in the *Manual for Complex Litigation (4th).*

To pass muster, a class definition ordinarily must satisfy several criteria. As an initial matter, the class definition should be sufficiently precise so that a court can ascertain the members of the class and thereby determine specifically who is bound by the ruling. For example, a class brought on behalf of individuals "active in the peace movement," or a class "affected" by the defendants' discharge of pollutants, may be viewed by a court as too vague, because words like "active" and "affected" can mean different things to different people. Similarly, the class definition should not turn on each class member's subjective state of mind (for instance, all persons who "believe" that the defendant's emissions harmed their real property). Likewise, a class definition should not depend upon a resolution of the merits of the case (for instance, all persons who suffered illness "caused by" defendants' defective breast implants).

Generally, a class definition should focus on the defendant's alleged conduct and should include geographic, temporal, or other objective parameters that serve to limit the membership of the class.

The level of judicial scrutiny that courts give to class definitions depends in part on the type of class action involved. Thus, a damages "opt-out" class under Rule 23(b)(3) requires a very specific definition because notice to class members is required under Rule 23(c)(2), and class members must be given the chance to exclude themselves from the class. *See* pp. 169–170, *infra.* By contrast, the class definition in Rule 23(b)(1) or Rule 23(b)(2) cases seeking exclusively declaratory or injunctive relief need not be as precise. For instance, because notice is required under (b)(3) but generally not under (b)(1) and (b)(2), *see* pp. 160–161, 170–172, *infra*, a class definition that includes future members (*i.e.*, those who have not yet suffered injury but will do so in the future) is more likely to be upheld under Rule 23(b)(1) or (b)(2) than under Rule 23(b)(3).

§ 3.2 A Representative Who Is a Member of the Class

A second threshold requirement for class certification is that the class representative must be a member of the class that he or she seeks to represent. Although most courts recognize this requirement, there is a wide range of views regarding its precise source. Some courts derive the requirement from the opening clause of Rule 23(a), which states that "[o]ne or more members of a class may sue or be sued on behalf of the class." Some courts derive this requirement by implication from Rule 23(a)(2), which requires "questions of law or fact common to the class." Others derive the requirement from Rule 23(a)(3), which provides that "the claims or defenses of the representative parties [be] typical of the claims or defenses of the class." Others derive it from Rule 23(a)(4), which requires that "the representative parties will fairly and adequately protect the interests of the class." Finally, other courts derive the requirement from the constitutional mandate (U.S. Const. art. III § 2, cl.1)—fully applicable in class actions—that an individual must have standing to assert a claim. Despite the source cited in a particular court decision, the analysis employed by the courts is largely the same: Does the class representative have the same basic interests and the same alleged injuries as the class members?

A leading case applying the requirement of class membership is *East Tex. Motor Freight Sys., Inc. v. Rodriguez*, 431 U.S. 395, 403 (1977), which held that, because the named plaintiffs in an employment discrimination suit lacked the qualifications for the job positions at issue, they "were not members of the class... they purported to represent," and thus could not serve as class representatives. Similarly, a class of individuals complaining about the wording of a government notice (such as one describing the procedures for revocation of a driver's license) could not be represented by someone who did not receive the challenged notice; class members claiming antitrust injury from anticompetitive conduct could not be represented by someone who did not participate in the affected market; and a class of employees claiming discrimination on the basis of a certain disability could not be represented by an employee who did not suffer from that disability. The cases tend to be very fact-specific, however, and some courts are more rigorous than others in applying the membership requirement.

§ 3.3   A Claim That Is Not Moot

As a general matter, courts do not allow someone to serve as a class representative if his or her claim is moot. The mootness doctrine derives from Article III of the Constitution (U.S. Const. art. III, § 2, cl. 1) and requires that the litigant have a personal stake in the outcome in the form of a live controversy. As applied in various class action circumstances, however, the mootness doctrine is extremely complex.

For instance, the Supreme Court has held that if a class representative's claim becomes moot after a class is certified, the class action itself is not rendered moot. *Sosna v. Iowa*, 419 U.S. 393 (1975). Likewise, if a class representative's claim becomes moot after class certification is *denied* (for instance, a prisoner challenging parole guidelines is released from incarceration after the denial of certification), the class representative may still appeal the denial of class certification. *United States Parole Comm'n v. Geraghty*, 445 U.S. 388 (1980). And under the exception to the mootness doctrine that allows review of claims that are "capable of repetition yet evading review," even if a class representative's claim becomes moot *prior* to a ruling on class certification, the class representative may be able to serve in that capacity if other class members' claims are likely to become moot in a short time frame as well. *Gerstein v. Pugh*, 420 U.S. 103 (1975). On the other hand, if the "capable of repetition" doctrine does not apply and the class representative's claim becomes moot before class certification, then the entire suit is deemed moot and should be dismissed unless a new class representative with a live claim can be added to the case.

Another application of the mootness doctrine that sometimes arises in class actions is when the defendant voluntarily ceases the conduct challenged by the plaintiff, and the plaintiff seeks no damages for prior wrongdoing. The case will not become moot, however, unless the defendant can demonstrate that the wrongdoing is not likely to be repeated. Courts closely scrutinize the defendant's motivation to determine if the defendant deliberately mooted the controversy to evade judicial review of its conduct. Accordingly, the court has discretion in deciding whether to declare a case moot based upon the defendant's assurances that the wrongdoing will not recur.

II.   RULE 23(a)

Rule 23(a) sets forth four explicit requirements that must be satisfied in every federal class action. These are generally known as numerosity, commonality, typicality, and adequacy of representation. Failure to satisfy any of these four requirements is fatal to class certification.

§ 3.4   Numerosity

A.   OVERVIEW

Rule 23(a)(1) provides that "[o]ne or more members of a class may sue or be sued as representative parties on behalf of all only if ... the class is so numerous that joinder of all members is impracticable...." This requirement—commonly known as "numerosity"—is at the heart of a class action. If joinder under Rule 19 or Rule 20 is practicable (*see* pp. 368–385, *infra*), then there is no need for a representative action; each allegedly aggrieved individual can sue as part of a collective, non-class case. The numerosity standard requires only that joinder be impracticable or difficult; joinder need not be impossible. In determining whether Rule 23(a)(1) has been satisfied, the trial judge is given considerable discretion and will not be reversed absent an abuse of that discretion.

B. SIZE OF THE POTENTIAL CLASS

Rule 23 imposes no requirement of a minimum number of claimants necessary to bring a class action. Thus, absent a separate statutory requirement (such as the requirement of at least 100 class members to invoke federal jurisdiction under the Class Action Fairness Act), numerosity must be evaluated on a case-by-case basis. Cases can be found certifying classes with fewer than twenty known members, whereas other cases can be found holding that numerosity is *not* satisfied with more than three hundred members. Some courts have suggested that classes of twenty-five or more are generally sufficiently numerous to satisfy Rule 23(a)(1). Other courts have stated that focusing on numbers alone is improper, and that all relevant factual circumstances must be examined. Courts generally agree that small numbers are more acceptable in cases seeking only injunctive relief because the benefits of injunctive relief run to individuals not formally included within the suit.

In many cases, particularly those that indisputably involve large numbers of class members, the defendant will not contest that numerosity is satisfied. Attorneys in such cases reason that they would have no chance of succeeding under the governing law and would only undermine their credibility when they contend that other Rule 23 criteria have not been met.

In some cases, however, there may be a genuine issue as to how many individuals are actually in the class. In that event, the plaintiff may not rest on mere speculation but instead must offer some basis to estimate the number of class members. In some instances the proof may be indirect. For example, in a securities fraud case, plaintiffs may offer evidence as to the large number of stock trades during the class period in lieu of identifying the specific number of class members.

C.   POSSIBLE FUTURE CLAIMANTS

In addition to evaluating the size of the potential class, courts sometimes factor into the analysis possible future claimants. For example, in a class suit claiming discrimination against women in intercollegiate athletics, a court might look not only at the existing students claiming injury, but at the likelihood that future students will be subjected to the same discrimination. *See Pederson v. Louisiana State Univ.*, 213 F.3d 858 (5th Cir. 2000). Thus, the existence of unknown, future claimants makes it easier for plaintiffs to satisfy numerosity: Such claimants necessarily increase the sheer numbers and also confirm the impracticability of joinder.

D. OTHER FACTORS BEARING ON NUMEROSITY

In addition to size, other factors may in some cases be given significant weight. This is because the touchstone of the analysis is impracticability of joinder, not mere numbers.

One such factor is the geographic dispersion of the class. Obviously, if a class is spread out, joinder is more difficult than if a comparable class were limited to a small geographical area. For example, because of the difficulty in coordinating claims of plaintiffs dispersed throughout the country, a putative class of twenty-five dispersed class members could easily satisfy numerosity. On the other hand, if all twenty-five class members lived in the same city, joinder would be far less difficult because a small number of lawyers in that city could coordinate—and hence join—plaintiffs with similar claims.

Similarly, some courts reason that impracticability of joinder is more easily satisfied when each potential class member's claim is small, or when the potential class members lack the resources to pursue their claims individually. In these circumstances, class members are unlikely to litigate *at all* unless a class is certified, thus making joinder in the absence of a class all but impossible. Such cases—in which the claims likely would not be brought in the absence of a class action—are commonly referred to as "negative value" claims.

The facts of a specific case may indicate other reasons why joinder is impracticable. For example, impracticability of joinder may be found where employees fear reprisals from suing their employer individually. Likewise, impracticability may be shown where claimants alleging police brutality are reluctant to come forward and identify themselves because the events occurred in a homosexual bar, and "the potential social prejudice against homosexuals ... may deter class members from suing in their own name." *Patrykus v. Gomilla*, 121 F.R.D. 357, 361 (N.D.Ill. 1988). And joinder is often deemed impracticable, even in relatively small classes, when the class members are poor, uneducated, or otherwise not inclined or able to bring individual actions. Furthermore, a court may deem joinder impracticable if several of the putative class members reside outside the court's jurisdiction. These kinds of facts will frequently tip the scale in favor of finding numerosity in cases in which sheer numbers alone would be insufficient.

E. APPLICABILITY TO SUBCLASSES

When a court is considering whether to certify subclasses under Rule 23(c)(4)(B), each subclass must independently satisfy Rule 23(a)(1) (along with the other elements of Rule 23(a) and (b)). For example, when multiple subclasses are proposed based on the nature of the class members' injuries, numerosity is more difficult to satisfy because sheer numbers are reduced (by being spread out among subclasses).

F.   RE–EVALUATION OF NUMEROSITY

Satisfaction of numerosity at the outset of a case does not necessarily mean that the issue is resolved for the entire litigation. For instance, a large number of class members "opting out" might disqualify a class that at one time satisfied Rule 23(a)(1). On the other hand, the entry of numerous intervening parties may render a case sufficiently large to qualify under Rule 23(a)(1), even when the case previously did not so qualify. Therefore, courts will sometimes revisit the numerosity issue (as well as other Rule 23 requirements) during the course of the litigation.

§ 3.5   Commonality

A.   OVERVIEW

Rule 23(a)(2) states that a class action may not be certified unless the case presents "questions of law or fact common to the class." This requirement, known as "commonality," focuses upon the group of persons who would make up the class and requires a court to assess whether the group shares one or more issues relevant to the dispute that could be adjudicated on a collective basis. Although most actions brought as class actions easily satisfy the commonality requirement, some courts have applied Rule 23(a)(2) to reject class action treatment when collective adjudication would not achieve the efficiencies that the class action device is designed to achieve, or if those efficiencies would be achieved at too great a cost in terms of substantive and procedural fairness to the litigants.

B. WHETHER MORE THAN ONE COMMON LEGAL OR FACTUAL ISSUE IS NECESSARY

The language of Rule 23(a)(2) presents a threshold issue: By its use of the plural (questions), it appears to provide that a court may not find commonality satisfied unless there is *more than one* common question of law or fact. By contrast, Rule 20(a) (permissive joinder), Rule 24(b) (permissive intervention), and Rule 42(a) (consolidation) all make it clear that only a single common legal or factual question is required. Nonetheless, the overwhelming majority of cases that have addressed commonality have found, either explicitly or implicitly, that Rule 23(a)(2) is satisfied if a proposed class action provides even a single common question of law or fact.

C. CORE FOCUS OF RULE 23(a)(2)

The "commonality" requirement of Rule 23(a)(2) seeks to ensure that group adjudication will achieve efficiencies without unfairness to the litigants. Like the numerosity requirement—but unlike the typicality and adequacy requirements, *see* pp. 44–66, *infra*, which both focus upon the individual class representatives—the commonality requirement focuses upon the *group* that seeks to proceed as a class. But because both commonality and typicality ultimately focus upon similarities and differences among representatives (and thus the class as a whole), the Supreme Court has observed that commonality and typicality "tend to merge." *General Tel. Co. of the Sw. v. Falcon,* 457 U.S. 147, 158 n.13 (1982).

A potential class does not have to present identical issues of law and fact for commonality to be satisfied. Nor does the group even have to be similar in most respects. Rule 23(a)(2) instead requires the court to determine whether the group presents one or more questions of law or fact (1) that are susceptible to adjudication by representatives of that group and (2) that would materially advance the litigation if adjudicated on a classwide basis.

If a proposed class consists of individuals whose legal claims share either common legal theories or common factual circumstances relevant to their claims for relief, adjudication of their claims may achieve efficiency without imposing substantial unfairness on either class members or their opponents. If, however, a proposed class is diverse with respect to critical facts, or if the legal theories presented by putative class members are dissimilar, trying the claims on a representative basis may be both inefficient and unfair.

D. LAW *OR* FACT

It is also evident from Rule 23(a)(2) that the commonality requirement may be satisfied by presentation of a common issue of law *or* fact. That means that common questions of law, as well as fact, will satisfy the rule. Thus, many courts have found that commonality has been satisfied where all of the plaintiffs are suing under the same legal theory or theories. Some courts, however, have resisted finding commonality based solely on questions of law, such as whether the statute of limitations barred the class members' claims, or whether punitive damages would be available, ruling instead that such questions do not satisfy Rule 23(a)(2).

E. OTHER PURPOSES UNDERLYING RULE 23(a)(2)

In addition to achieving efficiencies, the commonality requirement serves other purposes as well. By focusing the court's and litigants' attention on whether the proposed class presents common issues, Rule 23(a)(2) helps to refine the definition of the class itself. The commonality inquiry also influences the determination of "typicality" under Rule 23(a)(3), since a potential class representative must present the allegedly "common" issues in a way that makes the claims or defenses being asserted "typical" for the class as a whole.

F. APPROACHES TO COMMONALITY

Most putative class actions present at least one common question of law or fact. Thus, it is not unusual for defendants to concede that commonality is satisfied.

When commonality is disputed, courts take a variety of approaches in addressing the issue. Some courts find that commonality is satisfied without performing any substantial analysis. Other courts find that commonality is satisfied if the potential class members generally seek the same remedy under the same legal theories.

Still other courts, however, apply a more rigorous approach to commonality. Some courts hold that for commonality to be satisfied, relief must turn in whole or in part upon the common questions; other courts hold that the common issues must be of sufficient importance to demonstrate that class treatment is the most efficient method of adjudicating the claims; and various courts look at whether the case presents at least one common question that, if resolved, would materially advance the litigation.

Courts applying these more stringent commonality tests appear to be motivated, either explicitly or implicitly, by a concern that unless significant common issues exist, the costs of a class action will outweigh the benefits.

G. DIFFERENCES FROM "PRE-DOMINANCE" INQUIRY OF RULE 23(b)(3)

Rule 23(a)(2) is sometimes confused with the "predominance" requirement for certain types of classes (Rule 23(b)(3) classes, discussed on pp. 96–99, *infra*). Under a predominance inquiry, common legal or factual issues must *predominate* over individual issues. This analysis requires a court to weigh both the common and the individual issues. Rule 23(a)(2), by contrast, simply asks whether there are *any* common legal or factual issues. That subdivision does not require a court to weigh those issues against the individual issues in the case.

H. EXAMPLES OF COMMONALITY AND LACK OF COMMONALITY

Although each case turns upon its particular facts, courts readily find that Rule 23(a)(2) has been satisfied in various situations. For example, commonality is likely to be found if a group of plaintiffs sues upon identical contractual provisions. Similarly, courts often find commonality when a plaintiff alleges that members of a class were victims of a common course of conduct by a defendant (such as an employer who allegedly applied the same discriminatory testing procedures to a group of persons of a particular race), or if many people were injured in the same catastrophic event.

By contrast, courts have found commonality lacking when questions of law presented by different plaintiffs in the potential class would have to be determined under the laws of numerous jurisdictions. Courts have also found that commonality is not satisfied when exposure to the same alleged toxin occurred in different amounts, at different times, to different plaintiffs, causing different types of injuries; when resolution of a "common" question will not materially advance the adjudication (because it is not relevant to the issues ultimately in dispute or because it is too abstract to be meaningful to the litigation); or when the legal theory under which the class members are proceeding (such as oral contract or estoppel) requires inherently individualized determinations of fact. Some of the foregoing decisions appear to confuse commonality with the more exacting "predominance" test under Rule 23(b)(3).

Ultimately, cases addressing commonality are very fact-specific. Courts that are inclined not to certify a class will sometimes seize upon factual differences and find that commonality is not satisfied. By contrast, courts that are inclined to favor certification can usually find numerous common issues.

§ 3.6 Typicality

A. LACK OF CONSENSUS ON MEANING

Rule 23(a)(3) provides, as a prerequisite to class certification, that "the claims or defenses of the representative parties [must be] typical of the claims or defenses of the class...." This requirement first appeared in the 1966 amendment to Rule 23. The 1938 version of Rule 23 did not contain a typicality requirement but simply required adequacy of representation: "one or more [representatives], as will fairly insure the adequate representation of all...." The Advisory Committee Notes to the 1966 amendment provide no guidance on the intent or meaning of Rule 23(a)(3). Courts have thus struggled to interpret the typicality requirement, resulting in confusion and a lack of consensus.

Some courts have stated that the typicality requirement has no independent meaning and should simply be ignored. But even these courts do not agree on *why* typicality should be ignored. Some have said that it is simply the same as commonality; others have said that it is the same as adequacy; others have said that Rule 23(a)(3) merely repeats the requirement that the class representative be a member of the class that he or she purports to represent; and still others have said that typicality is just another label for determining whether individual issues predominate over common issues. In 1997, the Supreme Court stated that adequacy, typicality, and commonality " 'tend[] to merge' " and that all of these requirements " 'serve as guideposts for determining whether ... maintenance of a class action is economical and whether the named plaintiff's claim and the class claims are so interrelated that the interests of the class members will be fairly and adequately protected in their absence.' "

Amchem Prods., Inc. v. Windsor, 521 U.S. 591, 626 n.20 (1997) (citation omitted).

Despite this confusion, a substantial number of courts, applying the canon of construction that portions of a statute or rule should not be rendered meaningless, have attempted to give independent significance to the typicality requirement. As a result, Rule 23(a)(3) has occasionally been invoked by courts as a reason to deny class certification.

B.   GENERAL APPROACH BY COURTS GIVING SEPARATE MEANING TO TYPICALITY

A number of cases state that the core of typicality is a comparison of the claims and defenses of the representative with those of the class. This comparison involves many inquiries: Is the class representative challenging the same alleged misconduct as the unnamed class members? Is he or she advancing the same legal theory based on the same type of injuries? Is the class representative's claim subject to unique defenses or other factual or legal flaws not present in the claims of unnamed class members? Ultimately, the inquiry is designed to ensure that a representative, in pressing his or her claims, is also pressing the claims of the other class members.

Courts that focus on comparing the representative's claim with those of the other class members nearly always hold that a representative's claims need not be identical to those of unnamed class members, but only substantially similar. Factual differences do not destroy typicality unless they cast serious doubt on the representative's ability to prosecute the claims of class members.

C. UNIQUE DEFENSES

An important inquiry under typicality is whether the class representative is subject to unique defenses that threaten to divert the focus of the litigation from the classwide claims to the detriment of the class as a whole. The concern is that the entire class will be bound by an adverse ruling that may turn on a defense specific to the representative. To destroy typicality, however, such a defense must be unique to the representative—or at least limited to a small segment of the class. A defense that can be asserted against the entire class—for example, that *every* class member's claim is barred by the statute of limitations—does not raise a typicality problem. Likewise, the purportedly unique defense must be supported by the record. Purely speculative defenses will not render a representative atypical.

Some courts are reluctant to view unique defenses as an impediment to class certification, reasoning that to do so would be to improperly decide the merits of the case at the certification stage. Other courts, however, hold that there is no need to resolve the merits of the defense: As long as the defense—meritorious or not—is likely to occupy a considerable amount of trial time, to the detriment of the class as a whole, then a typicality problem exists. In addition, there is growing recognition that courts may address merits issues that overlap with the class certification requirements. *See* pp. 140–143, *infra.*

In all events, courts agree that a unique defense must be serious to justify disqualification of someone as a class representative. The defense must, in other words, be likely to become a significant issue at trial. Examples of representatives with unique defenses that could defeat typicality are:

- A representative in an employment discrimination suit who, according to the defendant employer, was terminated not because of race but because he was caught stealing money from the company and covering up the theft by falsifying records.

- A representative in a securities fraud suit who purchased large volumes of the company's stock *after* the alleged fraud was disclosed.

- A representative in a mass tort property damage case whose property value actually increased when the defendant opened its neighboring manufacturing plant.

- A representative in a consumer protection case who admitted to friends that he knew the alleged dangers of a product *before* purchasing it.

In each of these cases, the representative would be subject to substantial cross-examination on these unique facts, and those facts could jeopardize the outcome of the case for the entire class. Each situation must be evaluated on its own facts, however, and courts differ as to how rigidly they approach the issue. For instance, some courts hold that a representative who is subject to a statute of limitations defense cannot represent a class, while other courts refuse to view a statute of limitations defense as disqualifying.

D. PLAINTIFF SEEKING RECOVERY AGAINST ONLY ONE OF SEVERAL DEFENDANTS

Ordinarily, the class representatives as a group must have a viable suit against every defendant named in the complaint in order to satisfy typicality. For example, a class representative who bought illegally overpriced airline tickets from only one of ten defendants in a case normally would not be typical of the class as a whole. There are, however, cases holding that this requirement need not be satisfied when the defendants are alleged to have engaged in a conspiracy to injure the class, or where they are linked in some special way (for instance, by being part of a common organization or otherwise acting in concert). *See* pp. 337–338, *infra.*

E. FACTUAL DISPARITIES DEFEATING TYPICALITY

Some courts apply a typicality analysis in holding that factual differences from one class member to another defeat class certification. For example, if the various class representatives allege different injuries from a chemical exposure (*e.g.,* some claiming breathing problems, others claiming headaches, still others claiming property damage), some courts hold that no class member's claim is "typical." Other courts, however, find no typicality problem in these circumstances, reasoning that mere differences in damages do not defeat typicality. Such courts hold that as long as the class members are all challenging the same alleged misconduct and are relying on the same legal theories, typicality is satisfied. For instance, in one case involving an alleged fraudulent scheme against life insurance policyholders, the court found that typicality was satisfied even though the class members alleged a wide variety of fraudulent sales practices. The court reasoned that the claims arose from the same fraudulent course of conduct and involved similar legal theories. *In re Prudential Ins. Co. America Sales Practices Litig. Agent Actions*, 148 F.3d 283 (3d Cir. 1998), *cert. denied*, 525 U.S. 1114 (1999).

One possible approach to factual disparities—and thus to potential typicality problems—is to form subclasses. If each subclass has at least one representative with facts typical of those of the members of the subclass, then the typicality concerns will have been resolved. In some instances, however, courts hold that there are too many factual differences even *within* a proposed subclass to declare any member "typical."

§ 3.7   Adequacy of Representation

A.   OVERVIEW

Rule 23(a)(4) requires that, before a class may be certified, a court must find that "the representative parties will fairly and adequately protect the interests of the class." This requirement—which applies to both the class representatives and class counsel—is based on fundamental principles of due process: A ruling cannot bind absent class members if the representatives were inadequate. *Hansberry v. Lee*, 311 U.S. 32 (1940). Rule 23(a)(4) requires only *adequate* class representatives and counsel; it does not require that the best possible plaintiffs and counsel be selected.

A court's determination of adequacy is not simply a threshold one. The court has a continuing duty to monitor the adequacy of the class representatives and class counsel. Moreover, Rule 23(d)(2) allows the court to give notice to class members "of the opportunity . . . to signify whether they consider the representation fair and adequate," thus giving class members a role in supervising the adequacy of representation.

Rule 23(a)(4) is not the only subdivision of Rule 23 that addresses adequacy. As discussed below (pp. 63–65, *infra*), in 2003, a new subdivision (Rule 23(g)) was added that specifically addresses the criteria for appointing class counsel.

B.   CHALLENGES TO ADEQUACY
RAISED BY DEFENDANTS

The law governing adequacy of representation reveals an apparent anomaly: In most cases the *defendants* are the ones who seek to challenge adequacy. But do defendants really *want* to exclude inadequate representatives or class counsel? Or would they prefer weak, ineffective representatives and class counsel? (The same tension exists with respect to typicality: Do defendants want to exclude atypical representatives who, for example, are subject to unique defenses?) It is undoubtedly true that, in some cases, a defendant's motivation is not to secure the substitution of adequate plaintiffs and counsel, but to obtain dismissal of the class suit altogether. On the other hand, defendants have an important interest in ensuring that, if a class action goes forward, the class members are represented by adequate named plaintiffs and counsel. If defendants secure a favorable verdict with inadequate representatives, the class members will have a strong argument that they are not bound by the judgment. *See* pp. 235–237, *infra*. Thus, the absence of adequate representation can be a no-win situation for defendants: If defendants lose, the entire class benefits, but if defendants win, they risk having their success disappear through collateral attacks on the judgment based on lack of adequate representation. Nonetheless, while defendants have legitimate reasons for challenging the adequacy of class representatives and class counsel, courts sometimes view defendants' challenges with skepticism, reasoning that defendants' real goal is not to protect the welfare of absent class members, but to see that no class is certified. Other courts, by contrast, do not question the sincerity of defendants' challenges. Moreover, many courts give conclusive weight to a defendant's *failure* to contest adequacy—even absent a strong affirmative showing of adequacy by the plaintiff—and do not conduct any independent scrutiny when defendants do not object.

C.   ADJUDICATING THE ADEQUACY OF CLASS REPRESENTATIVES

The adequacy of class representatives is an issue for the trial court and is reviewed only for abuse of discretion. Most courts hold that plaintiffs bear the burden of persuasion, but some courts require defendants to establish inadequacy. Adequacy encompasses numerous components, discussed below, although many courts focus entirely on whether class representatives suffer from a conflict of interest, and do not require proof of other indicia of adequacy (*e.g.,* knowledge of the case, good moral character). Courts usually require serious deficiencies before finding that a class representative is inadequate. The ultimate inquiry is whether the representative's interests are so antagonistic or detrimental to those of the class that effective representation would be jeopardized. When a case involves multiple representatives, Rule 23(a)(4) is satisfied if any one representative is adequate;

there is no requirement that each representative satisfy Rule 23(a)(4), although a proposed class representative who fails to satisfy the adequacy requirements cannot continue to serve in that role.

D. VIGOROUS PROSECUTION

A number of courts state that a class representative must vigorously prosecute the claims of the class. This means, for example, that he or she must be committed to the claim, believe in its merit, prosecute the case in a timely manner, and supervise the conduct of class counsel. Also, a class representative must have the necessary time and resources to devote to the case and not be hampered by severe and disabling physical or mental problems. A representative's failure to attend important court hearings or respond to critical discovery may provide strong evidence of inadequacy. Likewise, a representative's failure to move promptly for class certification may cast doubt on that person's adequacy. In addition, the size of a representative's claim may bear on adequacy: If a representative has only a small stake in the outcome, he or she generally will be less inclined to commit the time and resources necessary to be vigorous and effective. No particular factor is dispositive; instead, courts evaluate the totality of the circumstances to determine whether a representative is so deficient that, even with adequate counsel, the interests of the class members will be seriously jeopardized. Few cases actually reject class representatives on this basis.

E. KNOWLEDGE OF THE CASE

Numerous courts indicate that a class representative must have at least some knowledge of the facts, parties, and basic issues in the case and must stay in contact with class counsel. This requirement ensures that the class representative is an active participant, not a meaningless figurehead in a lawyer-driven suit. On the other hand, many courts recognize that class representatives cannot be expected to have precise knowledge of all of the factual or legal issues involved, particularly when the case is complicated or highly technical, such as an antitrust or securities fraud case. Thus, courts frequently find that a representative is competent if he or she has some basic knowledge of the case. Such courts recognize that clients necessarily look to counsel to understand the factual and legal intricacies. Cases actually finding inadequacy on this ground are rare: They generally involve representatives who cannot even articulate the claims or grievances at issue and have little or no knowledge of the parties, remedies sought, or responsibilities of class representatives.

F. HONESTY, GOOD CHARACTER, AND CREDIBILITY

Several courts state that a class representative must have good moral character. For instance, a representative who gives materially false testimony, or who otherwise acts dishonestly in the litigation at issue, may be found inadequate, whereas minor inconsistencies in memory or testimony are permitted. The issue is less clear when the misconduct occurred in an unrelated case or circumstance, although serious misconduct in another context may render a representative inadequate by substantially undermining the person's credibility. Depending on the circumstances, a prior criminal record may or may not render a class representative inadequate. Again, few courts have disqualified class representatives on this ground.

G. LACK OF CONFLICTS

A class representative should not have interests that significantly conflict with those of the other class members. For example, if the representative has a financial interest in a particular company that allegedly was involved in the claimed wrongdoing, plaintiff's failure to sue that company along with the other defendants may raise serious adequacy concerns. Likewise, adequacy issues would be raised with respect to a class representative who is a relative of the opposing party or the opposing party's counsel. In some circumstances, conflicts of interest may also arise if the representative is related to class counsel. In all instances, however, the issue must be decided based on the particular facts. Not all business or family relationships with the opposing side (or one's own) are disqualifying.

Many cases addressing adequacy (as well as typicality, *see* pp. 44–50, *supra*) have focused on potential conflicts between the class representative and unnamed class members. Indeed, this is by far the most common reason for rejecting class representatives. As noted above, many courts make alleged conflicts the sole focus of the inquiry into a representative's adequacy and do not even consider issues of knowledge or character. It is easy to understand why a representative having serious conflicts cannot be deemed adequate. For example, in a discrimination case, a person seeking to represent a class of African–American terminated employees might have a fatal conflict of interest if he also claims that his termination was based on age discrimination. To win his age discrimination case, he might need to show that he was replaced by a younger black man, and that an older white man was also passed over for the job. Such evidence, while advancing the representative's own age discrimination claim, undercuts the unnamed class members' claims of race discrimination. Similarly, in a securities fraud suit, a conflict might exist if a named plaintiff sold—rather than purchased—stock at a time when, according to the complaint, the defendant corporation was falsely painting a rosy picture of the company's future prospects. Likewise, a named plaintiff who purchased large quantities of stock following the disclosure of an alleged fraud might well be an inadequate representative of class members who claim that, but for the fraud, they never would have purchased any shares of the company's stock. These latter facts may also subject the class representative to the argument that he or she should be disqualified on typicality grounds because of unique defenses. (*See* pp. 47–49, *supra.*)

Likewise, a class representative who has a personal relationship with class counsel (*e.g.*, a parent, child, or spouse) might be more concerned about maximizing counsel's fees than about maximizing the recovery for individual class members.

A related type of potential conflict occurs when the named plaintiffs' claims differ from those of the class. For example, in *Amchem Prods., Inc. v. Windsor*, 521 U.S. 591 (1997), and again in *Ortiz v. Fibreboard*, 527 U.S. 815 (1999), the Supreme Court made clear that class representatives who allegedly suffered injury from exposure to asbestos could not represent class members who had been exposed but had not yet suffered injury. The Court noted that the goal of the class representatives—to maximize recovery for those who had already suffered injury—conflicted with the goal of those who had not yet suffered injury—to preserve the maximum amount possible to compensate for future injuries.

Courts have indicated that "minor conflicts" will not demonstrate inadequacy. Rather, "the conflict must be a 'fundamental' one going to the specific issues in controversy." *Valley Drug Co. v. Geneva Pharms. Inc.,* 350 F.3d 1181, 1189 (11th Cir. 2003) (citations omitted).

H. UNIQUE DEFENSES

The existence of unique defenses that threaten to become a major focus of trial is relevant not only to typicality but also to adequacy. If a representative must devote time and attention to defenses unique to the representative's own case, that is time taken away from representing the interests of the class as a whole.

I.   ABILITY TO FINANCE THE CLASS ACTION

A few courts have held that a class representative's inability to finance the litigation renders the representative inadequate. Most courts, however, do not strike class representatives on this ground, at least when class counsel is able and willing to fund the litigation. The issue turns in part on the applicable code of ethics. In some states, it is unethical for an attorney to advance litigation costs without any expectation of repayment, while in other states such conduct is permissible. *See* discussion on pp. 362–363, *infra*.

When a court views a class representative's financial resources to be relevant, it generally looks to whether the representative has sufficient resources to pay for class notice and other reasonable costs. The issue of a named representative's financial resources is sometimes a subject of pre-certification discovery.

J.   MEMBERSHIP IN THE CLASS

It is fundamental that a class representative must be a member of the class that he or she seeks to represent. As explained above (pp. 30–31, *supra*), the textual basis (if any) of this requirement is unclear. Many courts, however, have identified Rule 23(a)(4) as the authority for this requirement on the ground that someone who lacks the characteristics—and has not suffered the injury—of other class members cannot be an adequate representative of those absent class members.

K. ADEQUACY OF CLASS COUNSEL

Although successful challenges to the adequacy of class counsel are very rare, they do exist. Courts examine a variety of factors in asserting adequacy of counsel. Rule 23(g)—enacted in 2003 and discussed below—may focus greater judicial attention on the criteria necessary for adequate class counsel.

Qualifications. Courts look at the qualifications, experience, and reputation of counsel, particularly in handling class actions or other complex cases, or in handling other cases involving the same subject matter (such as similar types of antitrust cases). It is relatively rare for a class attorney to have such meager qualifications as to fail Rule 23(a)(4) on this basis. Frequently, lawyers lacking significant class-action experience will affiliate with more experienced counsel to assist in the representation.

Performance. Courts also look at the performance of counsel in the litigation at issue. An attorney who has repeatedly missed deadlines, failed to pursue discovery in a vigorous manner, filed substandard pleadings or briefs, or otherwise exhibited lackluster performance may be found inadequate. A few courts take the view that Rule 23(a)(4) mandates a high standard of performance by class counsel. Other courts, however, merely seek to ensure that counsel's performance is minimally competent.

Involvement of Class Representatives. A class action attorney may be found inadequate if he or she does not keep the class representatives informed of important matters and does not allow them to review and comment on significant court filings. For instance, a class representative's failure to review the complaint before it is filed bears not only on the adequacy of the class representative but also on the adequacy of counsel.

Unlawful or Unethical Conduct. Courts further examine whether counsel has committed legal or ethical violations, either in the case at issue or in other cases. Courts are particularly unwilling to tolerate attorneys who encourage or elicit false testimony or who destroy pertinent evidence. Some courts also disqualify counsel who advance litigation costs in violation of governing ethical rules.

Conflicts of Interest. Courts also examine whether attorneys have conflicts of interest with respect to the litigation. For example, class counsel must not have a financial or other relationship with any defendant, and must not be simultaneously serving as counsel for any of the defendants in any other case. A close relationship between class counsel and a class representative—such as a family relationship or significant business relationship—may also render both counsel and the representative inadequate.

Likewise, class counsel may be unsuitable if he or she is a member of the putative class at issue. In addition, class counsel may have a conflict when he or she attempts to represent two separate classes against the same defendant or attempts to represent two potentially conflicting groups in the same case, such as holders of present tort claims (with existing physical injuries) and holders of future claims (involving exposure to a substance but no physical injury). *Ortiz v. Fibreboard*, 527 U.S. 815 (1999).

L.   DUTY OF COUNSEL TO EDUCATE REPRESENTATIVES AND IDENTIFY INADEQUATE REPRESENTATIVES

A few courts have held that class counsel have a duty, throughout a class action, to ensure that class representatives understand their obligations and are performing them properly. If class representatives are not performing adequately, class counsel must bring these problems to the attention of the court. Failure to adhere to these duties may render class counsel inadequate.

M.   FAILURE TO BRING CERTAIN CLAIMS TO IMPROVE LIKELIHOOD OF CLASS CERTIFICATION

Assume that a case raises a number of potential causes of action. Some can be litigated without significant individual issues. Others, however, such as fraud—which requires each class member to prove reliance (*see* pp. 99–100, *infra*)—raise myriad individualized questions. If class counsel and the representative choose not to bring claims that are not suitable for class certification, do they risk being challenged on adequacy grounds? In the view of some courts, *res judicata* would bar class members from later bringing those omitted claims. (*Res judicata* applies to claims that were *or could have been* brought.) Thus, some courts have found adequacy concerns because class members will lose the chance to bring potentially valuable claims, solely to enable the case to be brought as a class action. Other courts, however, have held that, because the omitted claims could not have been brought as part of the class action, class members are free to bring those claims individually, and thus the class representatives and counsel are not inadequate for failing to assert them as part of the class action.

N.   RULE 23(g)

Rule 23(g)—which relates to court appointment of counsel—recognizes the critical role that class counsel plays in ensuring fair treatment of class members. Rule 23(g)(1)(A) states that "[u]nless a statute provides otherwise, a court that certifies a class must appoint class counsel." Codifying the case law, Rule 23(g)(1)(B) specifies that class counsel "must fairly and adequately represent the interests of the class." Rule 23(g)(1)(C)(i) then provides criteria that the court must consider in appointing class counsel: (i) counsel's work "in identifying or investigating potential claims in the action"; (ii) "counsel's experience in handling class actions, other complex litigation, and claims of the type asserted in the action"; (iii) "counsel's knowledge of the applicable law"; and (iv) "the resources counsel will commit to representing the class[.]" In addition, Rule 23(g)(1)(C)(ii) permits the court to "consider any other matter pertinent to counsel's ability to fairly and adequately represent the interests of the class[.]" Rule 23(g)(1)(C)(iii) provides that, in selecting counsel, the court may, *inter alia*, order counsel to "provide information on any subject pertinent to the appointment" and may require counsel "to propose terms for attorney fees and nontaxable costs[.]"

Rule 23(g)(2)(A) provides that, before appointing counsel, the court may designate interim counsel. When only one applicant seeks appointment as class counsel, the court must still find that counsel satisfies the criteria of Rule 23(g)(1)(B) and (C). Under Rule 23(g)(2)(B), if more than one adequate counsel applies, the court "must appoint the applicant best able to represent the interests of the class." And Rule 23(g)(2)(C) provides that, in appointing class counsel, the court may include provisions regarding attorneys' fees and nontaxable costs.

The cases to date provide little insight as to whether Rule 23(g) will significantly alter the approach taken by courts in assessing adequacy of counsel. Some courts have continued to find class counsel adequate with only minimal scrutiny. A few courts, however, have rigorously scrutinized the qualifications of counsel based on the Rule 23(g) criteria.

O. SOLUTIONS TO INADEQUATE REPRESENTATION

Courts have taken a variety of approaches in addressing inadequacy of class representatives and class counsel. If an adequacy problem arises before a class action is certified, the court may either deny class certification or permit the substitution of an adequate representative or counsel. Alternatively, the court may narrow the class to encompass only those individuals who would be adequately represented. If an adequacy problem arises after certification, the court may likewise allow substitution of new representatives or counsel, narrow the class, or, in extreme cases, decertify the class. In no event should a court allow the case to proceed in the absence of at least one adequate representative and one adequate attorney for each subclass in the case.

Two circuit court cases exemplify the various approaches that courts have taken. In *Birmingham Steel Corp. v. TVA*, 353 F.3d 1331 (11th Cir. 2003), the Eleventh Circuit held that the district court abused its discretion in decertifying the class based on a representative's inadequacy without providing an opportunity for a new class representative to be substituted. The court emphasized that, at the time of the finding of inadequacy, "discovery had been completed, numerous pretrial motions had been resolved, and the case was ready for trial...." *Id.* at

1342. It is not clear whether the result would have been the same had the adequacy concerns arisen earlier in the case. By contrast, one federal appeals court has upheld decertification without giving counsel time to find a new representative, finding that there was no evidence that any class member "ha[d] any interest beyond that of a curious onlooker in pursuing the litigation." *Culver v. City of Milwaukee*, 277 F.3d 908, 913 (7th Cir. 2002).

P.   COLLATERAL ATTACKS ON ADEQUACY

Courts and commentators are sharply divided over whether class members must raise adequacy issues in the class action suit itself or are permitted to raise the issues in a collateral attack. Those issues are discussed in Chapter 8 (pp. 235–237, *infra*).

CHAPTER 4

CLASS CERTIFICATION REQUIREMENTS: RULE 23(b)

In addition to satisfying all of the implicit requirements for certification and all four requirements of Rule 23(a), a class action must also satisfy at least one of the four categories of Rule 23(b): (b)(1)(A), (b)(1)(B), (b)(2), or (b)(3). A court is not restricted to one category but may certify a case under multiple subdivisions of Rule 23(b)—for instance, Rule 23(b)(2) and Rule 23(b)(3). The Rule 23(b) categories can be difficult to apply. Moreover, the case law is often conflicting and confusing, and the text of Rule 23 fails to provide clear guidance.

§ 4.1 Rule 23(b)(1)(A) Classes

Rule 23(b)(1) is divided into two subsections, (b)(1)(A) and (b)(1)(B). Each has different purposes and requirements. A class that satisfies *either* (b)(1)(A) or (b)(1)(B) may proceed as a (b)(1) class action, assuming that the implicit requirements and those of Rule 23(a) are met.

A. THE PURPOSES OF RULE
23(b)(1)(A) CLASSES

Rule 23(b)(1)(A) focuses on the party opposing the class—typically the defendant. (By contrast, Rule 23(b)(1)(B) is a mirror-image provision that focuses on protecting the interests of class members.) Rule 23(b)(1)(A) authorizes a class action if:

> [T]he prosecution of separate actions by or against individual members of the class could create a risk of . . . inconsistent or varying adjudications with respect to individual members of the class which would establish incompatible standards of conduct for the party opposing the class. . . .

The purpose of Rule 23(b)(1)(A) is to protect a party (usually a defendant) who is litigating against several parties in related suits (or is faced with the threat of multiple suits) from being subject to a series of contradictory court orders. One example cited in the Advisory Committee Notes is "litigation of. . . landowners' rights and duties respecting a claimed nuisance," a situation that "could create a possibility of incompatible adjudications."

To illustrate, if a factory is sued for nuisance by numerous neighbors seeking different forms of relief, the landowner could be subjected to incompatible adjudications. Some neighbors may be seeking shutdown of the plant; others may be seeking only that certain air quality standards be met; and still others may be seeking yet other forms of relief.

Another example of the need for (b)(1)(A) classes is cited in the Advisory Committee Notes: "Separate actions by individuals against a municipality to declare a bond issue invalid or condition or limit it...." Here, too, absent a Rule 23(b)(1)(A) class, the municipality could be subject to inconsistent adjudications. For instance, some courts might order the municipality to revoke the bond issue; others might order the municipality to impose conditions (and those conditions might conflict from one case to another); and still other courts might approve the bond issue. A (b)(1)(A) class would prevent the municipality from having to face these inconsistent adjudications.

Although one of the purposes of a (b)(1)(A) class is to protect the party opposing the class, most courts do not require that such party acquiesce in class certification. In other words, most (but not all) courts will certify a (b)(1)(A) class to protect a defendant against inconsistent adjudications even if—as is true in most cases—the defendant *opposes* class certification.

B. REQUIREMENTS FOR CERTIFICATION UNDER RULE 23(b)(1)(A)

To qualify under Rule 23(b)(1)(A), the parties seeking class certification must establish a realistic probability that the party opposing the class will face separate actions that will likely result in varying adjudications. As the Advisory Committee Notes state: "The class action device can be used effectively to obviate the actual or virtual dilemma which would thus confront the party opposing the class." To qualify under Rule 23(b)(1)(A), the risk of separate actions may not be hypothetical or speculative. Furthermore, there is authority holding that in situations in which many potential claimants have very small individual claims (thus making all suits other than class actions cost prohibitive), the separate actions requirement of Rule 23(b)(1)(A) is not satisfied because, apart from the class action suit, the defendant does not, in fact, face a likelihood of separate actions. *Eisen v. Carlisle & Jacquelin*, 391 F.2d 555 (2d Cir. 1968).

C. CERTIFICATION UNDER RULE 23(b)(1)(A) IN CASES SEEKING MONETARY DAMAGES

Even if a litigant faces numerous related suits, Rule 23(b)(1)(A) does not automatically apply to certify all of those party opponents as a class. The outcome frequently turns on the type of relief sought by the claimants. Most courts hold that Rule 23(b)(1)(A) applies only to actions for declaratory or injunctive relief, *not* to actions seeking only compensatory damages, reasoning that having to pay damages to some plaintiffs but not others does not subject the defendant to inconsistent standards of conduct. For instance, in *In re Dennis Greenman Sec. Litig.*, 829 F.2d 1539 (11th Cir. 1987), the court held that (b)(1)(A) certification was improper because the class members, all of whom were suing an allegedly dishonest stockbroker, were seeking only damages.

Even declaratory relief is sometimes improper for certification under Rule 23(b)(1)(A). For example, in *McDonnell Douglas Corp. v. United States District Court,* 523 F.2d 1083 (9th Cir. 1975), plaintiffs sought class certification under Rule 23(b)(1)(A) in an air crash disaster in which the complaint requested damages and a declaration of liability. The Ninth Circuit held that the claim for damages did not raise the possibility of inconsistent adjudications, and that the prayer for declaratory relief—a request for a finding of liability—was nothing more than a request for damages.

Many courts hold that an action under Rule 23(b)(1)(A) for compensatory damages can be certified, as long as the class also seeks injunctive or declaratory relief. Of course, the injunctive or declaratory remedy must expose the party opposing the class to varying adjudications and incompatible standards. Furthermore, a few courts have permitted Rule 23(b)(1)(A) class actions to be maintained for compensatory damages in mass tort cases, reasoning that inconsistent damages awards could lead to uncertainty about how the defendant should conduct itself in the future.

D. CERTIFICATION OF MEDICAL MONITORING CLASSES UNDER RULE 23(b)(1)(A)

Some court decisions have applied Rule 23(b)(1)(A) to medical monitoring cases. Medical monitoring is a process whereby a class of individuals who have been exposed to a dangerous condition that could cause latent diseases or injuries seek to have the defendant provide them with periodic medical checkups (or establish a fund to use to pay for such checkups) to determine whether any dangerous symptoms have developed. In some cases, medical monitoring is brought as a separate cause of action. In others, it is sought as an element of damages. Some courts have held that a Rule 23(b)(1)(A) class is appropriate in medical monitoring cases because separate judicial orders in individual cases could result in different types of medical monitoring regimens, making it difficult or impossible for a defendant to comply. Other courts, however, have refused to certify Rule 23(b)(1)(A) classes in medical monitoring cases, because the plaintiffs did not show how separate actions could result in incompatible standards of conduct for the defendant. Such courts have noted that any medical monitoring programs ordered would turn not on different standards but on individual factors, such as exposure level and family history. Thus, separate actions would not subject the defendants to inconsistent or varying adjudications.

E.   OTHER KINDS OF CASES INVOLVING RULE 23(b)(1)(A)

In addition to the cases discussed above, Rule 23(b)(1)(A) has also been applied in cases by patent owners against alleged patent infringers; in actions for declaratory relief against government agencies; in actions by professional athletes against their players' league challenging a proposed merger with a rival team; and in actions by employees against their employer for recovery of benefits.

One interesting case under (b)(1)(A) involved a suit by Hispanic prisoners challenging the constitutionality of a policy barring alien prisoners from transferring to minimum security facilities. In certifying the class, the court reasoned that individual lawsuits could have created conflicting rules as to the permissibility of such transfers. *See Franklin v. Barry,* 909 F.Supp. 21 (D.D.C. 1995).

Some courts have declined to certify Rule 23(b)(1)(A) classes against government entities involving the validity of statutes on the ground that all government officials would be bound by the ruling in a single-plaintiff case. Similarly, some courts hold that incompatible standards are not threatened if inconsistent trial court rulings likely will be resolved by the appellate courts.

§ 4.2   Rule 23(b)(1)(B) Classes

A.   OVERVIEW OF RULE 23(b)(1)(B)

Rule 23(b)(1)(B) authorizes class actions if

the prosecution of separate actions by or against individual members of the class could create a risk of ... adjudications with respect to individual members of the class which would as a practical matter be dispositive of the interests of the other members not parties to the adjudications or substantially impair or impede their ability to protect their interests....

The Advisory Committee Notes state in part:

[Rule 23(b)(1)(B)] takes in situations where the judgment in a nonclass action by or against an individual member of the class, while not technically concluding the other members, might do so as a practical matter.... This is plainly the case when claims are made by numerous persons against a fund insufficient to satisfy all claims....

As the Advisory Committee Notes reveal, the purpose of (b)(1)(B) is to protect the members of the class. It is, therefore, the mirror-image of Rule 23(b)(1)(A), which is designed to protect those who oppose the class. Under the most common usage of (b)(1)(B), in the "limited fund" cases discussed below, class certification is designed to avoid depletion of the fund by those who are first to secure a judgment.

B.   *STARE DECISIS* EFFECT INSUFFICIENT TO SATISFY Rule(b)(1)(B)

To obtain certification under Rule 23(b)(1)(B), the party seeking certification must show the risk of prejudice to the class members in the absence of a class. Courts generally hold, however, that the possibility that an action will have a precedential (or *stare decisis*) effect on later cases (and thereby indirectly threaten the class) is not a sufficient reason to invoke Rule 23(b)(1)(B). The rationale of these cases is that, were Rule 23(b)(1)(B) to apply simply because of *stare decisis* effects, the other subdivisions of Rule 23(b) would be rendered superfluous. Since any class must have common issues (Fed.R.Civ.P. 23(a)(2)), any individual class member's suit could conceivably have a *stare decisis* effect on other class members' claims in the absence of a class action. Thus, any case satisfying commonality would satisfy Rule 23(b)(2)(B), a conclusion that the drafters of Rule 23 could not have contemplated.

C.   REQUIREMENTS FOR "LIMITED FUND" TREATMENT

As noted above, the most common use of Rule 23(b)(1)(B) is in so-called "limited fund" cases. Limited fund cases are those in which all of the parties seeking recovery must obtain damages from a finite source of assets that will be exhausted before all expected claims are paid. Examples of limited funds include trust funds, bank accounts, insurance policies, and assets of an estate.

In *Ortiz v. Fibreboard Corp.*, 527 U.S. 815 (1999), the Supreme Court articulated the standards that govern whether a class action qualifies for certification under the "limited fund" doctrine. *Ortiz* involved a large national class of asbestos-related claimants whose claims amounted to potentially billions of dollars. The defendant, Fibreboard Corporation, had a net worth of approximately $235 million. Although the defendant had exhausted much of its insurance coverage because of massive asbestos claims during the 1980s, it claimed to have insurance coverage remaining through two carriers on policies that were issued in the 1950s. That coverage was being disputed by the insurance carriers in litigation in California state court.

In the early 1990s, Fibreboard undertook to settle hundreds of thousands of potential asbestos claims. Fibreboard approached a group of asbestos-plaintiff lawyers, with a goal that these attorneys would bring a "limited fund" class action under Rule 23(b)(1)(B) consisting of all asbestos claims, and that Fibreboard would then enter into a settlement. Fibreboard wanted a (b)(1)(B) class because that subdivision does not provide for opt outs, thereby ensuring that there would be a cap on its liability. These negotiations continued throughout the early 1990s. Fibreboard's insurance carriers, having lost at the trial level in the coverage litigation, joined in the settlement negotiations in 1993. As negotiations over a "global settlement" continued in 1993, plaintiffs' counsel began to settle their cases that were already then pending (the so-called "inventory" claims), with fifty percent of the settlement funds being conditioned on Fibreboard's either achieving a "global" settlement or prevailing on its California insurance cases. On the eve of an appellate argument in the California coverage cases, the negotiating parties agreed upon a $1.535 billion settlement, with virtually all of the money coming from Fibreboard's insurance carriers (and with Fibreboard retaining all but $500,000 of its net worth). Days later, plaintiffs' counsel filed an action in the Eastern District of Texas seeking to certify a class that essentially consisted of all asbestos claimants everywhere who had not yet filed suit against Fibreboard. Over the objections of several intervening class members, the district court certified a Rule 23(b)(1)(B) class, and the Fifth Circuit affirmed.

The Supreme Court reversed. 527 U.S. at 830–865. The Court first noted that "limited fund" class actions in equity had three characteristics that the Advisory Committee must have considered in drafting (b)(1)(B): (1) the fund available to satisfy all claims is inadequate to pay the claims; (2) "the whole of the inadequate fund [is] devoted to all the overwhelming claims"; and (3) the claimants to the fund are "treated equitably among themselves."

With regard to the first element, the Court faulted the district court for simply accepting the parties' settlement agreement figure without making an independent determination that a "limited fund" in fact existed. While not ruling out the possibility that a settlement amount could form the basis of a "limited fund" determination, the Court noted that the settlement figure here could not be relied upon because of the conflicting interests of class counsel, who had also negotiated settlements of inventory cases (not included within the class) that were tied to the success of a global settlement. As the Court noted, "[c]lass counsel thus had great incentive to reach any agreement in the global settlement negotiations that they thought might survive" court approval.

With respect to the second element, the Court stated that classic "limited fund" cases ensured claimants the "best deal," and did not result in the defendant being better off under the class action than if individual suits had been filed. The Court found it troubling that Fibreboard would be able to emerge from the settlement with virtually all of its net worth intact. The Court, however, did not base its holding on this part of the test, and specifically reserved the question of whether a defendant could retain any of its net worth in a (b)(1)(B) settlement.

With respect to the third element, the Court faulted the class action settlement as being inequitable because it treated claimants with unequally valuable claims identically. The Court noted that, under the terms of the disputed insurance coverage, claimants exposed to asbestos after 1959 could end up receiving much less were they forced to litigate, since the major insurance policy expired in 1959. Lumping these claimants together with the pre–

1959 claimants and giving them an equal share of the limited fund was an inequitable allocation of the fund. The Court also faulted the fact that holders of present claims (those with actual physical injuries) and those with future claims (no physical injury) were lumped together without separate counsel and subclasses to protect their respective interests.

The Court identified, but did not decide, several additional arguments that were made by objectors to the proposed limited-fund settlement, including (i) the denial of due process and Seventh Amendment jury trial rights stemming from the inability of class members to opt out of the settlement; and (ii) potential Article III standing issues involving "exposure-only" class members, who had not suffered physical injury.

As a result of *Ortiz,* the vast majority of courts have refused to certify mass tort cases under Rule 23(b)(1)(B).

D.   RULE 23(b)(1)(B) AND PUNITIVE DAMAGES

The prospect of significant punitive-damage awards in factually related cases may be a basis for certification under Rule 23(b)(1)(B). Punitive damages present a special problem because, as a remedy, they are intended not to compensate the plaintiff to whom they are awarded, but to punish the defendant. Punitive damages awarded by juries often exceed the compensatory damages that a plaintiff can recover. Courts tend to focus upon two issues with respect to punitive damages and Rule 23(b)(1)(B). First, if individual litigants will each be able to claim significant punitive damage awards, even the wealthiest defendants likely will not have assets sufficient to pay all of the awards. Second, if litigants individually sue a defendant in related but separate suits, some courts may be reluctant to authorize the award of punitive damages against a defendant who has already sustained a series of punitive-damage awards for the same misconduct in earlier cases. Indeed, some litigants have argued that there are due process restrictions against imposing multiple punitive-damage awards for the same conduct.

Courts have developed two theories under Rule 23(b)(1)(B) to deal with punitive damages. Under the first theory, certification of a punitive damages class is appropriate to protect claimants because the assets of the defendant may not be enough to satisfy multiple, large punitive damage awards (or because of due process limits to multiple awards). The second theory, which has been called the "limited generosity" theory, invokes certification under Rule 23(b)(1)(B) out of a concern that late arriving plaintiffs will be less likely to obtain awards of punitive damages against a defendant who has already had to pay punitive damages for the same conduct. In general, plaintiffs have had only mixed success in asserting either theory. The Supreme Court's decision in *Ortiz v. Fibreboard*, 527 U.S. 815 (1999), which states that courts should be reluctant to stray from the "historical limited fund model," makes it even less likely that many courts will adopt these or other creative limited fund theories. Illustrative of the caution shown by courts in the wake of *Ortiz* is *In re Simon II Litig.*, 211 F.R.D. 86 (E.D.N.Y. 2002), *rev'd*, 407 F.3d 125 (2d Cir. 2005). There, the district court certified a nationwide smoker class action under (b)(1)(B) solely on claims for punitive damages out of concern that "the first plaintiffs may recover vast sums while others who arrive later are left with a depleted fund against which they cannot recover." 211 F.R.D. at 190. The Second Circuit reversed, holding under *Ortiz* that "[t]he fund . . . is not easily susceptible to proof, definition, or even estimation, by any precise figure," and "the record . . . does not evince a likelihood that any given number of punitive awards to individual claimants would be constitutionally excessive, either individually or in the aggregate, and thus overwhelm the available fund." 407 F.3d at 138.

E.   OTHER TYPES OF RULE 23(b)(1)(B) CASES

Rule 23(b)(1)(B) is not restricted to limited fund cases. As the Advisory Committee Notes point out, "[s]imilar problems . . . can arise in the absence of a fund either present or potential." For example, "[a] negative or mandatory injunction secured by one of a numerous class may disable the opposing party from performing claimed duties toward the other members of the class or materially affect his ability to do so." Here, adjudication as to one or more class members would significantly affect the interests of other class members, rendering a (b)(1)(B) class action appropriate.

F. COMPARISONS BETWEEN RULE 23(b)(1)(B) AND OTHER JOINDER DEVICES

Courts and commentators have noted the functional similarities between the certification of a class under Rule 23(b)(1), joinder under Rule 19 (*see* pp. 377–385, *infra*) and interpleader under Rule 22 (*see* pp. 393–398, *infra*). Indeed, the Advisory Committee Notes to Rule 23(b)(1) state that "the considerations stated under clauses (A) and (B) are comparable to certain of the elements which define the persons whose joinder in an action is desirable as stated in Rule 19(a), as amended."

As with interpleader, Rule 23(b)(1)(B) focuses on prejudice to absent parties in the case of a limited fund. Moreover, like Rule 19(a), Rule 23(b)(1)(B) focuses on impairment of interests of non-parties. Compulsory joinder and interpleader are discussed on pp. 377–385 and 393–398, *infra*.

G. PREFERENCE BETWEEN MANDATORY AND OPT-OUT CLASSES

In many instances, an action may qualify for certification under Rule 23(b)(1)(A)—or (b)(1)(B)— as well as other subdivisions of Rule 23(b). The choice between subdivisions can be of great significance because it may determine whether class members receive notice and the right to opt out of class membership. *See* pp. 161–174, *infra*. The rule applied by most courts is that if an action can qualify under both Rule 23(b)(1) and Rule 23(b)(3), the action is generally certified under Rule 23(b)(1), and an inquiry under (b)(3) will not be undertaken. By taking this approach, the courts avoid burdening litigants with notice requirements that go along with a certification under (b)(3). As discussed below (pp. 172–173, *infra*), however, in cases seeking monetary relief, mandatory classes may raise serious due process issues because of the absence of notice and opt-out rights.

H.   OPTING OUT OF A RULE 23(b)(1) CLASS

Despite the fact that Rule 23(b)(1), as discussed above, establishes a mandatory class, courts have occasionally permitted claimants to opt out of Rule 23(b)(1) classes because of due process concerns. In certain circumstances, however, such as limited fund classes, opt outs could defeat the entire purpose of certifying a case as a class action. The issue of opt-out rights in (b)(1) and (b)(2) class actions is addressed on pp. 172–174, *infra*.

§ 4.3 Rule 23(b)(2)

A. OVERVIEW

Rule 23(b)(2) authorizes a class action if:

the party opposing the class has acted or refused to act on grounds generally applicable to the class, thereby making appropriate final injunctive relief or corresponding declaratory relief with respect to the class as a whole. . . .

Class actions under Rule 23(b)(2) were conceived to facilitate awards of injunctive or declaratory relief against defendants whose actions affected an entire class of individuals. As the 1966 Advisory Committee Notes indicate, Rule 23(b)(2) was envisioned as a device for civil rights cases to enjoin unlawful discrimination against a class. Although most courts were willing to certify civil rights cases as class actions even prior to Rule 23(b)(2), a few courts had taken the view that civil rights cases were not appropriate for class certification. Since its enactment in 1966, Rule 23(b)(2) has been utilized by numerous courts to certify civil rights class actions.

As the Advisory Committee Notes also indicate, however, Rule 23(b)(2) was not intended exclusively for civil rights cases. The Notes refer to patent suits and suits alleging unlawful pricing practices as two examples. Additional examples include due process, First Amendment, and other constitutional challenges (in cases not involving discrimination claims); suits seeking enforcement under federal or state statutory entitlement programs; and mass tort suits seeking injunctive relief.

B.   GENERAL REQUIREMENTS

By its terms, Rule 23(b)(2) contains two requirements. Both must be satisfied before a Rule 23(b)(2) class can be certified.

First, the party opposing the class must have "acted or refused to act on grounds generally applicable to the class...." This requirement is rather vague, and courts have been satisfied with a pattern or practice that is generally applicable to a class as a whole. In fact, the defendant's conduct challenged by the Rule 23(b)(2) action need not even be directed to, or cause damage to, every member of the class. According to the Advisory Committee Notes, "[a]ction or inaction is directed to a class within the meaning of [Rule 23(b)(2)] even if it has taken effect or is threatened only as to one or a few members of the class, provided it is based on grounds which have general application to the class."

The second requirement of Rule 23(b)(2) is that final injunctive relief or corresponding declaratory relief must be "appropriate ... with respect to the class as a whole." As the Advisory Committee Notes point out, the injunctive or declaratory relief must "settl[e] the legality of the behavior with respect to the class as a whole...." Moreover, the Advisory Committee Notes state—in language that has been critical to the outcome of many court decisions—

that Rule 23(b)(2) "does not extend to cases in which the appropriate final relief relates exclusively or predominantly to money damages."

C.   WHETHER THE PARTY SEEKING CERTIFICATION MUST SHOW PRE-DOMINANCE OR SUPERIORITY

Historically, courts have declined to read any requirements into Rule 23(b)(2) that are not evident from its text. Most importantly, unlike Rule 23(b)(3) (discussed on pp. 96–99, *infra*), neither the text of Rule 23(b)(2) nor the Advisory Committee Notes provide that common legal or factual issues among the claimants must predominate over individual issues. Consistent with the language of Rule 23(b)(2), the vast majority of courts have held that Rule 23(b)(2) does not require the plaintiff to satisfy this sort of predominance inquiry.

Most recent decisions adhere to this analysis. For instance, in *Walters v. Reno*, 145 F.3d 1032 (9th Cir. 1998), *cert. denied*, 526 U.S. 1003 (1999), the Ninth Circuit upheld the district court's certification of a class consisting of approximately 4,000 aliens who had been adjudicated as deportable without constitutional due process under a provision of the Immigration and Naturalization Act of 1990. In certifying the class pursuant to Rule 23(b)(2), despite the government's objection that certification would lead to thousands of individualized administrative proceedings, the Ninth Circuit stated:

The government's dogged focus on the factual differences among the class members appears to demonstrate a fundamental misunderstanding of [Rule 23(b)(2)]. Although common issues must predominate for class certification under Rule 23(b)(3), no such requirement exists under 23(b)(2). It is sufficient if class members complain of a pattern or practice that is generally applicable to the class a whole. 145 F.3d at 1047.

A decision from the Third Circuit, however, has taken a different approach. In *Barnes v. The American Tobacco Co.*, 161 F.3d 127 (3d Cir. 1998), the court of appeals approved a district court's decertification of a Rule 23(b)(2) class consisting of potentially thousands of Pennsylvania smokers. As relief, the plaintiffs sought a court-supervised medical monitoring fund that would pay for medical examinations designed to detect latent disease caused by smoking. While acknowledging that Rule 23(b)(2) does not require that common issues predominate over individual issues, the court nonetheless invoked a "cohesiveness" requirement to deny certification of the class of smokers under Rule 23(b)(2). The court noted that "a (b)(2) class may require more cohesiveness than a (b)(3) class" because (b)(2) classes do not permit opt outs. Referring to the many individual issues in the case, the court concluded that "a class action [would] devolve into a lengthy series of individual trials...." *Id.* at 142, 149. *Barnes* illustrates that, even under Rule 23(b)(2), courts will occasionally focus explicitly on whether a class action would be efficient in light of the individualized issues that are likely to arise.

Courts are also divided over whether (b)(2) contains a manageability requirement. Some courts have held that issues of manageability and judicial economy are not relevant under (b)(2) because (b)(2), unlike (b)(3), does not specifically require a determination of manageability. *E.g., Elliott v. Weinberger,* 564 F.2d 1219 (9th Cir. 1977); *Forbush v. J.C. Penney Co., Inc.,* 994 F.2d 1101 (5th Cir. 1993). Other courts, however, have held that, because the purpose of a class action is to achieve efficiency, a court may assess manageability and efficiency in evaluating certification under (b)(2). *E.g., Shook v. El Paso County Bd. Of County Comm'rs,* 386 F.3d 963 (10th Cir. 2004), *cert. denied,* 544 U.S. 978 (2005); *Lowery v. Circuit City Stores, Inc.,* 158 F.3d 742 (4th Cir. 1998).

D.   REQUIREMENT THAT NON–MONETARY RELIEF PREDOMINATE OVER DAMAGES

Although many courts addressing (b)(2) have refused to assess whether common issues predominate over individual issues, there is a different kind of predominance analysis that is universally applied by the courts: The non-monetary relief sought must predominate over any damages sought. As noted above, the Advisory Committee Notes specifically caution that Rule 23(b)(2) does not apply to cases in which the relief sought is "predominantly" money damages.

As an initial matter, courts view some forms of monetary awards as equitable remedies that can be pursued in a (b)(2) class. For example, many courts have held that back pay relief sought by class members in employment discrimination cases constitutes equitable restitution, not legal damages. Some courts have determined that other forms of financial restitution, such as the repayment of welfare benefits, constitute equitable relief that can be sought in a (b)(2) class action.

In cases seeking both equitable relief and damages, courts have traditionally applied Rule 23(b)(2) by weighing the importance of the monetary damages sought against the importance of the injunctive or declaratory relief at issue. Under this approach, if the principal focus is on monetary relief, then these courts deny (b)(2) certification. For example, when the declaratory relief sought is simply a declaration of a defendant's liability for damages, courts have little difficulty holding that damages are the primary relief sought. On the other hand, when significant injunctive or declaratory relief is sought wholly apart from damages, courts are willing to conclude that injunctive relief predominates, even if the monetary relief requested is more than incidental. Finally, some courts will use a "hybrid" approach, certifying the equitable claims under (b)(2) and evaluating the damages claims under another subdivision of Rule 23(b), usually (b)(3).

In *Allison v. Citgo Petroleum Corp.*, 151 F.3d 402 (5th Cir. 1998), the Fifth Circuit took a different approach. In *Allison*, a group of Citgo employees brought a (b)(2) class action under Title VII claiming race discrimination. The named plaintiffs sought certification of a class of potentially 1,000 members to recover for defendant's allegedly discriminatory employment practices. In addition to seeking declaratory relief, the putative class sought compensatory and punitive damages, remedies that, according to the Fifth Circuit, were made available in Title VII cases pursuant to federal legislation enacted in 1991. The district court refused to certify the class under Rule 23(b)(2), holding that the monetary relief requested by the class was not sufficiently incidental to the injunctive relief to warrant (b)(2) certification. The Fifth Circuit, over a vigorous dissent, affirmed, holding that (b)(2) does not apply if the monetary claims are more than incidental. As the court noted:

Ideally, incidental damages should be only those to which class members automatically would be entitled once liability to the class (or subclass) as a whole is established.... Moreover, such damages should at least be capable of computation by means of objective standards and not dependent in any significant way on the intangible, subjective differences of each class member's circumstances. Liability for incidental damages should not require additional hearings to resolve the disparate merits of each individual's case.... Thus, incidental damages will, by definition, be more in the nature of a group remedy, consistent with the forms of relief intended for (b)(2) class actions. *Id.* at 415.

The Fifth Circuit noted that the claims for compensatory and punitive damages at issue did not qualify under (b)(2) because they would require individualized proof of injury to establish how each class member was personally affected by the discriminatory conduct.

Several circuits, including the Third and Eleventh, have followed *Allison*. Some circuits have not yet opined on the issue. Other circuits, however, have explicitly refused to follow *Allison*. The most notable case rejecting *Allison* is *Robinson v. Metro–North Commuter R.R.*, 267 F.3d 147 (2d Cir. 2001), *cert. denied,* 535 U.S. 951 (2002). In rejecting *Allison*'s "incidental damages" approach, the Second Circuit noted that when a (b)(2) action seeks both injunctive relief and non-incidental monetary damages, a district court must assess whether (b)(2) certification is appropriate in light of "the relative importance of the remedies sought, given all of the facts and circumstances of the case." Under this so-called *"ad hoc"* approach the court should thus consider whether: (1) "reasonable plaintiffs" would pursue the case for injunctive or declaratory relief "even in the absence of a monetary recovery," and (2) "the injunctive or declaratory relief sought would be both reasonably necessary and appropriate were the plaintiffs to succeed on the merits." In the Second Circuit's view, as long as injunctive or declaratory relief is "predominant" in terms of its value to the class, a court may certify a class that also seeks compensatory and punitive damages, even if those damages cannot be characterized as incidental. 267 F.3d at 164.

There can be no doubt that in those circuits following *Allison*, plaintiffs will have a difficult time obtaining (b)(2) certification when they seek significant monetary damages.

E. MEDICAL MONITORING UNDER RULE 23(b)(2)

Certification of a medical monitoring class pursuant to Rule 23(b)(1)(A) is discussed on p. 72, *supra*. In some instances, potential medical monitoring classes also seek certification under Rule 23(b)(2). For purposes of Rule 23(b)(2), the critical question to some courts is whether medical monitoring constitutes monetary or injunctive relief. Such courts are likely to view a request for money to pay for medical monitoring as monetary relief, but may view a request for a court-supervised program as a claim for injunctive relief. Other courts, however, have viewed a medical monitoring claim as primarily one for damages, even if the class is requesting a court-supervised program. These courts are concerned that permitting (b)(2) classes for medical monitoring would enable the class to circumvent the more exacting requirements of (b)(3).

F. NOTICE AND OPT–OUT RIGHTS

In contrast to Rule 23(b)(3) classes, Rule 23 does not mandate that class members in (b)(2) actions be notified that a class has been certified, and does not give (b)(2) class members a right to "opt out" of the class. Nonetheless, courts have occasionally ordered notice and opt-out rights in (b)(2) classes as a matter of discretion. Rule 23(b)(2)'s approach to notice and opt out, and the potential due process issues raised by a mandatory class seeking money damages, is discussed on pp. 172–174, *infra*.

G.   CLASSES APPROPRIATE FOR CERTIFICATION UNDER BOTH RULE 23(b)(2) AND RULE 23(b)(3)

As noted on pp. 82–83, *supra*, when a class qualifies for certification under both Rule 23(b)(1) and Rule 23(b)(3), courts usually prefer certification under (b)(1) rather than (b)(3), because the latter contains notice and opt-out requirements that inevitably lead to fewer people being bound. Put another way, mandatory classes achieve a greater scope of finality. Courts generally prefer (b)(2) classes over (b)(3) classes for the same reasons. Some courts, however, have stated that the issue of (b)(2) versus (b)(3) must be decided on a case-by-case basis after considering, among other things, the fairness to the class members under each approach.

H.   DEFENDANT CLASSES UNDER RULE 23(b)(2)

The courts are sharply divided over whether class action lawsuits can be filed *against* a class under

Rule 23(b)(2). The various approaches are discussed on pp. 341–342, *infra*.

I.   WHETHER RULE 23(b)(2) CONTAINS A "NECESSITY" REQUIREMENT

Many courts in (b)(2) cases have considered situations in which, because of the nature of injunctive or declaratory relief sought, the outcome of a lawsuit will have essentially the same effect upon all class members regardless of whether the court certifies the case as a class action. A good example would be an action challenging the constitutionality of a city ordinance, when the defendant locality acknowledges that the result of the litigation will bind it with respect to all citizens. In light of the city's acknowledgment, it is not clear whether a class action serves any purpose. Likewise, if a single plaintiff seeks a declaratory judgment that a statute or contract has a particular meaning or is unenforceable, a class action may not be necessary for similarly situated individuals to benefit from the ruling. Many defendants have thus attempted to invoke the doctrine of "necessity" as a reason to deny class certification: If a class suit is not necessary to achieve the desired result, then there is no reason to go through the time and effort of proceeding as a class action. This argument—which finds no explicit basis in the text of Rule 23—has usually been unsuccessful. Most courts hold that, if the requirements of Rule 23 are otherwise met, lack of necessity cannot be a reason to deny class certification. Of course, in some instances, it will not be clear whether the defendant would voluntarily comply with its duties to all class members in the absence of a classwide judgment. In those situations, in which the defendant refuses to concede that it will treat all class members the same, the defendant cannot plausibly argue that a class action is unnecessary.

§ 4.4   Rule 23(b)(3)

A.   OVERVIEW

When Rule 23 was revised in 1966, many scholars viewed Rule 23(b)(3) with particular skepticism. Rule 23(b)(3) replaced the old "spurious" class action with a new, untested "opt-out" class. Although the new (b)(3) purported to contain specific criteria for evaluating whether to certify a class, those criteria were—and remain today—vague and difficult to apply.

Rule 23(b)(3) states that a class action is maintainable if:

the court finds that the questions of law or fact common to the members of the class *predominate* over any questions affecting only individual members, and that a class action is *superior* to other available methods for the fair and efficient adjudication of the controversy (emphasis added).

Rule 23(b)(3) thus requires a court to make two inquiries: (1) Do the common issues "predominate" over issues affecting only individual members? (2) Is class treatment "superior" to other alternative methods for adjudicating the controversy? In articulating Rule 23(b)(3)'s purposes, the Advisory Committee Notes state:

> In the situations to which this subdivision relates, class-action treatment is not as clearly called for as in those described above [(b)(1) and (b)(2)], but it may nevertheless be convenient and desirable depending upon the particular facts. Subdivision (b)(3) encompasses those cases in which a class action would achieve economies of time, effort, and expense and promote uniformity of decision as to persons similarly situated, without sacrificing procedural fairness or bringing about other undesirable results.

B.   DEFINING PREDOMINANCE

The "predominance" inquiry arises because a court can assess the efficiencies of a putative class action only by considering the extent to which the common issues would advance the case overall. This analysis involves weighing and evaluating both the common and individualized issues. Neither Rule 23(b)(3) nor the Advisory Committee Notes define "predominance," and courts and commentators have struggled with how to apply that concept. Although courts and commentators agree that the predominance criterion is more rigid than merely showing the existence of a common legal or factual issue, *see* p. 43, *supra*, there is disagreement over what precisely is encompassed by predominance.

Some courts have stated that, although adjudication of common questions need not resolve the entire litigation, common questions predominate if resolving those questions at least signals the beginning of the end of the litigation. Other courts have applied a more lenient standard, finding that common questions may predominate if the litigation as a whole is materially advanced by resolving the common questions. Still other courts consider the extent to which individualized proof or arguments must still be made after resolution of the common issues. Under that approach, "[w]here, after adjudication of the classwide issues, plaintiffs must still introduce a great deal of individualized proof or argue a number of individualized legal points to establish most or all of the elements of their individual claims, such claims are not suitable for class certification under Rule 23(b)(3)." *Klay v. Humana, Inc.,* 382 F.3d 1241, 1255 (11th Cir. 2004), *cert. denied,* 543 U.S. 1081 (2005).

By contrast, however, some courts have resisted attempts to define the predominance inquiry in terms of quantity or quality of issues. Instead, they have recognized that the issue should be, in essence, a gut-level decision by the trial court upon consideration of how the case would actually be litigated.

At least one court has held that, in deciding predominance, a court is not limited to contested issues. Thus, for example, even if a defendant concedes classwide issues of liability, those issues may be counted in weighing whether common issues outweigh individual issues. *In re Nassau County Strip Search Cases*, 461 F.3d 219 (2d Cir. 2006). According to the Second Circuit, "[e]liminating conceded issues from Rule 23(b)(3)'s predominance calculus would undermine the goal of efficiency by requiring plaintiffs who share a 'commonality of the violation and the harm,' nonetheless to pursue separate and potentially numerous actions because, ironically, liability is so clear." *Id.* at 228.

One area in which individualized issues often exist is in determining damages for each class member. Many courts hold that the need to calculate damages on an individual basis does not preclude a finding of predominance, given the importance of the liability questions being resolved. This is particularly true when damages calculations are largely mechanical. Some courts, however, have rejected certification when individual damage calculations would have been exceedingly complex. Such concerns have been raised, for example, in complicated antitrust cases.

In calculating individual damages pursuant to a class action, courts have adopted a number of devices, such as using special masters or magistrates or employing separate juries to decide damage issues. Using special masters or magistrates over a party's objection raises Seventh Amendment right to jury trial issues. In addition, the practice of using multiple juries has recently been questioned in some contexts on Seventh Amendment "reexamination" grounds. *See* pp. 242–246, *infra*.

C. SPECIAL ISSUES REGARDING FRAUD AND RELIANCE

Plaintiffs often seek Rule 23(b)(3) certification in cases involving fraud or other torts sounding in fraud. The problem in such cases is that, because each member of the plaintiff class has been exposed to differing representations, individual issues may predominate over common issues. Defendants routinely contend that resolving the issue of reliance depends upon proving what representations were made to each plaintiff, what information was available to the plaintiff at the time of the representations, and whether each plaintiff actually—and reasonably—relied upon the representations. The difficulties surrounding fraud claims are discussed in the Advisory Committee Notes:

> [A] fraud perpetrated on numerous persons by the use of similar misrepresentations may be an appealing situation for a class action, and it may remain so despite the need, if liability is found, for separate determination of the damages suffered by individuals within the class. On the other hand, although having some common core, a fraud case may be unsuited for treatment as a class action if there was material variation in the representations made or in the kinds or degrees of reliance by the persons to whom they were addressed.

Many courts hold that the existence of individualized issues of reliance in a fraud case weighs against class certification. Indeed, the Fifth Circuit in *Castano v. American Tobacco Co.*, 84 F.3d 734 (5th Cir. 1996), articulated a bright-line rule that "a fraud class action cannot be certified when individual reliance will be an issue." *Id.* at 745. Several other courts have concluded that the presence of individualized reliance issues is fatal to class certification. A few courts, however, have taken the view that individualized reliance issues do not defeat class certification.

Some plaintiffs have avoided reliance issues by suing under consumer protection statutes that permit recovery for fraudulent conduct without proof of reliance. Other plaintiffs have argued that reliance issues should not foreclose class certification when the alleged misrepresentations were uniform across the members of the class.

D.   SUBMISSION OF A TRIAL PLAN

An important consideration under Rule 23(b)(3) is whether plaintiffs have proposed a viable plan to try the case. As the Advisory Committee Notes to the 2003 amendments point out, "[a]n increasing number of courts require a party requesting class certification to present a 'trial plan' that describes the issues likely to be presented at trial and tests whether they are susceptible of class-wide proof." Examples of such cases include *Wachtel v. Guardian Life Ins. of America,* 453 F.3d 179 (3d Cir. 2006), which quotes the Advisory Committee Notes with approval, and *Feder v. Electronic Data Systems Corp.*, 429 F.3d 125 (5th Cir. 2005), in which the court noted that a trial plan must be developed before certification when there are "potential trial complications."

E.   SECURITIES CASES: SPECIAL SITUATIONS IN WHICH A COURT MAY PRESUME RELIANCE

In securities fraud cases, courts have held that reliance should be *presumed* in certain circumstances. Courts have relied heavily on two seminal Supreme Court cases: *Basic v. Levinson,* 485 U.S. 224 (1988), and *Affiliated Ute Citizens v. United States*, 406 U.S. 128 (1972). A discussion of reliance in the securities fraud context is contained on pp. 323–329, *infra*.

It should be emphasized that, outside the securities area, courts have been reluctant to presume reliance under *Basic, Affiliated Ute*, or other doctrines.

F.   PREDOMINANCE AND MASS TORTS

"Mass torts" are discussed comprehensively on pp. 295–310, *infra*, but the subject of mass torts is significantly intertwined with the analysis of predominance under Rule 23(b)(3). Indeed, many of the most important (b)(3) cases in recent years have been mass tort cases, such as cases involving exposure to asbestos or injuries from allegedly defective products. As discussed on pp. 297–303, *infra*, several recent appellate court cases have raised concerns about permitting class certification in mass tort cases.

G. RULE 23(b)(3) PREDOMINANCE AND CHOICE-OF-LAW CONCERNS IN MULTI–JURISDICTIONAL CLASS ACTIONS

As discussed in detail below (*see* pp. 190–194, *infra)*, classes that consist of members from multiple states (or from different countries) implicate the predominance inquiry by creating potentially difficult choice-of-law issues. This is because many Rule 23(b)(3) class actions involve state-law claims that are being litigated in federal court pursuant to diversity jurisdiction. In those cases, the state whose law applies may vary from class member to class member. Under *Erie R.R. v. Tompkins*, 304 U.S. 64 (1938), and *Klaxon Co. v. Stentor Elec. Mfg. Co.*, 313 U.S. 487 (1941), federal courts in diversity cases must apply the choice-of-law rules of the state in which the court sits. In cases in which the classes at issue consist of claimants from all fifty states and the District of Columbia, there conceivably could be, depending upon the applicable choice-of-law rules, up to fifty-one different sources of law governing the claims (all 50 states plus the District of Columbia). This would be true, for example, when the applicable choice-of-law rules require the court in a nationwide class action to apply the law of the place of injury. Applying so many laws can be an onerous task, particularly in the context of a jury trial. Numerous courts have found that the need to apply so many different laws makes individual issues predominate over common issues, thus defeating class certification under (b)(3). Some courts, however, have certified classes notwithstanding the presence of such issues. *See* pp. 192–193, *infra*.

H.   SUPERIORITY IN RULE 23(b)(3) CLASSES: ALTERNATIVE METHODS FOR RESOLVING THE DISPUTE

In addition to predominance, Rule 23(b)(3) requires a court addressing a motion for class certification to assess whether class treatment is "superior to other available methods for the fair and efficient adjudication of the controversy." As the wording of (b)(3) reveals, courts must consider alternative methods of litigating a dispute, including the various methods discussed on pp. 367–429, *infra*. Such alternative methods include:

- Individual actions;

- Compulsory or permissive joinder under Rules 19 and 20, respectively;

- Intervention of nonparties under Rule 24;

- Consolidation under Rule 42(a);

- Multi-jurisdictional coordination, such as coordinated pretrial proceedings through the Judicial Panel on Multidistrict Litigation;

- Deferring to another judicial forum (federal or state court), or deferring to an administrative forum; or

- Employing a test case or bellwether approach, in which a small number of class members try their cases individually, with or without the defendant's agreement that, if the plaintiffs prevail, the defendant will not relitigate common issues when the remaining claimants bring suit.

The issue in each instance is whether some device other than a class action can resolve the cases fairly and efficiently, without the complexities inherent in a class action.

I. ASSESSING SUPERIORITY IN RULE 23(b)(3) CLASSES USING ENUMERATED FACTORS

In making an assessment of superiority, courts consider a wide variety of factors. These include the four that are listed in the text of subdivision 23(b)(3) itself:

(A) the interest of members of the class in individually controlling the prosecution or defense of separate actions;

(B) the extent and nature of any litigation concerning the controversy already commenced by or against members of the class;

(C) the desirability or undesirability of concentrating the litigation of the claims in the particular forum;

(D) the difficulties likely to be encountered in the management of a class action.

No single element listed in the rule is determinative, and as the Advisory Committee Notes make clear, the court may consider other factors when making a superiority determination.

The following sections discuss the four factors listed in Rule 23(b)(3) and other factors that courts have considered.

(1) Rule 23(b)(3)(A): Interest in Individual Control of Litigation

The first superiority factor listed in Rule 23(b)(3) is the "interest of members of the class in individually controlling the prosecution or defense of separate actions." Class actions are often justified on the ground that they permit the aggregation of claims of a group of people who may be similarly wronged, when each injured person's limited damages would make individual litigation cost-prohibitive. Courts have labeled such situations "negative value" suits.

Litigants occasionally try to certify class actions when each class member is alleged to have suffered significant damages. Courts are much more reluctant to certify such classes (as opposed to classes in which relief sought by individual class members is less substantial) because, given the large individual claims, each class member has a greater interest in controlling the litigation. Furthermore, given that each individual case could result in large damages, it is frequently economically viable for individual plaintiffs to obtain separate counsel. This point was made by the Fifth Circuit in *Castano v. American Tobacco Co.*, 84 F.3d 734 (5th Cir. 1996), as a reason for overturning the certification of a smoker class action. Statutes that permit the award of attorneys' fees may also lead a court to conclude that a class action is not superior, since the ability to recover legal costs may make individual litigation economically viable.

Ultimately, the inquiry under (b)(3)(A) is case-specific. As the Advisory Committee Notes explain:

> [T]he court should inform itself of any litigation actually pending by or against the individuals. The interests of individuals in conducting separate lawsuits may be so strong as to call for denial of a class action. On the other hand, these interests may be theoretic rather than practical; the class may have a high degree of cohesion and prosecution of the action through representatives would be quite unobjectionable, or the amounts at stake for individuals may be so small that separate suits would be impracticable. The burden that separate suits would impose on the party opposing the class, or upon the court calendars, may also fairly be considered.

Accordingly, the court must make a practical, realistic assessment of whether, among other things, the class members would prefer to litigate separately or collectively.

(2) Rule 23(b)(3)(B): Extent and Nature of Pending Litigation

Rule 23(b)(3)(B) requires a certifying court to consider "the extent and nature of any litigation concerning the controversy already commenced by or against members of the class." The rule does not make clear, however, whether the presence of other litigation is a factor in *favor* of class treatment or *against* it. Accordingly, the rule has been interpreted to call for a variety of different—and sometimes contradictory—assessments. For example, the presence of similar litigation has been viewed by some courts as showing the superiority of a class action (because the cases can be heard together). Other courts, however, have viewed the *absence* of similar litigation as favoring superiority (because individuals do not have enough at stake to bring their own claims).

Conversely, the absence of similar suits has been used as a reason to deny classes as non-superior. As the Fifth Circuit noted in *Castano,* "[o]ur specific concern is that a mass tort cannot be properly certified without a prior track record of trials from which the district court can draw the information necessary to make the predominance and superiority [analysis] required by rule 23." *Id.* at 747. Some courts have held, however, that the *presence* of similar suits makes the suit fail the superiority test (because the individual suits show that plaintiffs have sufficient incentives to sue without the need for a class).

If the other lawsuits pending are themselves class actions, courts are much less likely to find a new class action to be superior. On the other hand, even the pendency of a multi-jurisdictional class action will not necessarily deter a court from certifying a smaller class, particularly if the larger class has not yet been certified.

(3) Rule 23(b)(3)(C): Desirability or Undesirability of Concentrating the Litigation in the Particular Forum

Rule 23(b)(3)(C) requires a court considering class treatment to assess "the desirability or undesirability of concentrating the litigation of the claims in the particular forum." Courts sometimes reject certification under this subdivision if parties, witnesses, and evidence are dispersed throughout the nation. Courts have also frequently held, however, that concentration of the claims in the court's forum was desirable, despite dispersion of parties, witnesses, and evidence, either because the key facts complained of occurred in the forum state, or because inconvenience to many parties and witnesses was inevitable regardless of the forum chosen for the litigation.

(4) Rule 23(b)(3)(D): Manageability Issues

Rule 23(b)(3)(D) requires a court to consider "the difficulties likely to be encountered in the management of a class action." Of the four superiority factors specifically listed in Rule 23(b)(3), this factor has received the most attention from litigants and courts. As discussed on pp. 253–256, *infra*, however, when a class is being certified solely for settlement, a court need not inquire whether a case, if *tried*, would present serious manageability problems, since there will not be a trial. *Amchem Prods., Inc. v. Windsor*, 521 U.S. 591 (1997).

A significant focus under (b)(3)(D) involves how to identify and provide notice to members of the class. By virtue of the notice requirements imposed upon Rule 23(b)(3) classes by Rule 23(c)(2), *see* pp. 164–165, *infra*, a court must sometimes attempt to notify large classes dispersed throughout the country, with little or no information to go on. The difficulty of notifying any significant percentage of the class on an individual basis may counsel against certifying the class.

Although courts are reluctant to certify classes whose members would be difficult to communicate with or identify, the sheer size of a class does not necessarily result in the denial of certification. For example, the district court in *In re Domestic Air Transportation Antitrust Litigation*, 137 F.R.D. 677 (N.D.Ga. 1991), certified a class involving an estimated 12.5 million unidentified purchasers of airline tickets during a four-year period. The district court concluded that a class action was the only fair approach because the individual claims were so small that, in the absence of a class action, most claims would not be pursued. On the other hand, some courts have found that sheer numbers may make a class unmanageable. In *In re Hotel Telephone Charges*, 500 F.2d 86, 91 (9th Cir. 1974), for example, the Ninth Circuit held that a putative class of 40 million hotel guests was " 'beyond [a court's] capacity to manage or effectively control.' " (Citations omitted.)

As noted above, choice-of-law concerns with respect to multi-jurisdictional class actions impact a court's predominance inquiry under Rule 23(b)(3). These concerns also affect a court's manageability inquiry pursuant to Rule 23(b)(3)(D). This is because the existence of a class in which members' claims will be litigated pursuant to many different jurisdictions' laws makes the litigation much more difficult to administer. Similarly, although certification usually should not be denied solely on the ground that class members will have to prove their damages claims on an individualized basis, the difficulty in calculating damages may be a factor in assessing manageability, particularly if there are other manageability concerns as well.

J.   ASSESSING SUPERIORITY IN RULE 23(b)(3) CLASSES USING FACTORS OTHER THAN THOSE ENUMERATED

Courts are not limited to the four factors enumerated in Rule 23(b)(3), and have thus considered a variety of others in analyzing superiority. These factors have included whether an alternative regulatory mechanism exists and whether a class action would achieve significant judicial efficiencies.

CHAPTER 5

LITIGATING A CLASS ACTION

Litigating a class action is a multi-step process that begins with a complicated array of strategic decisions. Once those initial decisions have been made, the parties must then marshal their evidence to address the critical issue of class certification. Discovery is ordinarily central to this evidence-gathering function. If a class is certified, the parties must then address the multitude of case management and trial tasks necessitated by a class action. This chapter addresses these various strategic and legal issues that attorneys and parties must face in litigating a class action lawsuit.

§ 5.1 Strategic Considerations in Class Action Litigation

At the outset of a class-action suit, both the plaintiff and the defendant must consider a variety of strategic issues. These initial decisions frequently determine the ultimate success of the litigation. These decisions, of course, will be informed by the class action rule (Federal Rule 23 or its state counterpart), the relevant case law, and any applicable local rules.

111

A. PLAINTIFF'S PERSPECTIVE

Whether to Pursue a Class Action. A threshold decision of plaintiffs' counsel is whether to pursue a class action at all. In some instances, many of the benefits of a class action can be obtained by joinder of multiple plaintiffs (*see* pp. 368–377, *infra*), Rule 42 consolidation (*see* pp. 407–410, *infra*), the use of a test case with potential *res judicata* or collateral estoppel effects, or other approaches. Although a class action has certain advantages, such as the coercive effect that a certified class has on a defendant's willingness to settle, plaintiffs' counsel becomes a fiduciary to all potential members of the class by filing a class action suit. Thus, settling on behalf of individual plaintiffs becomes more difficult once a putative class action is certified.

Whom to Sue. Plaintiff must make an initial determination of which defendant(s) to name in the case. The issue cannot be determined merely by the simplistic rationale that more defendants are better because more money is available. Rather, plaintiff must evaluate the strategic implications of adding additional defendants. Each additional defendant potentially creates additional individualized issues that could be used by the defendant to defeat class certification. Also, multiple defendants may potentially utilize their collective resources to overwhelm the plaintiff and make the case difficult to prosecute effectively.

Where to Sue. This decision is often critical to the case. In general, plaintiffs' attorneys prefer state court and defense attorneys prefer federal court. The perception is that state court judges (many of whom are elected) are more willing than federal judges to certify sprawling class actions in the face of potential management issues. For that reason, the business community overwhelmingly supported legislative efforts (culminating in The Class Action Fairness Act ("CAFA")) to transfer most interstate class actions to federal court, whereas the plaintiffs' trial bar has overwhelmingly opposed such efforts. This general preference is not absolute, however, and plaintiffs' counsel must analyze the precise circumstances involved. For example, selecting a state court may mean giving up potentially viable federal causes of action, since the assertion of a federal claim will allow the defendant to remove the case to federal court. If plaintiffs' counsel selects state court, he or she must be careful to structure the case so that defendants cannot successfully remove the case on diversity jurisdiction or other grounds. The ability to structure a massive class action to avoid federal jurisdiction is now particularly challenging in light of CAFA. *See* pp. 214–227, *infra.*

In choosing a forum, it is important for parties to consider the specific procedural and substantive laws that are potentially involved. For example, Mississippi state procedural rules do not provide for a class action device as such, so the decision to stay in Mississippi state court as a practical matter means mass joinder rather than a class action. Also, state-specific restrictions on class certification may, in a particular case, render a federal forum more attractive than a state forum. *See* pp. 195–198, *infra*.

What Claims to File. As with deciding which defendants to sue, it is not necessarily true that more claims are better. Some claims are particularly susceptible to classwide determination, while other claims are often laden with individualized issues. For example, numerous courts have declined to certify fraud cases because of individual issues of reliance. *See* pp. 99–100, *supra*. Accordingly, when other viable claims exist, plaintiffs' counsel may decide to omit a fraud claim from the complaint to avoid the potential adverse ramifications from a class certification standpoint. Of course, plaintiffs' counsel must consider whether the omission of viable claims will raise adequacy of representation concerns. *See* pp. 62–63, *supra*.

How to Define the Class. This issue, likewise, must be decided by weighing the pros and cons of various alternatives. Although a broad class may have pecuniary or tactical advantages, it is not always true that a broader class is better. An expansive nationwide class action suit may entail so many individualized issues—such as complicated choice-of-law issues—that such a suit would be destined to fail as a class action. In addition, under CAFA, the scope of the class may affect the ability of plaintiffs to remain in state court. A more limited statewide class, in which only one state's law controls, may have a better chance of certification. Likewise, a class that is defined more narrowly in terms of the number of people and time period involved may have more chance of succeeding than an unwieldy class involving hundreds of thousands (or even millions) of people.

Which (and How Many) Representatives To Select. Careful consideration needs to be given to selecting class representatives. The threshold decision of how many representatives to utilize is a difficult one. On the one hand, having more than one representative helps ensure that the class action may continue if one of the representatives is found to be inadequate or atypical (or if that representative's claims become moot during the pendency of the action). On the other hand, having multiple representatives may give the defense the opportunity to demonstrate conflicts among the class representatives (and thus conflicts among the class members) or to show why individual issues for each representative (and thus each class member) would predominate over common issues. Another disadvantage of multiple representatives is the difficulty of preparing all of these plaintiffs for depositions.

The qualifications of the class representatives must be carefully scrutinized. Counsel must ensure that the representatives do not have negative characteristics—such as unsavory backgrounds or prior disapproval from other courts, particularly in the class action context—that could raise problems. Potential conflicts of interest could exist as well. In addition, the representatives must be individuals who will invest the time and effort necessary to learn the basic facts of the case and be effective witnesses.

When to Move for Class Certification. As discussed on p. 137, *infra*, many jurisdictions—both federal and state—have specific rules on when a plaintiff must move for class certification. In the absence of such a rule, plaintiffs' counsel faces the tactical issue as to whether to move for class certification early in the case or wait until a later point in time, such as after substantial discovery has taken place. This tactical decision will depend, in part, on whether, absent discovery, the defendant is likely to possess evidence showing individualized issues, such as evidence showing that class members suffered various types of injuries at different points in time. If discovery will permit defendant to make a better showing against the suitability of class certification, then plaintiff may well prefer to seek an early ruling on certification.

B.   DEFENDANT'S PERSPECTIVE

Defense counsel faces an equally challenging series of strategic issues. Many of these mirror those faced by plaintiffs' counsel.

Whether to Seek a Different Forum. Like plaintiffs' counsel, defense counsel must carefully analyze the pros and cons of a particular forum. Thus, defense counsel must evaluate whether, if the case is filed in state court, there are legal grounds for removing the case to federal court under CAFA (pp.

214–227, *infra*), under supplemental jurisdiction (pp. 208–213, *infra*), or otherwise. If there are such grounds, counsel must then decide whether, as a strategic matter, the defendant would be better off in federal or state court. Defense counsel must also decide whether a particular venue is preferable and, if so, whether legal arguments may be made to support that choice of venue.

Whether to Challenge the Viability of the Complaint at the Outset or Challenge the Class Allegations. One of the most difficult issues for defense counsel is whether to seek dismissal of the case at the outset or first obtain a ruling on class certification issues. A dismissal on the merits prior to certification binds only the class representative. If a defendant's position on the merits is extremely strong, defense counsel may in a rare case choose to play out the certification issue first—or even acquiesce in certification—so that the favorable decision on the merits will bind the entire class.

On the other hand, a decision certifying a case could have potentially disastrous consequences for the defendant, particularly if there is a significant risk that the defendant will lose the case at trial. In that event, a better option may be to seek dismissal on the merits first, before litigating the certification question. If the dismissal motion is successful, defense counsel can use the ruling as persuasive precedent in any future class or individual suit raising similar issues. If the dismissal motion is unsuccessful, the defendant can still contest class certification.

Whether to Challenge Class Certification Prior to the Initiation of Class Discovery. As discussed on pp. 120–122, *infra*, it is theoretically possible to challenge class allegations prior to any discovery. Defense counsel must decide whether to attempt to defeat class allegations on the pleadings or instead develop an evidentiary record after full discovery. If the class certification issues turn on factual matters, then it is obvious that an attack on the pleadings will not prevail. Moreover, if an initial motion challenging the class allegations on the pleadings is unsuccessful, that ruling could make the trial court skeptical when the defendant later challenges class certification after discovery. On the other hand, a successful motion early in the case would eliminate expensive and time-consuming discovery.

How to Attack the Class–Certification Issue. Defense counsel must decide whether to attack class certification based on the inability to satisfy Rule 23(b), on deficiencies with respect to class representatives (such as adequacy or typicality problems), or on other grounds. An attack focused exclusively on the class representatives could ultimately lead nowhere, because plaintiffs' counsel may simply substitute other representatives. Moreover, if there are other strong grounds for challenging class certification—such as a clear predominance of individualized issues—focusing on characteristics of the representatives could be viewed as nitpicking and could undermine the force of the predominance challenge.

On the other hand, challenging the class representatives could be effective if plaintiffs' counsel has few actual clients and has apparently chosen the best ones to serve as representatives. In that circumstance, successfully challenging the representatives could, as a practical matter, end the entire lawsuit.

§ 5.2   Discovery in Class Actions

This section addresses discovery in the class action context. Class discovery occurs at two stages: (1) at the pre-certification stage in connection with whether to certify a class; and (2) in connection with the merits of the lawsuit. In each of these contexts, several important issues arise.

A.   CLASS CERTIFICATION DISCOVERY

(1) Overview

The determination of whether a class should be certified is frequently the most important issue in the case. A plaintiff who fails to secure class certification may find that the case is financially impracticable to pursue on an individual basis. By the same token, a defendant who fails to defeat class certification may be forced to settle the case for a substantial sum or face the risk of economic devastation (and perhaps bankruptcy). In many instances, the most crucial factor in resolving whether class certification will be granted is the evidence each side marshals. The discovery process, of course, is crucial to this evidence-gathering process. Aggressive, thorough discovery is frequently decisive in class certification battles.

(2) Granting or Denying Class Certification Without Discovery

It is useful at the outset to discuss the circumstances in which courts may rule on class certification without discovery. Although pre-certification discovery often provides a court with important information bearing on the Rule 23(a) and (b) criteria, the decision whether to permit *any* discovery prior to the certification decision rests within the trial court's discretion. In some instances, a court may deny any discovery because it believes that it can determine, based solely on the pleadings, whether the requirements of Rule 23(a) and (b) are satisfied.

For example, if a case seeks certification for personal injuries and property damage on behalf of millions of people throughout the nation, a court may determine from the face of the complaint that the individualized issues—including choice-of-law questions, plaintiff-specific medical issues, causation issues, and so forth—are so pervasive that common issues cannot predominate. Alternatively, the requirements of Rule 23 may be so clearly satisfied on the face of the pleadings that a court may grant class certification without discovery. This could be the case, for example, in a securities fraud suit involving alleged misstatements in a prospectus by a major Fortune 500 company in which there are no individual issues of reliance and the defendant does not challenge the adequacy of the class representatives or class counsel. Likewise, class certification may be granted or denied without discovery when the opposition to certification is based solely on legal—as opposed to factual—arguments, such as an argument that class actions are barred by a specific statute for the claims at issue.

Courts usually do not grant or deny class certification without discovery. In circumstances in which the viability of class claims depends heavily on facts outside the pleadings, some appellate courts have held that the failure to allow any discovery is an abuse of discretion. Nonetheless, there is also authority for courts to take a restrictive view on class-certification discovery in certain circumstances. The *Manual for Complex Litigation (4th)* states that "[d]iscovery may not be necessary when claims for relief rest on readily available and undisputed facts or raise only issues of law (such as a challenge to the legality of a statute or regulation)." § 21.14. The *Manual* goes on to note, however, that "[s]ome discovery may be necessary ... when the facts relevant to any of the certification requirements are disputed" or "when the opposing counsel contends that proof of the claims or defenses unavoidably raises individual issues." *Id.* In some instances, parties may choose to rely almost entirely on evidence gathered outside of formal discovery. It is not uncommon for parties to submit extensive expert declarations and supporting material, even when little formal discovery has taken place. More often, however, the record will include both declarations and materials obtained during class-certification discovery.

(3) Conditional Certification or Deferral of Certification Pending Discovery

When the court finds that the pleadings are not adequate to decide the class certification issue, the usual approach is to defer ruling on the issue until discovery has been conducted. A few courts have taken a different approach: conditionally certifying the class, while preserving the opportunity to re-examine the initial determination if discovery reveals information suggesting the inappropriateness of class certification. These courts rely on the pre–2003 version of Rule 23(c)(1), which permitted "conditional certification" and provided that the ruling could be amended before a decision on the merits. Most courts recognized, however, even prior to the 2003 amendments, that a class should not be even conditionally certified unless a *prima facie* showing had been made that the case satisfied Rule 23(a) and (b). The 2003 amendments to Rule 23(c) delete the language permitting "conditional" certification, thus making clear that premature certification is inappropriate. As the Advisory Committee Notes to the amendment explain, "[a] court that is not satisfied that the requirements of Rule 23 have been met should refuse certification until they have been met." As discussed on pp. 146–147, *infra*, however, even after the 2003 amendments, there is some authority authorizing conditional certification.

The amendment retains the language that a certification order "may be altered," but sets the cutoff at "final judgment," rather than a "decision on the merits," to avoid ambiguity (*e.g.*, to confirm that alteration may be made even after liability, if remedial proceedings are still pending).

(4) Discovery of Merits Issues Before Class Certification

Merits discovery is discussed later in this chapter. One merits discovery issue, however, is directly linked to certification discovery: the permissibility of merits discovery before a ruling on class certification.

On the one hand, several courts have stated that, at the certification stage, the underlying merits of plaintiffs' claims should not be adjudicated. Instead, the scope of discovery should be limited to whether plaintiffs meet the requirements of Rule 23(a) and (b). A court may not require a plaintiff to prove its case on the merits to show that a class should be certified. *Eisen v. Carlisle & Jacquelin*, 417 U.S. 156 (1974).

On the other hand, courts making class-action rulings almost invariably conduct inquiries that relate to the merits of an action, particularly when class issues are inextricably linked with merits issues. For example, without information regarding the nature of different plaintiffs' claims, defendants normally cannot contest the plaintiffs' contention that common questions exist and that the named representatives' claims are typical of those of the class. Thus, as one court has recognized, discovery into the substantive nature of the claims may be necessary to determine whether the requirements of Rule 23 are satisfied. *Szabo v. Bridgeport Machs., Inc.*, 249 F.3d 672 (7th Cir. 2001) (discussed on pp. 142–143, *infra*).

Although some issues may relate to both certification and the merits, courts are usually able to distinguish between issues that are relevant solely to certification (or, perhaps, to both certification and the merits) and issues that are entirely merits-based. But this does not mean that courts universally forbid pure merits discovery before certification. In fact, courts occasionally open up all discovery even prior to certification. Many courts, however, bifurcate class and merits discovery, reasoning that the merits of the claims are not relevant at the certification stage. Some courts also reason that merits discovery could end up being wasteful: Absent certification, the case may not go forward at all, or it may go forward with the issues greatly narrowed. The *Manual for Complex Litigation (4th)* takes a cautious approach with respect to precertification merits discovery. It notes that "[a]llowing some merits discovery during the precertification period is generally more appropriate for cases that are large and likely to continue even if not certified." § 21.4. By contrast, the *Manual* states that, "in cases that are unlikely to continue if not certified, discovery into aspects of the merits unrelated to certification delays the certification decision and can create extraordinary and unnecessary expense and burden." *Id*. Ultimately, the decision whether to bifurcate class and merits discovery must be made on a case-by-case basis. As the Advisory Committee Notes to the 2003 amendments state, "[a]ctive judicial supervision may be required to achieve the most effective balance that expedites an informed certification determination without forcing an artificial and ultimately wasteful division between 'certification discovery' and 'merits discovery.'"

One tactical issue plays heavily in the debate about certification discovery versus merits discovery: One or both parties may want to use certification discovery as an opportunity to preview the opponent's case (or even to secure damaging substantive admissions). As a related matter, the parties may view certification discovery as an opportunity to obtain, at an early stage of the case, information that could facilitate a prompt, favorable settlement. Because of such strategic considerations, it would be overly simplistic to state that defendants always want class discovery and plaintiffs always oppose it (or vice versa). In some cases, plaintiffs may be the ones who are aggressively pursuing discovery, and defendants may be the ones who are resisting; in other cases, the positions may be reversed.

(5) Types of Pre–Certification Discovery

Depositions are frequently appropriate at the class certification stage, particularly when the person deposed is a proposed class representative or a defendant with critical information. In some instances, however, courts may require that a party initially seek discovery through written means (interrogatories, document requests, requests for admission) and pursue deposition discovery only upon a showing of good cause. Obviously, the limitations imposed will depend in part on the complexity of the case, the size of the putative class, the nature of relief sought (*i.e.,* damages, injunctive relief, or declaratory relief), and the amount of money at stake. Limitations on discovery may also reflect the "maturity" of the litigation. For instance, if the case involves a novel or untested theory or claim, a court may be more flexible in allowing discovery. On the other hand, if there is extensive information in the public domain as a result of prior trials or other proceedings involving similar claims and issues, a court may impose greater restrictions.

(6) Limitations on the Scope of Class Certification Discovery

Trial courts have wide discretion over the scope of discovery. In general, discovery regarding class certification issues is governed by Rules 26 through 37 of the Federal Rule of Civil Procedure, the same rules that govern discovery in all federal civil cases. As with discovery generally, the scope of class discovery under Rule 26 is limited to "any matter, not privileged, which is relevant to the subject matter involved in the pending action. . . ." If a court limits discovery to class certification issues, that limitation necessarily circumscribes the scope of what is relevant.

Class certification discovery may be relevant to a number of issues, such as numerosity, the adequacy or typicality of the class representatives, the appropriateness of the class definition, the existence and predominance of common issues, and other matters addressed by Rule 23(a) and (b). In applying the relevancy standard to class certification discovery, some courts have considered (1) the court's needs; (2) the amount of time discovery would entail; and (3) the probability that discovery would be helpful in resolving the issue of class certification. Courts also look at whether the discovery would be unduly burdensome.

The goal of trial courts in overseeing class discovery is to define discovery that is sufficiently broad to allow the parties to address the class certification requirements, but also is tailored to protect both sides from burdensome or privileged requests. Some common types of class discovery include: depositions of class representatives (particularly on the issues of adequacy and typicality) to probe their backgrounds, their familiarity with the case, and the existence of any unique or individualized defenses; depositions of corporate officials on the issue of Rule 23(b)(3) superiority to ascertain the existence of other similar lawsuits and the results in such cases; depositions of experts proffered to demonstrate or refute the existence of common issues; and discovery regarding plaintiffs' proposed trial plan for the case.

A court may restrict the scope of discovery in a variety of ways, particularly when the discovery sought would be unusually expensive or burdensome. Such restrictions include the following:

Geographic and Time Restrictions. A common restriction used by courts is to limit discovery to a particular geographic area (for instance, limiting discovery in an occupational exposure toxic tort case involving 300 different facilities to those where the named plaintiffs worked). Similarly, courts may restrict discovery by limiting the time frame for which information can be sought.

The Number of People Against Whom Discovery is Sought. Another common restriction is to limit discovery to a set number of people, a percentage of the group of targeted individuals, or a random sampling of the group. A court may also limit the discovery to particular classifications of people, such as limiting plaintiffs' discovery in an employment discrimination case to immediate supervisors of the named plaintiffs.

The Defined Class. Although courts generally allow discovery consistent with the breadth of the class definition, this is not true when the class definition is unreasonably broad. In that event, a court might limit discovery to a class that is at least potentially viable. For example, if a plaintiff files a putative nationwide class and the court is convinced at the outset that *at most* a statewide class would be warranted, the court might restrict discovery to claims and plaintiffs within a particular state.

Financial Issues. Courts are cautious about allowing wholesale discovery concerning the named plaintiffs' finances. Some courts, however, have permitted such discovery when it is necessary to evaluate whether the named plaintiffs possess the financial resources necessary to provide adequate representation to the class. Of course, this rationale is subject to the recognition that, as a practical matter, class counsel, not the representatives, are the ones who usually fund the case.

Courts are also cautious in allowing pre-certification discovery into the contingent fee or other fee arrangements between the named plaintiffs and their counsel or the arrangements for payment of costs and expenses. Here, too, discovery may be allowed when the information sought can be linked to the adequacy of class counsel or another Rule 23 requirement.

Other Limitations. Courts also commonly restrict class certification discovery by imposing strict schedules for completing discovery; limiting the number of depositions, interrogatories, and document requests; and limiting the length of depositions. In addition, as noted above, courts may restrict the types of discovery devices that can be used.

(7) Discovery of Names of Absent Class Members

Names Sought by Plaintiff. Plaintiffs frequently seek the identities of putative class members when such information is in the possession of defendants. For example, in an employment discrimination case, the defendant employer presumably can identify every person of a particular minority group who was laid off during a given period. The names of putative class members are certainly relevant at the notice stage. Rule 23(c)(2)(B) requires the court to "direct to class members the best notice practicable under the circumstances, including individual notice to all members who can be identified through reasonable effort."

The Supreme Court has indicated that courts may require a defendant to help identify the class members to whom notice must be sent by compiling a list of names and addresses. *Oppenheimer Fund, Inc. v. Sanders*, 437 U.S. 340 (1978). At the precertification stage, however, defendants are likely to contend that plaintiffs do not need to obtain the *identities* of class members but only information about the *numbers* of class members. Courts often refuse to allow discovery of the class members' identities at the pre-certification stage, sometimes out of concern that plaintiffs' attorneys may be seeking such information to identify potential new clients, as opposed to using the information to establish the appropriateness of certification.

Names Sought by Defendant. Courts are likewise reluctant to require plaintiffs, at the pre-certification stage, to provide defendants with the names and addresses of putative class members. Because discovery of putative class members is susceptible to being used by defendants to harass and embarrass potential class members, courts have frequently imposed limits on the scope of such discovery. Some courts have also noted concerns that, if given names of potential class members, defendants might approach identified individuals and attempt to compromise or settle their claims outside the context of the case. Although defendants have frequently tried to justify the need for names by pointing to the Rule 23 criteria, courts have generally not been receptive to arguments that the identification of unnamed class members is relevant to such issues as numerosity, typicality, commonality, and adequacy.

Other courts, by contrast, have been more lenient in permitting such discovery, particularly when the defendant is willing to receive the information pursuant to a protective order that limits (1) the persons who may receive the information and (2) the uses that may be made of it.

(8) Pre–Certification Discovery Directed at Absent Class Members

Although the issue of discovery directed at absent class members usually arises at the merits discovery phase following class certification, it also may arise prior to certification. While such discovery is not *per se* unavailable prior to class certification, courts generally disfavor it. Courts must balance the competing interests of the absent class members in remaining passive and those of the defendant in acquiring information to defeat class certification.

Courts considering the scope of discovery against absent class members generally will permit such discovery only if: (1) the defendant demonstrates a clear need for the information in order to litigate class issues; (2) the court is satisfied that the discovery requests are narrowly tailored to their purpose; (3) the discovery requests are tendered in good faith and are not unduly burdensome; and (4) the information is not available from the representative parties.

Some courts prefer document requests and interrogatories over depositions because the former are often less intrusive. Accordingly, the party seeking discovery will in many instances bear a heavier burden to justify depositions.

The type of plaintiff involved may affect a court's willingness to allow pre-certification discovery from absent class members. For instance, a court may be more inclined to allow such discovery when the absent class members are organized groups and businesses rather than individuals with small claims and limited means. One approach that some courts have adopted is to allow discovery—written discovery and, perhaps, depositions—from a sample of absent class members.

(9) Expert Discovery and Judicial Gatekeeping

In *Daubert v. Merrill Dow Pharmaceuticals, Inc.,* 509 U.S. 579 (1993), the Supreme Court recognized that trial courts must serve a gatekeeping function by ensuring that scientific expert testimony is both relevant and reliable. The Supreme Court subsequently held that *Daubert* applies not only to scientific expert testimony but also to other expert testimony involving technical or specialized knowledge. *Kumho Tire Co. v. Carmichael,* 526 U.S. 137 (1999).

Whether *Daubert* and *Kumho* apply with full force at the class certification stage is unclear. The Second Circuit has noted that *Daubert* "involves an inquiry distinct from that for evaluating expert evidence in support of a motion for class certification. . . ." *In re Visa Check/MasterMoney Antitrust Litig.,* 280 F.3d 124, 132 n.4 (2d Cir. 2001). Nonetheless, even at the class certification stage, the court must assess the testimony of all experts proffered. As the *Visa* court noted, "[a] district court must ensure that the basis of the expert opinion is not so flawed that it would be inadmissible as a matter of law." But, according to the *Visa* court, "a district court may not weigh conflicting expert evidence. . . ." *Id.* at 135. Rather, "[t]he question for the district court at the class certification stage is whether plaintiffs' expert evidence is sufficient to demonstrate common questions of fact warranting certification of the proposed class, not whether the evidence will ultimately be persuasive." *Id.* (Later Second Circuit authority, rendered as this text was going to press, has retreated from *Visa* and has indicated that a court may need to weigh conflicting expert testimony in ruling on class certification.) In contrast to *Visa,* some courts have taken a very active role in scrutinizing (and even striking) expert testimony at the class certification stage. The trend clearly favors the latter approach.

B. POST–CERTIFICATION MERITS DISCOVERY IN CLASS ACTIONS

(1) General Principles

Although full-blown post-certification merits discovery is normally allowed against class representatives, courts generally limit merits discovery against absent class members. Courts are sensitive to the fact that an absent class member's role is very different from that of a class representative. The latter expects to be subjected to considerable discovery, including document requests, interrogatories, and (in many cases) depositions. Absent class members, by contrast, normally assume that their role in the case will be largely passive, at least in the early stages of the case. Nonetheless, if the trial court concludes that discovery of absent class members would be relevant to the issues for trial and is not being sought for harassment purposes, the court has discretion to order such discovery. Indeed, given the stakes in some class action trials, many courts are willing to allow at least some merits discovery against absent class members.

As is often true at the certification stage, courts may limit the discovery that may be directed to absent class members. *The Manual for Complex Litigation (4th)* provides several examples of such limitations, including restricting discovery to only a sample of class members, requiring the use of questionnaires as opposed to potentially more burdensome interrogatories, or severely limiting the number of interrogatories. And, as is often the case at the certification stage, courts often prefer written discovery over depositions.

(2) Discovery of the Unnamed Class Members' Individual Claims

One difference between merits discovery and certification discovery is that, at some point (if the class claims are successful after a classwide trial), individual class members will have to prove their membership in the class as well as their entitlement to damages. Obviously, at that stage of the case, defendants have a compelling argument for seeking discovery from all participating class members (who, at this point, are no longer absent but are coming forward to share in the recovery).

(3) Penalties for Noncompliance With Discovery Requests

Noncompliance with discovery by unnamed class members—particularly when specifically authorized by the court—has occasionally resulted in sanctions. The Seventh Circuit held in a leading case that unnamed class members who fail to respond to discovery are subject to all of the sanctions allowed under the Federal Rules of Civil Procedure, including dismissal of their claims with prejudice. *Brennan v. Midwestern United Life Ins. Co.*, 450 F.2d 999 (7th Cir. 1971). A few courts, however, have held that unnamed class members are not parties and thus cannot be sanctioned under Rule 37.

(4) Stay of Discovery Pending Dispositive Motions

If a defendant has filed a dispositive motion, such as a motion to dismiss for failure to state a claim, the defendant may be able to convince the court to stay all discovery pending a ruling on the motion. It is within the discretion of the court, however, to decide whether discovery should continue pending the court's ruling on a dispositive motion.

§ 5.3 The Class Certification Decision

A. OVERVIEW

Without question, the ruling on class certification is frequently the most important decision in a class action lawsuit. But even though the entire case may depend on the certification decision, there are few rules governing motions to certify a class. The following sections discuss the rules and practices relating to the certification decision.

B. TIMING OF CERTIFICATION DECISION

Prior to the 2003 amendments, Rule 23(c)(1) directed that the certification decision should be made by the court "[a]s soon as practicable after commencement of an action brought as a class action." Amended Rule 23(c)(1)(A) changes that language to state that "the court must—at an early practicable time—determine by order whether to certify the action as a class action." The Advisory Committee Notes indicate that the pre–2003 standard "neither reflect[ed] prevailing practice nor capture[d] the many valid reasons that may justify deferring the initial certification decision." For example, extensive, time-consuming discovery may be necessary before the decision can be made. In addition, the parties may need time, prior to the certification decision, to address how the proposed class action would actually be tried. The Advisory Committee Notes caution, however, that the court should "not unjustifiably delay[]" the certification decision.

The appellate courts generally leave the timing of the certification decision to the discretion of the trial courts. Many trial courts, however, have adopted time frames in their local rules specifying when motions for class certification must be made, typically thirty to ninety days after filing of the complaint. Some courts have strictly applied these time frames and refused to consider untimely class certification motions. Other courts hold that these time limits may be extended for good cause.

There is no rule of thumb regarding how long a trial court should take to rule on class certification. Some courts decide the issue relatively promptly, while others take many months (or even years) to decide the question.

The timing of class certification affects a variety of important litigation issues. An early ruling on certification helps define the structure of the litigation, the parties, the motion procedures to be followed, and the approach to settlement negotiations. Additionally, the denial of class certification usually means that the clock begins running again on the statute of limitations applicable to the unnamed class members' individual claims. *See* pp. 194–204, *infra.*

The timing of the certification decision also affects the defendant's decision whether and when to make a motion to dismiss on the merits. Courts are split over the advisability of ruling on dispositive motions prior to ruling on class certification. Some courts hold that dispositive motions prior to certification are permissible and will rule on these motions prior to certification. Other courts, while not entirely prohibiting the resolution of dispositive motions prior to certification, reason that pre-certification resolution of dispositive motions may be problematic and discourage the practice. The disadvantage to the defendant of making a motion on the merits prior to certification is that, even if the motion is successful, it will bind only the named plaintiffs, not any of the unnamed class members.

C.   RAISING THE CERTIFICATION ISSUE

In general, the named plaintiff raises the issue of class certification in a motion to the court (usually accompanied by supporting briefs, declarations, and exhibits). The plaintiff has the burden of establishing that a class action is proper and that the requirements of Rule 23 are satisfied.

The defendant, however, need not wait for the plaintiff to raise the issue of class certification. The defendant may raise the issue through a motion to deny class certification or a motion to strike the class allegations. When the defendant makes such a motion, the motion is frequently accompanied by a motion to dismiss or a motion for summary judgment.

As discussed on pp. 126–129, *supra*, the trial court has discretion regarding whether to permit discovery on class certification issues. When the court permits discovery on certification issues, it will often defer discovery on the merits until a later date.

D. COURT'S OBLIGATION TO RULE

The general rule is that, absent certification by the trial court, a suit may not properly proceed as a class action. One exception to that rule is when a class is implicitly certified. This arises when the court enters a judgment for classwide relief in the absence of making a formal determination as to class certification. This can occur, for example, where neither party moves for a determination as to class status, even though the complaint seeks classwide relief. Courts, however, will not permit an action to proceed as a class action when the plaintiff's complaint does not seek classwide relief. In other words, a court may not *sua sponte* convert an action brought in an individual capacity that does not seek classwide relief into a class action. Likewise, a court may not grant classwide relief that is not sought in the complaint.

When a plaintiff's complaint seeks classwide relief in addition to individual relief, but the plaintiff does not move for class certification, the question arises as to whether the trial court must nonetheless address the issue of class certification. In *Bieneman v. City of Chicago,* 838 F.2d 962, 964 (7th Cir. 1988), the Seventh Circuit held that the court must do so and cannot avoid the issue by assuming that the failure to raise the issue was, in effect, an amendment to delete class allegations.

E. APPROPRIATENESS OF INQUIRY INTO THE MERITS

The Supreme Court in *Eisen v. Carlisle & Jacquelin*, 417 U.S. 156 (1974), stated that "nothing in either the language or history of Rule 23 ... gives a court any authority to conduct a preliminary inquiry into the merits of a suit ... to determine ... [if] it ... may be maintained as a class action." *Id.* at 177. Thus, when determining if a class action may be maintained, a court should not inquire into whether plaintiffs have stated a cause of action or will prevail on the merits. Instead, the focus should be on whether the requirements of Rule 23 are satisfied. This general rule against reviewing the merits of the claims has been justified as necessary to protect the parties' interests, since a court at the certification stage is not bound by the rules of evidence or procedure that govern at trial and cannot know at certification what the ultimate proof will be.

Nonetheless, it is sometimes impossible to avoid all consideration of the merits, particularly when evidence may bear on both class certification *and* merits issues. For instance, an inquiry into the timeliness or validity of the class representatives' claims may be necessary to determine if the typicality and adequacy of representation requirements of a putative Rule 23(b)(3) class are satisfied. In *Castano v. American Tobacco Co.*, 84 F.3d 734 (5th Cir. 1996), the Fifth Circuit held that, in ruling on class certification, a trial court must look beyond the pleadings to understand the claims, defenses, factual allegations, and applicable substantive law. The court interpreted *Eisen* as not limiting the court's ability to look beyond the pleadings, but instead as restricting courts from using the *strength* of a plaintiff's claim as a basis for resolving class certification issues.

Some courts look beyond the pleadings to see if the litigation is "mature" prior to certifying a class. The concern is that, if a case does not involve a mature claim, a court cannot evaluate whether it would be appropriate for class certification. Litigation is "mature" when there have been a number of prior trials and verdicts that provide information for assessing the suitability of a case for class treatment. Looking at these prior verdicts involves at least some consideration of how prior similar cases have fared in the courts.

As a related matter, at least one court has explicitly analyzed the success of prior similar litigation to determine whether class action treatment is appropriate. In *In the Matter of Rhone–Poulenc Rorer, Inc.*, 51 F.3d 1293 (7th Cir. 1995), the Seventh Circuit found that a class action was inappropriate in part because only one out of thirteen individuals who had previously litigated the same claims to verdict had prevailed against the defendant. According to the court, this showed a "great likelihood that the plaintiffs' claims . . . lack legal merit," and thus demonstrated the unfairness that "jury number fourteen [the class action jury] may disagree with twelve of the previous thirteen juries—and hurl the industry into bankruptcy." *Id.* at 1299–1300.

A court may also need to consider the merits when determining whether to certify a Rule 23(b)(1)(B) class. In these cases, the defendants often have limited funds in relation to the judgments that plaintiffs are likely to receive, and early judgments may eliminate any chance of recovery by subsequent claimants. *See* pp. 73–83, *supra*. In assessing this probability, courts sometimes analyze facts regarding the assets available to satisfy a judgment (or judgments) and the amounts that the plaintiffs are likely to receive. Similarly, in determining whether a class representative is subject to a unique defense that would defeat typicality, it may be necessary to decide whether the representative's claim is barred by the statute of limitations. All of these examinations require inquiries into the merits of the litigation.

In an important decision, the Seventh Circuit has explicitly recognized that, in deciding class certification, a court will often need to address merits issues that also relate to certification issues. *Szabo v. Bridgeport Machines, Inc.,* 249 F.3d 672 (7th Cir. 2001). According to the court, "[t]he proposition that a district judge must accept all of the complaint's allegations when deciding whether to certify a class cannot be found in Rule 23 and has nothing to recommend it." *Id.* at 675. In the Seventh Circuit's view, "a judge should make whatever factual and legal inquiries are necessary under Rule 23," including inquiries "relevant to both the merits and class certification." *Id.* at 676–77. The court explained that, although *Eisen* bars a court from saying "I'm not going to certify a class unless I think the plaintiff will prevail," nothing in Rule 23 or in *Eisen* "prevents the district court from looking beneath the surface of a complaint to conduct the inquiries identified in [Rule 23] and exercise the discretion it confers." *Id.* at 677. A number of federal appellate and district courts have explicitly followed *Szabo*. Some courts, however, have adhered to the view that a court addressing class certification may not assess the merits but must accept the allegations of the complaint as true.

F.   THE CERTIFICATION HEARING

(1) Need for a Hearing on Class Certification

Rule 23 does not require a hearing when determining class certification, and some courts have held that parties are not entitled to a hearing unless they can show that they would be prejudiced absent a hearing. Nonetheless, courts generally hold some type of hearing before ruling on class certification issues, especially when a court determines that it must look beyond the pleadings. Some cases emphasize the need for a hearing before *denying* class certification. Courts have also noted the need for a hearing when factual disputes exist.

Even if a hearing is held, the litigants are not always allowed to put on evidence. Whether an evidentiary hearing is called for (and, if so, what evidence will be allowed) depends upon the particular case. In many cases, oral argument (or even just written briefing) will suffice, particularly when the pertinent facts are undisputed. On the other hand, if the facts are complicated or hotly disputed, an evidentiary hearing may be essential.

(2) Burden of Proof and Procedures at the Hearing

At the hearing, the burden of establishing that all the requirements of Rule 23 are met and that a claim may proceed as a class action rests with the party seeking certification. Conclusory allegations will not satisfy plaintiffs' burden. Rather, courts require an adequate statement of facts indicating that each of the requirements of Rule 23 is met. Although some courts state that all doubts should be resolved in favor of certification, other courts emphasize that a rigorous analysis is required to determine if the requirements of Rule 23 are met.

With respect to procedures at the hearing, the *Manual for Complex Litigation (4th)* advises that the hearing should not be a mini-trial to adjudicate the merits of the action. Moreover, the court may control the nature of the hearing, limiting the number of witnesses and prescribing other procedures. Factual issues can often be narrowed by the submission of uncontradicted declarations, stipulations, and answers to requests for admission.

(3) Expert Testimony at the Class Certification Stage

As noted above (*see* pp. 132–134, *supra*), courts are not uniform with respect to the propriety of conducting a *Daubert* challenge to expert testimony at the class certification stage. Some have conducted full *Daubert* scrutiny, while others simply inquire whether the expert's methodology is so poor as to be "fatally flawed." *In re Visa Check/Master-Money Antitrust Litig.*, 280 F.3d 124, 135 (2d Cir. 2001).

(4) Reasons for the Certification Ruling

The determination of whether an action may be maintained as a class action is left to the discretion of the trial court and may be reversed on appeal only if the trial court abuses that discretion. Rule 23 does not on its face require that the certification order be accompanied by findings and conclusions. (The only exception is that a court certifying a Rule 23(b)(3) class must "find[]" that the predominance and superiority requirements are satisfied.) Nonetheless, as the *Manual for Complex Litigation (4th)* points out, "the court should enter findings of fact and conclusions, addressing each of the applicable criteria of Rule 23. Failure to do so may result in reversal or remand for further proceedings after interlocutory appeal under Rule 23(f)." § 21.21. Indeed, the Fifth Circuit has stated that "when certifying a class a district court must detail with sufficient specificity how the plaintiff has met the requirements of Rule 23." *Vizena v. Union Pacific R.R. Co.,* 360 F.3d 496, 503 (5th Cir. 2004). In addition, the Third Circuit has held that the class certification order or accompanying memorandum must provide "a clear and complete summation of the claims, issues, or defenses subject to class treatment . . . ." *Wachtel v. Guardian Life Ins. Co. of America,* 453 F.3d 179, 185 (3d Cir. 2006).

G. CERTIFICATION OPTIONS

(1) Conditional Certification

As discussed on p. 122, *supra*, before the 2003 amendments, Rule 23(c)(1) provided that an order certifying a class "may be conditional. . . ." The 2003 amendments deleted this language. According to the Advisory Committee Notes, "[a] court that is not satisfied that the requirements of Rule 23 have been met should refuse certification until they have been met." Despite the deletion of language permitting conditional certification, at least one court has indicated that the 2003 amendments do not foreclose the use of conditional certification. *Denney v. Deutsche Bank Sec., Inc.,* 443 F.3d 253 (2d Cir. 2006). *Denney* raised the question whether conditioning certification solely for settlement purposes was proper. In concluding that it was, the court stated: "[C]onditional certification survives the 2003 amendment to Rule 23.... [I]f the requirements of Rule 23(a) and (b) are met, certification may be granted, conditionally or unconditionally." *Id.* at 270.

In all events, most courts agree that, while the amended rule prohibits a court from certifying a class when there is doubt about whether the requirements for certification are met, it does allow the court to modify its ruling in the face of changed circumstances. Specifically, Rule 23(c)(1)(C) allows a court to alter or amend a certification order, provided that the court makes the change before rendering a final judgment in the case. The Advisory Committee Notes point out, for example, that the class definition may need to be altered (new notice and opt-out may be required), or the court may decide that decertification is necessary.

A party seeking revocation or modification of a class certification ruling must normally show newly discovered facts or an intervening change in the law to support the request. The court may modify its certification decision *sua sponte*, but usually will do so only if a significant change in the facts or law warrants such a modification.

(2) Use of Subclasses

Rule 23(c)(4) permits the use of subclasses to resolve problems relating to the Rule 23 requirements. Whether to permit subclasses normally rests with the discretion of the trial court, although in some circumstances subclasses may be required—such as when a case involves claims of exposure to a harmful substance by those who have suffered physical injuries and those who have not. *Ortiz v. Fibreboard*, 527 U.S. 815 (1999).

It is fundamental that each subclass must satisfy all of Rule 23(a) and at least one subdivision of Rule 23(b). The proponent of class certification bears the burden of showing that an action may be properly divided into subclasses.

Subclasses are often used to resolve difficulties that arise within classes after certification, and may also be used prior to certification of a larger class. In addition, subclasses are often required when it appears that the class representatives and class members have conflicting factual or legal positions. Subclasses have also been used when there are claims or theories of damages unique to certain class members. The *Manual for Complex Litigation (4th)* points out that "[s]ubclassing sometimes represents a workable solution for differences in substantive law and for choice-of-law difficulties." § 21.23.

On occasion, the use of subclasses may complicate rather than remedy the problems in a class action. For instance, multiple subclasses may lead to confusion and conflicts among the classes, their representatives, and their counsel, requiring greater judicial supervision (and possibly resulting in serious manageability problems). Moreover, if too many subclasses are created, plaintiffs may have difficulty showing that each subclass satisfies the numerosity requirement.

(3) Issue Certification and Bifurcation

Rule 23(c)(4)(A) permits class certification of particular issues. The court may grant partial certification *sua sponte* or upon the motion of one of the parties. The court may separate claims or issues within a complaint, certifying some as a class action and leaving others as individual claims or issues. Courts may also certify part of the action as a Rule 23(b)(3) class action with opt-out rights and another portion of the same action as a Rule 23(b)(1) or Rule 23(b)(2) class action, neither of which requires opt-out rights. Courts have also bifurcated the issues of liability and damages by certifying a class action for purposes of liability, leaving the individual class members to pursue their damage claims individually following a determination of the defendant's liability. The decision whether to bifurcate a class action is within the discretion of the trial court after conducting an inquiry into the factual and legal aspects of the case.

The requirements of Rule 23 must, of course, be met for the court to permit partial certification. Application of those requirements, however, has generated confusion, especially with respect to whether common issues "predominate" in a (b)(3) class action. Some courts have found that only the issue for which partial certification is sought should be examined to determine if all the requirements of Rule 23 have been fulfilled. *See, e.g., In re Nassau*

County Strip Search Cases, 461 F.3d 219 (2d Cir. 2006). These courts reason that, if an issue certified under Rule 23(c)(4)(A) had to predominate over all of the other issues in the case, Rule 23(c)(4)(A) would be superfluous. Other courts, however, hold that, in determining whether to grant partial certification, the entire cause of action must be examined and must satisfy the requirements of Rule 23. *See, e.g., Castano v. American Tobacco Co.,* 84 F.3d 734 (5th Cir. 1996). These courts reason that, absent such a rule, a court would be able to find some issue to certify in every class action, thereby nullifying the predominance requirement. Without explicitly weighing in on this conflict, the *Manual for Complex Litigation (4th)* notes that a Rule 23(c)(4)(A) certification should be granted only if it "materially advances the disposition of the litigation as a whole," and that "[i]f the resolution of an issues class leaves a large number of issues requiring individual decisions, the certification may not meet this test." § 21.24.

In ordering a bifurcation or partial certification, the trial court would normally try the common issues first, followed by trials of the individualized issues. Because of such bifurcation, the court should examine whether issue certification raises Seventh Amendment issues. *See* pp. 242–246, *infra.*

One important case upholding issue certification (without citing Rule 23(c)(A)) is *Mejdrech v. Met–Coil Sys. Corp.,* 319 F.3d 910 (7th Cir. 2003). There, in an opinion by Judge Posner, the court upheld certification of two issues in a case alleging groundwater contamination by a noxious solvent (TCE): (1) "whether [defendant] leaked TCE in violation of law," and (2) "whether the TCE reached the soil and groundwater beneath the homes of the class members." *Id.* at 911. The court recognized that, after the resolution of these common issues, "[t]he individual class members [would] still have to prove the fact and extent of their individual injuries." *Id.* at 911–12. But the existence of those individual issues did not prevent the certification of the two classwide issues.

(4) Multiple or Competing Classes

It is not uncommon for multiple class actions to be filed in various federal courts or in both state and federal courts. Sometimes the same class lawyers are involved; sometimes different lawyers are involved in the different cases. In some instances, the definitions and scope of the various cases are the same; in others, they differ substantially. The *Manual for Complex Litigation (4th)* contains a number of possible options for courts faced with such multiple class actions, including: asking the Judicial Panel on Multidistrict Litigation (*see* pp. 411–416, *infra*) to consolidate the federal cases before one federal judge for pretrial proceedings; coordinating with other judges (both state and federal) on class certification, discovery, and motions; defining the class to exclude members of an already-certified state court class; allowing an already-certified state court class to go forward without certifying a federal court class action; and expanding the federal case to take into account the claims and parties involved in other putative class actions.

When one of multiple class actions is resolved, either by trial or settlement, it may have *res judicata* implications for other pending class actions involving overlapping class members. *See* pp. 237–239, *infra.*

(5) Decertification

As part of the conditional nature of a certification decision, a court retains the power to decertify a class at any time prior to a final decision on the merits. Indeed, courts have occasionally decertified classes years into a lawsuit. For instance, decertification may be warranted if unanticipated complexities are revealed during discovery, or if the class representatives prove to be inadequate and no substitutes are readily available. Of course, decertification means that the parties and the court have wasted substantial resources on the case. Thus, courts should not rely on the possibility of decertification as a reason to avoid scrutinizing the appropriateness of class certification at the outset.

§ 5.4 Orders Controlling Class Proceedings

Rule 23(d) gives the court the discretion to make orders controlling class action litigation. The Advisory Committee Notes state that this subdivision "is concerned with the fair and efficient conduct of the action." Specifically, Rule 23(d) allows the court to issue the following types of orders: orders relating to the course of proceedings; requiring notice to class members; imposing conditions on the representative parties or intervenors; requiring amendment of pleadings to eliminate allegations as to class representation; and addressing similar procedural matters. Rule 23(d) contains five separate subdivisions, which are discussed below. It should be noted at the outset, however, that courts frequently enter orders authorized by Rule 23(d) without identifying the particular subdivision and often without identifying Rule 23(d) at all.

A.   RULE 23(d)(1)

Rule 23(d)(1) states that the court may make appropriate orders "determining the course of proceedings or prescribing measures to prevent undue repetition or complication in the presentation of evidence or argument." The court's power under this rule is often exercised in conjunction with other federal rules, such as Federal Rule of Civil Procedure 16, which governs pretrial conferences.

Courts have stayed proceedings and excluded intervenors under 23(d)(1). For instance, courts have stayed actions where similar actions are pending before several courts in order to await the outcome of the other litigation. Courts have also temporarily stayed actions in an effort to encourage alternative forms of resolution. In addition, courts have directed that a class be closed to future intervenors in order to simplify the litigation in accordance with the spirit of Rule 23.

Prior to the adoption of the amendments to Rule 23 in 2003, the general rule was that the class representatives controlled the decision to appoint lead counsel for the class. In some circumstances, courts used their power under (d)(1) to appoint lead counsel. Now, however, Rule 23(g) requires the court to appoint class counsel. *See* pp. 63–65, *supra*.

B.   RULE 23(d)(2)

Rule 23(d)(2) provides courts with the power to require that notice be given of any step in the litigation. Rule 23(d)(2) is addressed on p. 174, *infra*.

C.   RULE 23(d)(3)

Rule 23(d)(3) enables a court in a class action to make appropriate orders "imposing conditions on the representative parties or intervenors." The Advisory Committee Notes state that "[s]ubdivision (d)(3) reflects the possibility of conditioning the maintenance of a class action, *e.g.*, on the strengthening of the representation ... and recognizes that the imposition of conditions on intervenors may be required for the proper and efficient conduct of the action." The court has the full spectrum of judicial sanctions available for noncompliance with its orders under this subdivision.

Some courts have required the representative to divide one class action into multiple ones as a condition to maintaining a class action. This authority is related to the court's power to create subclasses and is often exercised at the certification stage of a class action. *See* pp. 147–149, *supra*. The court, however, may not require individuals to consolidate their individual actions into a class action.

Courts sometimes condition the maintenance of a class action upon strengthening class representation. For instance, a court may order intervention of another class member when concerns exist about the adequacy of the class representatives. Likewise, a court may require appointment of additional counsel when it has concerns over the adequacy of existing counsel.

As Rule 23(d)(3) itself contemplates, courts also impose conditions on intervenors in class actions. Such conditions are the same as the ones that a court would impose on intervenors in ordinary litigation, such as setting a final date for intervention or limiting the extent of participation by intervenors to particular issues. Courts may also impose conditions on communications between class counsel and potential class members. *See* pp. 177–182, *infra*.

D.   RULE 23(d)(4)

Rule 23(d)(4) authorizes the court to issue orders requiring amendment of the pleadings to eliminate allegations as to absent class members. This subdivision is often invoked in conjunction with a decision under Rule 23(c)(1) denying class certification. When the court denies certification, it may order the class allegations stricken from the complaint and permit the action to proceed in the plaintiff's individual capacity. The court may also order that the class allegations be amended to reduce the size of the class or to divide the class into subclasses. Additionally, the court may order separate trials of individual issues that are not capable of being handled on a classwide basis.

E. RULE 23(d)(5)

Rule 23(d)(5) authorizes the court to issue orders "dealing with similar procedural matters." Although this rule allows flexibility in controlling the conduct of class actions, courts generally interpret the words "similar procedural" to indicate that such orders must not alter the ability of parties to present their claims. Permissible powers under Rule 23(d)(5) clearly overlap with those under Rule 23(d)(1) through Rule 23(d)(4), and courts often do not indicate that they are relying on Rule 23(d)(5).

§ 5.5 Miscellaneous Trial Issues

Most class action cases settle prior to trial. Accordingly, there are relatively few instructive examples of class action trials.

In general, the trial court is given broad discretion in fashioning the course of trial proceedings in class actions. Some of the methods and tools used by trial courts in managing class actions are bifurcation (such as dividing the trial into liability and damages phases), Rule 23(d) orders, and the appointment of special masters. Some class action trials have also raised issues under the Seventh Amendment and the Due Process Clause. *See* pp. 242–248, *infra.*

An important issue that has arisen in recent years involves the permissibility of proving damages on an aggregate basis through the use of expert or statistical proof. Courts have taken various views on the propriety of dispensing with proof on a plaintiff-by-plaintiff basis. Some courts condemn the use of aggregate proof as a violation of due process, while other courts uphold the approach in certain kinds of complex cases. Because the issue has generally arisen in the mass torts area, it is addressed on pp. 307–310, *infra.*

§ 5.6   Alternative Dispute Resolution

Alternative Dispute Resolution ("ADR") is a process of private dispute resolution outside of court. It involves such procedures as arbitration, mediation, early neutral evaluation, summary jury trials, mini-trials, and negotiation. With the enactment of the Federal Alternative Dispute Resolution Act of 1998, 28 U.S.C. §§ 651–58, federal district courts are now required to authorize the use of ADR in civil proceedings (as well as in adversary proceedings in bankruptcy). A benefit in the class action context, as in many other contexts, is that ADR permits the parties to select neutral arbitrators or mediators with expertise to handle difficult (and often technical) issues in a case. ADR is particularly attractive in class actions because of the high stakes involved and the delays inherent in adjudicating such cases in court.

A related ADR tool is the use of court-appointed special masters. Special masters are usually lawyers or law professors with specialized knowledge who are appointed to assist the court. One type of special master used in class actions is a special settlement master, *i.e.*, an individual who coordinates and facilitates complex settlement agreements involving multiple defendants and plaintiffs. Special settlement masters have been used in a variety of class actions, including mass tort, securities fraud, and employment discrimination cases.

Issues involving arbitration in the class action context have appeared frequently in recent years. As an initial matter, if the arbitration agreement provides for classwide arbitration, courts will generally honor that agreement. The more difficult question is what happens when the arbitration agreement is silent with respect to class arbitration. For a number of years, courts had been divided on the issue: some courts held class arbitrations to be permissible, but others barred them in the absence of express authorization.

In *Green Tree Fin. Corp. v. Bazzle,* 539 U.S. 444 (2003), the Court reviewed the South Carolina Supreme Court's holding that, because the two contracts in question were silent on whether class arbitration was permissible, class arbitration was proper. (Based on that holding, the South Carolina Court upheld class arbitration awards of $9.2 million and $10.935 million.) The U.S. Supreme Court granted certiorari on the question of whether the South Carolina Court's ruling violated the Federal Arbitration Act, 9 U.S.C. § 1 *et seq.* A plurality of the Court decided that it first had to reach a threshold question of whether the agreements were in fact silent about the permissibility of classwide arbitration or instead prohibited classwide arbitration. The Court (the plurality plus Justice Stevens) determined that this threshold question should be made by the arbitrator, not by the courts.

Subsequently, in *Buckeye Check Cashing Inc. v. Cardegna*, 126 S.Ct. 1204 (2006), the Court held that the arbitrator, not the court, should decide whether a contract containing an arbitration clause was void for illegality. The challenge in that case was to the contract as a whole, not specifically to the arbitration clause. The Court reasoned that the arbitration clause was enforceable entirely apart from the provisions challenged as unlawful. Thus, the arbitrator, not the court, should rule on the lawfulness of the contract.

Following *Bazzle*, arbitration clauses barring class action arbitrations have become more common. Not surprisingly, therefore, another issue that the courts have addressed is whether an arbitration agreement that prohibits classwide arbitrations is enforceable. Although federal courts have overwhelmingly upheld the enforceability of such clauses, state courts are divided. One widely publicized case was decided by the California Supreme Court. *See Discover Bank v. Superior Court,* 113 P.3d 1100

(Cal. 2005). There, the court held that a waiver of class arbitration was unconscionable and as a result, a credit cardholder could seek classwide arbitration of a challenge to Discover Bank's practices regarding late payment fees. The court's ruling was limited to situations involving contracts of adhesion and consumers with small claims. Some courts, however, have refused to endorse the approach of *Discover Bank*, even in the narrow circumstances involved in that case. Some cases have ruled that clauses prohibiting class action arbitrations are enforceable and not subject to challenge as unconscionable.

CHAPTER 6

NOTICE, OPT–OUT RIGHTS, AND COMMUNICATIONS WITH CLASS MEMBERS

This chapter discusses three core issues of class action law and practice: (1) whether class members are entitled to notice that the class has been certified (as well as notice of other important events in the litigation); (2) whether the class members are entitled to opt out (*i.e.*, remove themselves from the class) and pursue their own individual actions; and (3) whether (and under what circumstances) communications with class members are proper. These issues have generated considerable controversy and a significant body of case law. Notice and opt-out rights are closely related to the due process requirements for binding absent class members, and thus should be considered together with the discussion of *res judicata* and collateral estoppel. *See* pp. 227–241, *infra*.

§ 6.1 Class Notice and "Opt–Out" Rights

A. NOTICE AND OPT–OUT RIGHTS IN RULE 23(b)(3) CLASS ACTIONS

Unlike classes under Rule 23(b)(1) and (b)(2), which generally are not subject to notice of certification or a right to opt out, class actions certified under Rule 23(b)(3) are subject to specific notice and opt-out requirements. Rule 23(c)(2)(B) provides that, in class actions maintained under Rule 23(b)(3), the court "must direct to class members the best notice practicable under the circumstances, including individual notice to all members who can be identified through reasonable effort." The notice shall advise each member "that the court will exclude from the class any class member who requests exclusion, stating when and how members may elect to be excluded...."

In *Eisen v. Carlisle & Jacquelin*, 417 U.S. 156 (1974), the Supreme Court addressed the notice requirements of Rule 23(c)(2)—the predecessor to amended Rule 23(c)(2)(B)—in a class action maintained under Rule 23(b)(3). In *Eisen*, the class certified by the district court included millions of buyers and sellers of small quantities of securities. Instead of requiring individual notice to all class members who could be reasonably identified, the district court adopted a less ambitious plan of requiring notice only to (1) all firms that were members of the New York Stock Exchange, (2) approximately 2,000 identifiable class members, and (3) 5,000 class members selected at random, coupled with publication in several national newspapers. Relying on Rule 23(c)(2), but also looking to due process case law for guidance, the Supreme Court rejected that approach. The Court held that individual notice was required for the 2,250,000 class members whose names and addresses were known or easily ascertainable. The Court relied upon the language of Rule 23(c)(2), as well as upon the Advisory Committee Notes to Rule 23, which state that the notice requirements of Rule 23(c)(2) are "not merely discretionary" and are designed to satisfy the due process requirements of class actions. The Court rejected the high cost of providing individual notice to 2,250,000 class members as a reason for departing from the express language and intent of Rule 23(c)(2). The Court also rejected the argument that adequate representation, not notice, was the "touchstone of due process in a class action." *Id.* at 176. It noted that "Rule 23 speaks to notice as well as to adequacy of representation and requires that both be provided." *Id.* Accordingly, the Court concluded that "Rule 23(c)(2) requires that individual notice be sent to all class members who can be identified with reasonable effort." *Id.* at 177.

Consistent with *Eisen*, the lower courts have required notice in Rule 23(b)(3) actions to all class members whose identities can be determined with reasonable effort. If some class members cannot be identified through reasonable effort, a class may still be certified, although the inability to identify a substantial percentage of the class may be a reason for denying class certification. In some cases, such as consumer cases involving potentially millions of consumers who purchased a product, individual notice to class members is not possible because their names and addresses are not reasonably ascertainable. In such instances, other forms of notice, such as newspapers, television, radio, or the Internet, may be used. Indeed, these other forms may sometimes be ordered as extra protection even when individual notice can be (and is) ordered. As an alternative to separate mailings, a court may sometimes order notice as part of a defendant's own mail distribution, such as an enclosure with bills or monthly statements.

B. METHODS FOR PROVIDING NOTICE IN RULE 23(b)(3) CLASS ACTIONS

In general, when a class member can be identified, notice by first-class mail is required. Occasionally, courts will allow bulk mailings or mailings to "occupant." Several courts have held that a class member need not actually receive the mailing to be bound, so long as the method chosen was reasonably calculated to provide notice. Courts have occasionally upheld notices that contained typographical errors or that omitted apartment numbers. Although the Supreme Court in *Phillips Petroleum Co. v. Shutts,* 472 U.S. 797 (1985), stated that "[t]he plaintiff must receive notice," *id.* at 812, the Court has not squarely addressed the circumstances in which a class member may be bound when notice has been sent out in good faith but not received.

For class members who cannot be identified through reasonable efforts, the usual method of notice is through newspaper or journal publications. Publications should be selected that are likely to be read by class members. This would include newspapers with wide circulation, publications targeted to class members' geographic area, and publications targeted to the particular backgrounds of the class members (such as financial publications when the class members are accountants or financial specialists). Other methods of notice include television, radio, the Internet, and bulletins (such as at the class members' place of employment).

C.   TIMING OF RULE 23(c)(2) NOTICE

Rule 23(c)(2) does not specify when notice should be sent, leaving the decision to the trial court's discretion. The rule does make clear, however, that individual notice should be given prior to the rendering of a judgment and should allow time for class members to decide whether they wish to opt out of the class. Courts should consider any harm that might result to a party as a consequence of delayed notice. For instance, as discussed on pp. 199–204, *infra,* the statute of limitations is normally tolled when a class action is filed, but it starts to run again when certification is denied. Also, as the *Manual for Complex Litigation (4th)* points out, "[i]f the certification order is amended to eliminate previously included class members," a notice might be "necessary to inform affected individuals who might have relied on the class action to protect their rights." § 21.311. Occasionally, there may be a reason for delaying notice. As the *Manual for Complex Litigation (4th)* points out, "[w]hen the parties are nearing settlement, ... a reasonable delay in notice might increase incentives to settle and avoid the need for separate class notices of certification and settlement." *Id.*

D. FORM AND CONTENT OF RULE 23(c)(2) NOTICE

Rule 23(c)(2)(B) sets forth the content of the notice for Rule 23(b)(3) class actions:

The notice must concisely and clearly state in plain, easily understood language:

- the nature of the action,
- the definition of the class certified,
- the class claims, issues, or defenses,
- that a class member may enter an appearance through counsel if the member so desires,
- that the court will exclude from the class any member who requests exclusion, stating when and how members may elect to be excluded, and
- the binding effect of a class judgment on class members under Rule 23(c)(3).

The notice should also provide information about the case in order to permit the class member to make an informed decision about whether to opt out. As the *Manual for Complex Litigation (4th)* notes, the notice should describe the positions of the parties, identify the parties, class representatives, and counsel involved, specify the relief sought, and explain the benefits and risks to class members of remaining in the case versus opting out. In addition, the notice should be written evenhandedly and should not attempt either to encourage or discourage participation in the class.

Before the notice is sent to class members, it normally is submitted to the court for review and approval. Rarely does the court itself actually draft the notice. The requirement that the notice be understandable to class members (*see* Rule 23(c)(2)(B)) may in some circumstances necessitate sending the notice in more than one language.

E. THE COST OF PROVIDING NOTICE IN RULE 23(b)(3) CLASS ACTIONS

The general rule is that the named plaintiff—not the defendant—should both administer the Rule 23(c)(2) notice and pay for it. As noted on pp. 362–363, *infra,* however, class counsel are entitled to advance the costs of notice, and under some ethical codes the representatives are not required to reimburse counsel for those costs.

The class representative, however, is not always required to perform all tasks incident to sending notice, such as ascertaining the identities of class members. Rule 23(d) gives the court discretion to "make appropriate orders" for the fair conduct of the action. Courts have relied upon this rule to require the defendant to perform tasks incident to providing notice when the court determines that the defendant can do so with less difficulty or expense than the class representative. When the court orders the defendant to perform notice-related tasks, such as identifying members of the class, the court has discretion to impose the cost on the party ordered to do the task, or to shift the cost to the party that benefits, generally the class representative.

In *Oppenheimer Fund, Inc. v. Sanders*, 437 U.S. 340 (1978), the Supreme Court addressed the allocation of costs incurred in sending class notice. The plaintiffs in that case moved for class certification, but before certification was granted, the plaintiffs moved to redefine the class to reduce its size. The district court denied plaintiffs' motion to redefine the class, which the defendant had opposed, but placed the cost of notifying the originally defined class on the defendant. The Supreme Court repudiated the district court's approach, holding that the cost should have been placed on the plaintiffs. The Court held that the district court erred in finding that the defendants should bear the cost of notification, even though the district court had found that the cost was minor in relation to the defendant's assets. While recognizing that the ability of a party to pay may in some circumstances be a consideration in determining who should bear the cost of notice, the Court stated that ability to pay was not the definitive test. Rather, "the test in this respect normally should be whether the cost is substantial; not whether it is 'modest' in relation to ability to pay." *Id.* at 361. The Court also rejected the argument that shifting the expense to the defendants was justified since they kept some of their records on computer tapes, which made it difficult for plaintiffs to retrieve the information. The Court pointed out that there was no indication of a bad faith effort to conceal information from the plaintiffs.

Following *Oppenheimer*, lower courts have generally imposed the costs of notice on plaintiffs. In exceptional circumstances, however, courts have shifted the cost of providing notice to the defendant when the defendant performs the tasks involved in the ordinary course of business and when the burden on the defendant would not be substantial. For instance, courts have sometimes required telephone companies to include class notices in monthly billing statements to customers. Courts have also sometimes shifted notice costs to the defendant when the plaintiff is indigent or when the defendant has engaged in wrongful conduct, such as deliberately failing to maintain proper records. Of course, even if plaintiff must initially incur the costs of notice, he or she may be able to recoup those costs if the case succeeds on the merits.

F.　ABILITY TO OPT OUT OF A RULE 23(b)(3) CLASS

In addition to requiring notice in Rule 23(b)(3) classes, Rule 23(c)(2)(B) also requires that Rule 23(b)(3) class members be given an opportunity to opt out. Apart from meeting the mechanical and timing requirements of the notice itself, a class member need not meet any standard in order to opt out. For example, the class member need not provide an explanation for his or her decision to opt out.

Opt-out rights serve two related functions. First, a class member's failure to opt out indicates consent to the jurisdiction of the court and consent to be bound by the court's judgment, at least if the class has been adequately represented. Second, opt-out rights provide procedural protection to class members who desire to pursue their claims individually.

Courts usually allow thirty to sixty days for a class member to opt out of the class. Opt-out papers returned by class members are usually filed with the court (although other procedures, such as a special address, may be adopted if the class is large and the opt-out process would be administratively cumbersome for the court). Courts have discretion to allow opt outs that were not filed in a timely manner, although normally a court should require good cause for deviating from the deadline set forth in the notice.

G. NOTICE IN 23(b)(1) AND 23(b)(2) CLASS ACTIONS

The notice provisions of Rule 23(c)(2)(B) do not apply to class actions certified under Rule 23(b)(1) or 23(b)(2). The only notice expressly required by Rule 23 for (b)(1) and (b)(2) classes is notice of a proposed settlement pursuant to Rule 23(e).

Courts agree that notice in Rule 23(b)(1) and Rule 23(b)(2) class actions is not required as a matter of due process when only injunctive or declaratory relief is sought. Since courts generally assume that a (b)(1) or (b)(2) class is homogeneous and lacks conflicts of interest, and since Rule 23(a)(4) requires that such classes be adequately represented, courts have usually found no unfairness in dispensing with notice. On the other hand, when the class action suit seeks damages as well as injunctive relief, such as in a discrimination action, some courts have held that due process requires notice and a right to opt out in order to bind class members' individual monetary claims. The Supreme Court has not squarely ruled on the issue. *See* pp. 172–173, *infra.*

In the past, courts that ordered notice in Rule 23(b)(1) or Rule 23(b)(2) classes usually relied upon Rule 23(d)(2), which provides that:

[T]he court may make appropriate orders: . . . (2) requiring, for the protection of the members of the class or otherwise for the fair conduct of the action, that notice be given in such manner as the court may direct to some or all of the members of any step in the action.

Notice under Rule 23(d)(2) is discretionary. Such notice may be advisable to identify and elicit conflicting interests among class members or to give unnamed class members the opportunity to monitor the adequacy of the class representatives or class counsel. When notice is ordered under Rule 23(d)(2), courts are not bound by the notice requirements of Rule 23(c)(2)(B) and may specify the type of notice appropriate for the particular case, such as ordering notice only by publication. Also, courts are not required to impose the costs of (d)(2) notice on the plaintiffs and may, in their discretion, impose such costs on the defendant.

The 2003 amendments to Rule 23 explicitly give courts discretion to order notice in (b)(1) and (b)(2) class actions. *See* Rule 23(c)(2)(A) ("For any class certified under Rule 23(b)(1) or (2), the court may direct appropriate notice to the class."). The Advisory Committee Notes to the amendments state that the discretion to order notice in a (b)(1) or (b)(2) class "should be exercised with care." According to the Notes, notice is generally less important in (b)(1) and (b)(2) actions because opt-outs are not permitted, and the costs of notice may "cripple actions that do not seek damages." The Notes further point out that, when notice *is* ordered in a (b)(1) or (b)(2) class, courts should exercise "discretion and flexibility" in the method of notice. "Informal methods," such as "[a] simple posting in a place visited by many class members, directing attention to a source of more detailed information, may suffice."

H.   OPT–OUT RIGHTS IN RULE 23(b)(1) AND RULE 23(b)(2) CLASSES

Rule 23(b)(1) and (b)(2) do not, by their terms, allow for opt outs, and courts agree that due process does not require opt outs when only non-monetary relief is sought. The more difficult question is whether notice and opt-out rights are required, even in a (b)(1) or (b)(2) class, when a significant component of the claim is for damages. In *Phillips*

Petroleum Co. v. Shutts, 472 U.S. 797 (1985), the Supreme Court stated that notice and opt-out rights were required in suits "wholly or predominately" for money damages, *id.* at 812, but left open whether notice and opt-out rights were required in (b)(1) or (b)(2) actions that also included monetary claims. In an important post-*Shutts* decision, the Ninth Circuit held, in the context of an antitrust settlement under (b)(1) and (b)(2), that class members could not be barred from bringing individual damages actions even though such claims had been settled as part of a mandatory class. *Brown v. Ticor Title Ins. Co.,* 982 F.2d 386 (9th Cir. 1992). The court reasoned that due process required notice and opt-out rights before monetary claims could be settled. The Supreme Court granted certiorari in the case but ultimately dismissed the writ on procedural grounds. The Supreme Court granted review in a later case to decide the issue, but ended up again dismissing the writ as improvidently granted. And, while the issue was raised by the petitioner in *Ortiz v. Fibreboard Corp.,* 527 U.S. 815 (1999) (*see* pp. 76–79, *supra*), the Supreme Court in *Ortiz* did not reach the due process issues but instead held that the class settlement violated Rule 23(b)(1)(B). As a result, this important issue remains to be addressed by the Supreme Court.

Because of these lurking due process issues, some courts in (b)(1) and (b)(2) actions permit opt outs, relying on their authority under Rule 23(d)(2) to issue notice to the class or their authority under Rule 23(d)(5) to issue appropriate procedural orders. Other courts certify "hybrid" classes—mandatory classes for non-monetary claims and opt-out classes for damages claims. Still other courts permit mandatory classes even when claims for money are involved because the monetary component is not substantial or does not depend on individualized circumstances of the class members.

I.   OTHER NOTICES PURSUANT TO RULE 23(d)(2)

Rule 23(d)(2) may be used for many notice purposes beyond simply notifying class members of (b)(1) or (b)(2) certification. For instance, the *Manual for Complex Litigation (4th)* suggests that (d)(2) may be used to notify class members if a previously certified class has been decertified or if the scope of a previously certified class has been narrowed. Rule 23(d)(2) may also be used to supplement, correct, or modify prior notices. (The *Manual* indicates that the party responsible for an error in a prior notice should bear the cost of a corrective notice.)

J.   NOTICE TO ABSENT CLASS MEMBERS OF A PROPOSED DISMISSAL OR COMPROMISE UNDER RULE 23(e)

Rule 23(e)(1)(B) provides that "[t]he court must direct notice in a reasonable manner to all class members who would be bound by a proposed settlement, voluntary dismissal, or compromise." Unlike Rule 23(c)(2)(B) notice, which applies only to classes certified under Rule 23(b)(3), Rule 23(e)'s notice provision contains no such limitation and thus applies to classes under (b)(1), (b)(2), and (b)(3).

Notice is required in cases when settlement occurs *after* certification, as well as in cases in which certification and settlement occur at the same time. Rule 23(e) does not articulate the contents or method of providing notice, leaving such matters to the court's discretion. Certain items, however, are common in a settlement notice. According to the *Manual for Complex Litigation (4th)*, the notice should define the class and any subclasses, and contain the terms of the settlement (including attorneys' fees), information about the settlement hearing (date, time, place), procedures for distributing settlement proceeds, any special benefits awarded to class representatives, options open to class members (and deadlines for acting), methods for objecting to the settlement, and ways of seeking additional information about the settlement.

One issue that previously divided courts was whether Rule 23(e) applied to settlements or dismissals of class actions *prior* to certification. Some courts held that actions commenced under Rule 23 should be treated as class actions for purposes of dismissal or settlement from the moment the action is commenced. As a result, these courts held that notice of a pre-certification settlement with the named plaintiffs must be given to all putative class members. Other courts, however, held that Rule 23(e) notice was not required in pre-certification settlements or dismissals unless collusion appeared to exist between the parties, or the rights of potential class members would be prejudiced by the dismissal or settlement. The 2003 amendments have resolved this issue by not requiring notice when only the class representatives are bound by a settlement. *See* pp. 250–253, *infra*.

K. NOTICE OF DECERTIFICATION

Assume that a class is certified and notice is provided to the class members. If the class is later decertified, must notice of the decertification be provided? The Seventh Circuit addressed this issue in *Culver v. City of Milwaukee*, 277 F.3d 908 (7th Cir. 2002). There, the court held that such notice was required. The court noted that the filing of a class action tolled the statute of limitations (*see* pp. 199–204, *infra*) but that the statute starts to run again upon decertification. "Unless [class members] are notified that the suit is dismissed, they may fail to file their own suits and ... find themselves time barred without knowing it." *Id.* at 914. The court qualified its ruling by stating that notice was not required if the class would not be prejudiced (*e.g.*, when the class likely "learn[ed] of [the decertification] through other channels ...." *Id.* at 915. A post-*Culver* case within the Seventh Circuit has held that notice of decertification is not required for mandatory classes, in which notice was not required at the time of certification, at least when the initial certification was not highly publicized. *Clarke v. Ford Motor Co.*, 228 F.R.D. 631 (E.D. Wis. 2005).

§ 6.2   Communications With Class Members

A.   CONTACTS WITH POTENTIAL CLASS MEMBERS BEFORE CLASS ACTION IS FILED

A court has no authority to regulate communications with potential class members until a class action suit is actually filed. Before filing, only the relevant rules of professional conduct regulate attorney contact with potential class members.

B.   COMMUNICATIONS WITH POTENTIAL CLASS MEMBERS BETWEEN FILING AND CLASS CERTIFICATION

(1) Reasons for Contacting Class Members

Plaintiffs, defendants, and their respective counsel have an interest in contacting potential class members after the lawsuit has been filed, but before the case has been certified as a class action. Plaintiffs and their counsel may seek to inform potential class members of the existence of the lawsuit, obtain information concerning the underlying facts from individuals who may be similarly situated to the class representatives, recruit additional class representatives, and obtain financial contributions for prosecuting the action. Defendants and their counsel may seek to obtain information concerning the underlying facts—such as conflicts among the class members—to bolster their opposition to class certification. They may also want to communicate with potential class members to obtain individual settlements or to encourage opt outs. The proper timing and content of communications with potential class members are subjects of significant debate, particularly given the serious potential for abuse when large numbers of unrepresented persons are the intended targets.

(2) Use of Rule 23(d) to Regulate Communications With Class Members

Rule 23(d) provides that the court may enter appropriate orders "imposing conditions on the representative parties or on intervenors," Rule 23(d)(3), and "dealing with similar procedural matters." Rule 23(d)(5). Courts have regulated communications with potential class members using Rule 23(d) to protect against: (1) solicitation of class members in violation of the ethical rules; (2) improper solicitation of funds from persons who are not formal parties; (3) unauthorized communications by counsel or parties that misrepresent the status, purpose, or impact of the litigation; and (4) attempts to persuade class members to opt out of the class. Because of these concerns, many courts routinely prohibited or limited contacts between counsel and absent class members prior to *Gulf Oil Co. v. Bernard,* 452 U.S. 89 (1981).

(3) The *Gulf Oil* Decision

In *Gulf Oil*, the Supreme Court invalidated a district court's protective order banning all communications between the parties (or their counsel) and potential or actual class members, without the court's prior approval. The district court made no findings of fact and did not write an opinion in support of its order. Without deciding whether the order violated the First Amendment as a prior restraint on free speech, the Supreme Court held that the order was an abuse of the district court's discretion under Rule 23(d). The Court noted that, while a trial court had discretion "to enter appropriate orders governing the conduct of counsel and parties, such discretion was 'not unlimited'. . . ." *Id.* at 100. Rather, orders restricting communications must be "based on a clear record and specific findings that reflect a weighing of the need for a limitation and the potential interference with the rights of the parties." *Id.* at 101. In addition, the balancing test "should result in a carefully drawn order that limits speech as little as possible, consistent with the rights of the parties under the circumstances." *Id.* at 102. Under the *Gulf Oil* facts, the Court found that, among other things, the district court's order impeded the ability of plaintiffs' counsel to inform potential class members of the existence of the lawsuit. Although the Court based its holding on Rule 23(d), it did note that the district court's order involved "serious restraints on expression."

(4) Developments After *Gulf Oil*

In light of *Gulf Oil*, most courts have invalidated local rules containing communication bans similar to the one struck down by the Supreme Court. A few courts have also continued to ban blanket restrictions of communications as unconstitutional prior restraints of free speech, the issue not reached by the Supreme Court in *Gulf Oil*.

Consistent with *Gulf Oil*, the *Manual for Complex Litigation (4th)* states that "[m]ost judges are reluctant to restrict communications between the parties or their counsel and potential class members, except when necessary to prevent serious misconduct." § 21.12. The *Manual* also notes that, although there is no formal attorney-client relationship between plaintiffs' counsel and potential class members prior to class certification, "an attorney acting on behalf of a putative class must act in the best interests of the class as a whole," and thus the court has authority to intervene in instances in which communications with class members are abusive. Plaintiffs' counsel should be free, however, to supply information, respond to inquiries, and obtain information necessary to represent the class. *Id.*

(5) Application of *Gulf Oil* to Defense Communications

Some courts have distinguished between communications by plaintiffs' counsel and those by defense counsel, holding that *Gulf Oil* does not protect the latter communications. Such courts reason that the Supreme Court in *Gulf Oil* was trying to protect the ability of plaintiffs' counsel to represent the class effectively. By contrast, a defendant's stated reason for contacting class members is generally to obtain information to defend the lawsuit, a need that can be satisfied through discovery. Other courts, however, use the *Gulf Oil* balancing test to evaluate all communications with potential class members, whether initiated by plaintiffs or defendants, and prohibit communications that are misleading or are designed to prevent participation in the class action. Some post-*Gulf Oil* courts have also regulated defendants' attempts to contact potential class members about settlement before a class is certified. Most courts, however, permit defendants to discuss settlement with unnamed class members as long as defendants do not provide false or misleading information or attempt to influence potential class members' decisions to opt out of the class. Of course, as the *Manual for Complex Litigation (4th)* notes, "[e]thics rules restricting communications with individuals represented by counsel may apply to restrict a defendant's communications" with named plaintiffs. § 21.12.

(6) Correcting Misleading or Otherwise Improper Communications

If a court determines that a communication by counsel is misleading or otherwise improper, it has authority under Rule 23(d)(2) to issue a corrective or clarifying notice. *See* p. 174, *supra*.

C. COMMUNICATIONS WITH CLASS MEMBERS AFTER CLASS CERTIFICATION

A basic rule of legal ethics is that, in representing a client, an attorney may not communicate regarding the subject matter of the representation with a party who is known to be represented by an attorney, absent the consent of that attorney. One issue that sometimes arises in class actions is whether this rule applies to unnamed class members after a class is certified. Most courts hold that upon certification of a class, an attorney-client relationship arises between plaintiffs' counsel and all members of the class. *See* p. 358, *infra*. Accordingly, once a class is certified, defense counsel must obtain the consent of class counsel before contacting class members. This principle applies even during the opt-out period following certification, in order to avoid undue influence in class members' opt-out decisions.

Because there is often an ongoing business relationship between a defendant and class members (for example, when class members are current employees or business affiliates of the defendant), courts have allowed post-certification communications between defendants and class members concerning day-to-day business operations. In such cases, defendants are generally prohibited from discussing the pending lawsuit.

CHAPTER 7

MULTI-JURISDICTIONAL AND STATE COURT CLASS ACTIONS

Nationwide or other multi-jurisdictional class actions enable a court to adjudicate, in a single proceeding, potentially millions of class members' claims. As a result, such class actions may be more efficient for the parties and the judicial system than a series of smaller class actions. In addition, nationwide class actions may allow the parties to achieve a uniform national result, as opposed to a series of potentially conflicting rulings. Yet, courts are generally cautious in utilizing such classes because of potentially difficult issues under Rule 23 and the Due Process Clause. This chapter addresses those issues.

Although many multi-state class actions are brought in federal court, plaintiffs in recent years have been filing an increasing number of such cases—as well as single-state class actions—in state court. Indeed, one of the leading Supreme Court cases on multi-jurisdictional class actions arose out of a state court proceeding. For that reason, this chapter also surveys how various state courts approach class action issues.

§ 7.1 Nationwide and Other Multi–Jurisdictional Class Actions

A. STANDARDS FOR CERTIFYING A MULTI–JURISDICTIONAL CLASS

The decision to certify any class, including a nationwide or other multi-jurisdictional class, is committed to the discretion of the trial court. In exercising that discretion, however, the court must recognize that the consequences of certifying—or not certifying—such a class may be profound. Certification of a multi-jurisdictional class results in only one trial to adjudicate claims that could involve millions of class members. On the other hand, not certifying such a class could potentially leave millions of people without an effective remedy.

Because of the high stakes involved in adjudicating a nationwide or other multi-jurisdictional class action, some defendants have tried to argue that such classes are never appropriate for certification. In *Califano v. Yamasaki*, 442 U.S. 682 (1979), the Supreme Court "decline[d] to adopt [such an] extreme position...." *Id.* at 702. The Court emphasized, however, that a district court should take special care to ensure that a nationwide class is indeed appropriate.

In certifying a multi-jurisdictional class, a trial court must examine all of the prerequisites required by Rule 23(a) and (b), as discussed in earlier chapters of this text. One important inquiry unique to such class actions is whether the claims are in fact multi-jurisdictional in scope. For example, in *State of Alabama v. Blue Bird Body Co.*, 573 F.2d 309 (5th Cir. 1978), the Fifth Circuit decertified a nationwide class in an antitrust action because the proof offered by plaintiffs to support a nationwide antitrust conspiracy was limited to a particular state, and there was no evidence of a single conspiracy that was national in scope.

An additional issue in a multi-jurisdictional class action is whether such a suit would frustrate other ongoing class-action litigation. Although it is not fatal that a multi-jurisdictional class could, in effect, swallow up smaller classes around the country, the court must determine whether one large class is the superior method for litigating the issues. Courts often refrain from certifying multi-jurisdictional classes out of deference to more limited suits already underway, such as class actions limited to a single state. For example, in *In re American Medical Systems, Inc.*, 75 F.3d 1069 (6th Cir. 1996), the Sixth Circuit granted mandamus and reversed a district court order certifying a national class of penile implant claimants, partly because there were "previously-filed cases at more advanced stages of litigation." *Id.* at 1088. The court noted that the certification order "threaten[ed] to throw preexisting cases into disarray," and "[t]he waste of judicial resources due to duplicative proceedings [was] plain and [was] not correctable on appeal." *Id.* Of course, numerous courts have certified multi-jurisdictional class actions notwithstanding the existence of other more limited class actions involving the same issues.

B. PROCEDURAL AND MANAGEABILITY ISSUES

(1) Overview

As discussed on pp. 108–110, *supra*, Rule 23(b)(3)(D) requires a court to consider "the difficulties likely to be encountered in the management of a class action." Two manageability issues are of particular concern in the context of multi-jurisdictional class actions: (i) due process constraints on binding out-of-state class members to a proceeding; and (ii) choice-of-law issues necessitated by the scope of the proposed class.

(2) Due Process Constraints on Multi–Jurisdictional Classes

A nationwide or other multi-jurisdictional class action will, by definition, involve claims of absent class members who do not reside in, or have any connection with, the state in which the case was brought. If these class members from distant states were individual *defendants*, due process would bar them from being bound by the forum court's judgment unless the defendants had "minimum contacts" with the forum state. *Int'l Shoe Co. v. Washington*, 326 U.S. 310 (1945). Although individual plaintiffs in non-class cases are not subject to a "minimum contacts" inquiry, since they are the ones who have *chosen* the particular forum, that rationale does not necessarily apply in multi-jurisdictional class actions. The unnamed class members likely had no say concerning where the class action suit was brought.

The Supreme Court addressed these concerns in *Phillips Petroleum Co. v. Shutts*, 472 U.S. 797 (1985). *Shutts* involved a state court class action that was brought under Kansas class action rules similar to Federal Rule 23. The suit was brought on behalf of thousands of royalty owners who claimed that they were entitled to interest on delayed royalty payments for natural gas produced by Phillips Petroleum. The class members resided throughout the United States and in several foreign countries, and the leases from which the natural gas was produced related to land located in multiple states. Less than one percent of the leases were on land located in Kansas, and only a small percentage of class members had any connection to Kansas. After the state trial court certified the class pursuant to Kansas' equivalent to Rule 23(b)(3), several thousand class members exercised their opt-out rights, and more than a thousand additional class members were excluded because notice could not be delivered. After finding the defendant, Phillips Petroleum, liable, the trial court applied Kansas substantive law in computing damages, regardless of where the individual plaintiffs or natural gas leases were situated, and regardless of whether the class members could have obtained similar damage awards in their home states. The Kansas trial court reasoned that, absent compelling circumstances (which it found did not exist), the law of the forum (*i.e.*, Kansas) controlled all claims. The trial court also justified its choice-of-law selection by noting that the class members had indicated a desire for Kansas law to apply by failing to opt out of the class.

The defendant objected to certification of the class and to the use of Kansas law to compute damages. It argued that, because most of the class members were not from Kansas, they lacked minimum contacts with the forum state, and thus were free to re-litigate the same issues if they were unhappy with the outcome. Both the trial court and the Kansas Supreme Court rejected these arguments. The U.S. Supreme Court granted certiorari to decide two questions affecting multi-jurisdictional class actions: (1) whether due process permits non-resident plaintiffs without minimum contacts to be included within a class; and (2) whether due process is violated if a court simply uses the substantive law of the forum state instead of conducting a more focused choice-of-law analysis.

With respect to the first issue, the Court held that the Due Process Clause does not require that absent class members in a class action receive the same procedural protections as out-of-state defendants. The Court observed that an absent class member is not subject to burdens that are typically put on a civil defendant: They do not need to hire separate attorneys, usually do not have to litigate any counterclaims or cross-claims, and rarely are liable for court costs or fees. Indeed, the Court observed that "an absent class-action plaintiff is not required to do anything." *Id.* at 810. The Court thus held that a forum state may exercise jurisdiction over the claim of an absent class member, even though that person does not possess the minimum contacts required for personal jurisdiction over a defendant. The Court went on to hold, however, that certain procedural due process protections must still be met. Specifically, in order to be bound, the class members must receive notice of the action (and an opportunity to be heard, in person or through counsel) and must be given "an opportunity to remove [themselves] from the class by executing and returning an 'opt out' or 'request for exclusion' form to the court." *Id.* at 812. Additionally, due process requires that the named plaintiff must adequately represent the interests of the class as a whole. The Court, however, rejected the contention that due process requires absent plaintiffs to affirmatively opt *into* a class instead of being included in the class unless affirmatively opting *out*. Moreover, in an important footnote, the Court stated that it was not deciding whether the same safeguards apply in classes seeking primarily non-monetary relief.

On the second issue, the Supreme Court held that it was a violation of due process for the trial court to apply Kansas law to the entire nationwide class when (1) most class members had no relationship to Kansas, and (2) Kansas law differed materially from the laws of various other states. The Court initially explained that the law of the forum *could* be applied "if it is not in conflict with that of any other jurisdiction connected to [the] suit." *Id.* at 816.

When there is a conflict, however, a forum's substantive law may be applied only if the forum has significant contacts with the transaction giving rise to the controversy, so that using the law of the forum is not arbitrary or fundamentally unfair. Noting that the laws of other states connected to the underlying transaction differed significantly from those of Kansas, and that Kansas had no interest in the vast majority of claims, the Court reasoned that the application of Kansas law to every claim in the case was "sufficiently arbitrary and unfair as to exceed constitutional limits." *Id.* at 822. The Court also stated that the class members' "desire for Kansas law" was entitled to "little relevance."

It is important to underscore that *Shutts*, by its terms, does not prohibit the application of a single state's law to a multi-state class action, provided the selection is not arbitrary or unfair. The question of what specific law(s) should apply depends on the choice-of-law rules of the state where the court is located. *See* p. 102, *infra. Shutts* merely insists that the application of the selected state(s)' laws not be arbitrary or unfair.

(3) Post-*Shutts* Choice-of-Law Issues in Multi–Jurisdictional Class Actions

In light of *Shutts*, a court in a multi-jurisdictional Rule 23(b)(3) class action may not resolve choice-of-law determinations by summarily concluding that one state's law should apply to all class members. As noted on p. 102, *supra*, federal courts in diversity cases must apply the law of the state whose law would govern if the case were being tried in state court. In some nationwide tort suits, for example, this could mean that the laws of as many as fifty states (plus the District of Columbia) could apply within a single lawsuit.

Numerous courts have addressed choice-of-law issues in multi-jurisdictional class actions. The Supreme Court in *Amchem Products, Inc. v. Windsor,* 521 U.S. 591 (1997), recognized that choice-of-law concerns could weigh against certification. Likewise, in *Castano v. American Tobacco,* 84 F.3d 734 (5th Cir. 1996), the Fifth Circuit stated that, "[i]n a multi-state class action, variations in state law may swamp any common issues and defeat predominance." *Id.* at 741.

Similar concerns were expressed by the Seventh Circuit in *In re Rhone–Poulenc Rorer Incorporated,* 51 F.3d 1293 (7th Cir. 1995). *Rhone-Poulenc* involved a nationwide class of hemophiliacs who contracted AIDS from contaminated blood transfusions in the early 1980s, prior to the discovery of AIDS, and claimed that various medical corporations were liable for negligence. Plaintiffs' theory was that, had the defendants done more to avoid the then-known risk of Hepatitis B, they would have avoided the AIDS infections as well. In certifying the class, the district court attempted to avoid choice-of-law issues by holding that a single body of negligence law would apply to all class members. As one of several grounds for decertifying the class, the Seventh Circuit ruled that, because of the novelty of the negligence issues, differences in the laws among the states (even in "nuance") could not be ignored, as the district court attempted to do.

More recently, in *In re Bridgestone/Firestone, Inc., Tires Products Liability Litigation,* 288 F.3d 1012 (7th Cir. 2002), *cert. denied,* 537 U.S. 1105 (2003), the Seventh Circuit held that the district court erred in applying the laws of Tennessee and Michigan, the headquarters of Firestone and Ford, respectively, to claims by a putative nationwide class involving alleged defects in certain Firestone tires and Ford Explorers. According to the court, applicable choice-of-law rules required that the law of each class member's place of injury should govern. Because the class included members from all 50 states, the District of Columbia, and various U.S. territories, the court held that the need to apply so many laws to numerous causes of action rendered the suit unmanageable.

By contrast, some courts have been receptive to certifying nationwide classes despite variations in state law. For example, in *In re School Asbestos Litigation,* 789 F.2d 996 (3d Cir. 1986), the Third Circuit affirmed the certification of a multi-jurisdictional class action, notwithstanding variations in state law, because the plaintiffs were able to group such laws into four categories. The Third Circuit subsequently ruled, in approving (for settlement purposes) a nationwide class alleging fraudulent sales practices against an insurance company, that choice-of-law issues did not present "insuperable obstacles." *In re Prudential Ins. Co. America Sales*

Practice Litig. Agent Actions, 148 F.3d 283 (3d Cir. 1998), *cert. denied*, 525 U.S. 1114 (1999). Another example of this more receptive approach is the decision by a Wyoming federal district court certifying a nationwide class action against a pharmaceutical company despite potential variations in state negligence and product liability law. *In re Copley Pharmaceutical, Inc.*, 161 F.R.D. 456 (D.Wyo. 1995). The court opined that choice-of-law issues do not necessarily make class actions unmanageable, and it concluded that the various state laws on negligence and strict liability were largely the same. Moreover, unlike *Firestone,* some courts have been willing to apply the law of a defendant's principal place of business even to class members residing in other states.

One important question is whether the Class Action Fairness Act will impact the reach of *Shutts*. As explained below (pp. 214–227, *infra*), the Class Action Fairness Act ("CAFA") will have the effect of shifting most multi-state class actions to federal court. Thus, to the extent that *Shutts* unleashed a wave of multi-state or nationwide class actions in state court, CAFA clearly will reverse that trend.

CAFA does not, however, address the due process or choice-of-law issues raised by *Shutts*. (Proposed amendments that sought to address choice-of-law issues were rejected.) Thus, federal courts, like state courts, will still have to ensure that the choice of state law to apply is neither arbitrary nor unfair. Prior to CAFA, federal courts, in diversity cases (like their state court counterparts) applied the choice-of-law rules of the state in which the court was located, as required by *Klaxon Co. v. Stentor Elec. Mfg. Co.,* 313 U.S. 487 (1941). Some commentators expect the same approach under CAFA, although other commentators contend that federal courts should have more flexibility.

§ 7.2   State Court Class Actions

A.   IMPORTANCE OF STATE COURT CLASS ACTIONS

The primary focus of this text is on federal class actions. As exemplified by *Shutts,* however, the vast majority of states allow class action suits to be brought in state courts. State court class actions are worthy of focus in this text for at least two reasons.

First, because various federal appellate courts have restricted certain kinds of class actions in recent years, state courts have become more attractive to plaintiffs. Many litigants believe that state courts are generally more receptive to class actions than are federal courts. One explanation offered by numerous commentators and practitioners is that most state court judges are elected and thus are motivated to make decisions that are politically popular.

Second, state court class actions are important because, under current diversity requirements, some class actions involving state law issues may *only* be brought in state court. Although the enactment of CAFA will severely reduce the number of multi-state class actions that proceed in state court (*see* pp. 214–227, *infra*), CAFA by no means eliminates state courts altogether as important venues for many significant class actions.

B. OVERVIEW OF STATE CLASS ACTION RULES

Because of the continuing importance of state court class actions, even after CAFA, it is instructive to survey some of the key differences between state and federal court class actions. A state-by-state survey of state court class action rules is beyond the scope of this text. This text simply highlights, in a general way, some of the areas in which class action rules and procedures may differ from one state to another. Students and practitioners analyzing state court class actions should consult the rules and case law applicable to the particular state at issue.

States Adopting the 1966 Version of Rule 23. About two-thirds of the states pattern their class action rules on the 1966 version of Rule 23. Many of these states look closely at federal case law in construing similarly worded state-law rules. Other Rule 23 states, however, do not always follow federal case law, particularly when the thrust of such case law is to restrict the availability of class actions. A number of state courts take the view that class actions should be certified whenever possible.

Among states that pattern their rules after Federal Rule 23, some do not have categories similar to (b)(1) and (b)(2), and thus allow certification only under standards similar to (b)(3). Moreover, states use a variety of criteria to determine whether a class action is "superior" to other methods of adjudication. The Michigan rule, for example, explicitly requires courts to consider, in addition to the (b)(3) criteria, (1) whether the claims of individual class members are insufficient in amount to warrant separate lawsuits; and (2) whether the amounts likely to be recovered by individual class members are large enough to justify a class action. In California, while the class action rule is much more succinct than Federal Rule 23, cases make clear that the requirements are very similar to those under Federal Rule 23(a) and (b).

States Not Adopting the 1966 Version of Rule 23. Several states have not adopted a rule similar to Federal Rule 23. Those states take a variety of approaches. For example, Mississippi and Virginia do not have specific rules authorizing class actions. In Virginia, class action-type suits may be brought only to the extent allowed by judicial decisions. In Mississippi, class actions do not exist, either by rule or by court decision.

The remaining states take a variety of approaches. A few states, including Nebraska and Wisconsin, pattern their class action statutes after the 1849 "Field Code," a code first enacted in New York that attempted to simplify civil procedure. Class actions under Field Code statutes differ from those under Rule 23. For example, Field Code states do not have different categories of class suits corresponding to Rule 23(b)(1), (b)(2), or (b)(3), but instead look to whether there is a "community of interest" among the class members. Taken literally, this requirement could foreclose class treatment, for example, in a contract suit in which the class members signed separate contracts with the same defendant. Nonetheless, some Field Code states have stated that their requirements are similar in application to those of Federal Rule 23.

North Carolina patterns its class action rule after the 1938 version of Rule 23. The North Carolina rule does not, however, refer specifically to "true," "hybrid," and "spurious" classes. *See* pp. 18–19, *supra*.

Approaches to Notice and Opt Outs. The vast majority of states require notice to the members of a putative class who can be reasonably identified, at least in Rule 23(b)(3)-type class actions. Some states, however, do not require notice (except for out-of-state class members in (b)(3)-type cases) but leave the decision to the discretion of the trial court. These courts reason that the Supreme Court's requirement of best practicable notice in Federal Rule 23(b)(3) actions, as set forth in *Eisen v. Carlisle & Jacquelin*, 417 U.S. 156 (1974), was based on Federal Rule 23, not on federal due process, and that the due process notice requirements in *Shutts* apply only to out-of-state class members.

With respect to opt outs, most states follow the Rule 23 approach and permit both opt-out classes and mandatory classes. Some states, however, have "opt-in" provisions for certain kinds of class actions. These provisions provide that, unless a potential class member takes affirmative steps to join the class, he or she will not be part of the case, and will not be bound by the judgment.

CHAPTER 8

CONSTITUTIONAL AND PROCEDURAL ISSUES

Previous chapters have discussed several concepts unique to class actions, such as numerosity, commonality, typicality, adequacy, notice, and opt-out rights. There are, however, a number of basic procedural and constitutional principles that apply in both class and non-class cases but that have special ramifications in the class action context. These include issues relating to statutes of limitations, subject-matter jurisdiction, and issue and claim preclusion, as well as constitutional due process and Seventh Amendment right-to-jury-trial issues. This chapter addresses these assorted issues.

§ 8.1 Statute of Limitations Issues in Class Actions

A. OVERVIEW OF "TOLLING" PRINCIPLES IN CLASS ACTIONS

The filing of a class action suit has important statute-of-limitations ramifications for prospective class members. In general, the filing of such a suit "tolls" the statute of limitations period (*i.e.,* stops it from running) for the entire class until class certification is denied. This is true regardless of whether the putative class member was even aware that a class action suit existed at the time it was pending.

The Supreme Court first announced a limited version of this tolling principle in *American Pipe & Construction Co. v. Utah,* 414 U.S. 538 (1974), stating that "the commencement of the original class suit tolls the running of the statute for all purported members of the class who make timely motions to intervene after the court has found the suit inappropriate for class action status." *Id.* at 553. The Court reasoned that, when a class action lawsuit is filed, the principal goals of limitations periods—putting defendants on notice of claims and discouraging plaintiffs from sleeping on their rights—are satisfied. The Court also reasoned that its approach was consistent with Rule 23, which is based on the premise that class members should rely on class representatives to press the claims of the entire class.

Nine years later, in *Crown, Cork & Seal Co., Inc. v. Parker*, 462 U.S. 345 (1983), the Court expanded the tolling rule to apply to all members of the putative class, including those who file separate suits, and not simply those who file timely motions to intervene after the denial of class certification.

For tolling to apply, the plaintiff must establish that his or her cause of action was within the definition of the class upon which the plaintiff relies for tolling. For example, a plaintiff suing for personal injuries based on a toxic spill would not be able to rely upon a prior class action that was limited solely to class members claiming property damage.

B.   WHEN TOLLING CEASES

When a putative class action is first filed, no one can say with certainty whether class certification will ultimately be granted or denied. For tolling purposes, however, courts presume at the outset that class certification will be granted. If and when class certification is denied, putative class members are expected either to seek to intervene in the case or to file separate actions. Accordingly, when certification is denied, the limitations period begins to run again.

One issue raised by *American Pipe* is ascertaining *when* certification is "denied" for purposes of when the limitations period begins to run again. Does it mean when class certification is denied by the trial court? Or is it when the denial of certification is ultimately upheld by the court of last resort? Courts that have addressed the issue have concluded that tolling ends when the *trial court* denies certification, even though there is still a remote possibility that the ruling will be reversed on appeal. As the Eleventh Circuit explained in *Armstrong v. Martin Marietta Corp.*, 138 F.3d 1374 (11th Cir.) (*en banc*), *cert. denied*, 525 U.S. 1019 (1998), because the trial court's denial of certification is a discretionary ruling that is generally upheld on appeal, continued tolling after the trial court's ruling is not necessary to protect the class members' reasonable reliance on the pendency of the class action suit.

C. LIMITATIONS ON THE *AMERICAN PIPE* TOLLING RULE

There are a number of restrictions on the *American Pipe* rule. Two of the most significant ones are discussed here.

First, courts generally hold that tolling should not be extended when successive class actions are filed. As one court reasoned, a contrary result would allow plaintiffs, even after a class action is found to be inappropriate, to "piggyback one class action onto another and thus toll the statute of limitations indefinitely." *Korwek v. Hunt,* 827 F.2d 874, 878 (2d Cir. 1987).

Some courts, however, have permitted putative class members to file nearly identical follow-up class actions when the reason for the original denial of class certification was not related to any substantive defect in the class claims as a whole. For example, courts may allow tolling with respect to a second class action when the original denial of certification was based on problems with the named plaintiffs, as opposed to the inherent impropriety of the substantive claims for class treatment. As one court has explained, "*American Pipe* tolling applies to the filing of a new class action where certification was denied in the prior suit based on the lead plaintiffs' deficiencies as class representatives, but

... does not apply where certification was denied based on deficiencies in the purported class itself." *Yang v. Odom*, 392 F.3d 97, 99 (3d Cir. 2004). The *Yang* court noted, however, that the courts were divided, on the issue, with some refusing in all circumstances to permit *American Pipe* tolling for successive class actions after the denial of certification in an earlier class action.

Second, some courts have held that *American Pipe* does not apply to state-law claims. When state-law claims are involved, the issue of tolling is determined by state law, not federal law. As a result, if a claim would be time-barred under state law notwithstanding the pendency of a class action, the fact that the case was brought in federal court does not change that result.

D.   APPLICATION OF *AMERICAN PIPE* TO OPT OUTS

As noted above, when class certification is denied, the clock starts to run again, and the individual plaintiffs must file their own claims before the limitations period expires. By contrast, if a timely-filed class action is certified, then the statute of limitations is not an issue for any class member who remains in the class. An issue arises, however, with respect to a class member who opts out of the class after receiving notice that certification has been granted. In that situation, courts hold that tolling ceases for that individual at the time of opt out and the clock starts to run again. Most courts hold that, prior to that time, that individual obtains the benefit of *American Pipe* tolling because the class representatives are deemed to have been pursuing that person's rights.

E.   AMENDING INDIVIDUAL ACTIONS TO ASSERT CLASS CLAIMS

An issue related to *American Pipe* is whether otherwise time-barred class claims will be deemed timely on the ground that they "relate back" to the filing of an individual claim. Federal Rule of Civil Procedure 15(c)(2) provides, in pertinent part, that "an amendment of a pleading relates back to the date of the original pleading when the . . . claim or defense asserted in the amended pleading arose out of the conduct, transaction, or occurrence set forth or attempted to be set forth in the original pleading."

A typical scenario is as follows: Plaintiff files an individual employment discrimination claim. After the statute of limitations has expired for similarly-situated employees who did not sue, plaintiff then attempts to modify his or her case to make it a class action suit, even though the putative class members would be time barred if they pursued their claims individually. In general, courts analyze this situation by evaluating whether the original complaint provided the defendant with notice that a class action could be pursued. If the defendant was aware, prior to the expiration of the statute of limitations, that classwide relief might be sought, or if the complaint itself describes a class that shares grievances similar to those of the plaintiff, courts are frequently willing to allow the class claims to relate back to the filing of the individual claim. On the other hand, when the individual complaint provides no such notice of classwide claims, courts generally hold that untimely class claims cannot be revived.

§ 8.2   Jurisdictional Issues: General Concepts

As noted on p. 194, *supra*, many plaintiffs' lawyers prefer to litigate class actions in state court. Defense counsel, by contrast, usually prefer a federal forum. If a case filed in state court raises federal-law questions, the defendant can remove the case to federal court. If a case filed in state court contains only state-law claims, the defendant may also have grounds to remove the case to federal court based on diversity of citizenship. Before CAFA, defense counsel faced two major impediments in many cases: (1) establishing the jurisdictional amount (under 28 U.S.C. § 1332(a)(1), only cases in which the amount in controversy exceeds $75,000 are removable); and (2) establishing complete diversity of citizenship (*i.e.,* that no plaintiff shares the same citizenship with any defendant). Although CAFA has relaxed these requirements in certain circumstances (*see* pp. 214–227, *infra*), an understanding of these historically critical diversity requirements is essential to appreciating of the genesis and importance of CAFA. Moreover, some cases may be removable under diversity even if they do not satisfy CAFA's requirements.

A. DETERMINING CITIZENSHIP FOR DIVERSITY PURPOSES

The federal diversity statute, 28 U.S.C. § 1332, requires (in addition to the $75,000 amount in controversy) complete diversity of citizenship. It is well established that, in the class-action context, the court should consider only the citizenship of the named plaintiffs and not the citizenship of the unnamed class members. *Supreme Tribe of Ben Hur v. Cauble*, 255 U.S. 356 (1921). This principle is extremely important. If the citizenship of each class member had to be considered, establishing complete diversity in a class action would have been impossible in classes that were nationwide in scope. Even the *Cauble* rule however, has posed serious impediments for defendants seeking to remove class actions to federal court.

Under *Cauble,* plaintiffs who wish to litigate in state court must scrutinize with care the citizenship of the named plaintiffs and defendants, to protect against removal to federal court based on diversity. This means that, if the key defendant is not a citizen of the same state as the named plaintiffs, then the risk of removal exists. Frequently, plaintiffs' lawyers have included in-state as well as out-of-state defendants, leading to claims by defendants that the in-state defendants were improperly joined and that their citizenship should be disregarded for diversity purposes. Defendants frequently argue, for example, that the defendant who would otherwise destroy diversity was "fraudulently joined" in the case and should be disregarded for diversity purposes. For instance, in a products liability suit by a Missouri plaintiff against a Michigan automobile manufacturer and a Missouri automobile dealership, the manufacturer may claim that the dealership was fraudulently joined to defeat diversity. Ordinarily, the fraudulent joinder doctrine applies in one of two circumstances: (1) when there is no possibility that the plaintiff can establish a cause of action against the non-diverse defendant or (2) when there is outright fraud in the pleading of jurisdictional facts (for example, when the complaint falsely alleges the citizenship of a particular defendant).

In some circumstances, plaintiffs will name a defendant who is liable, if at all, to only a small portion of the class. In such a case some defendants have argued that there is fraudulent joinder and that the residency of the particular defendant must be disregarded. The Eleventh Circuit faced that situation in *Triggs v. John Crump Toyota, Inc.*, 154 F.3d 1284 (11th Cir. 1998). In that case, defendants contended that 98 percent of the class members had no conceivable claim against the non-diverse defendant. Defendants thus argued that the non-diverse defendant had been fraudulently joined to defeat diversity. The court rejected this argument, holding that if the named plaintiff has the possibility of a claim against the defendant, diversity cannot be defeated on a fraudulent joinder theory merely because most unnamed class members have no claim against the defendant.

Because fraudulent joinder arguments are difficult to win, plaintiff lawyers have had much success
in joining in-state defendants in large, multi-state
class actions, thereby preventing defendants from
successfully removing such cases to federal court.
As discussed below, CAFA has modified the rule of
complete diversity in certain class actions, permitting removal based on minimal diversity (*i.e.*, any
plaintiff or class member with citizenship that differs from that of any defendant).

B.   AGGREGATION OF CLAIMS FOR PURPOSES OF JURISDICTIONAL AMOUNT

Before CAFA, plaintiffs tried to use the $75,000
jurisdictional amount as a vehicle to preclude diversity jurisdiction, while defendants argued that the
requirement was not an impediment. Specifically,
plaintiffs' attorneys took the position that the
$75,000 amount-in-controversy requirement needed
to be satisfied for *each* class member. By contrast,
defense counsel seeking to remove the case to federal court looked for ways to argue that the amount
in controversy *exceeded* $75,000, either on an indi-
vidual class member basis or through some theory
of aggregating class members' claims. With respect
to aggregation, the question arose whether a court
may add up the claims of prospective class members
to establish jurisdictional amount. For example, if
the damages claimed for each class member in an
80,000–member class are $1,000, then the jurisdic-

tional amount would be established if the damages could be aggregated.

The Supreme Court addressed this issue in *Zahn v. International Paper Co.*, 414 U.S. 291 (1973). In *Zahn*, the Court held that, to satisfy the amount in controversy requirement, each class member in a class action must have individual damages exceeding the jurisdictional amount. Thus, as a general rule, the claims of the individual class members cannot simply be added up to ascertain whether they exceed $75,000; rather, each class member's claim must exceed $75,000. Even before CAFA, however, several arguments could still be made, notwithstanding *Zahn*, in cases that appeared to involve less than $75,000 per plaintiff.

First, defense counsel have argued when appropriate that, in addition to seeking compensatory damages, each plaintiff is also seeking punitive damages, and that the total amount of damages awarded to each plaintiff could reasonably exceed $75,000. Whether this argument has merit depends upon the particular facts (as well as the applicable substantive law of punitive damages).

Second, defense counsel have argued that, when equitable relief is sought in addition to damages, courts should assess the value of equitable relief sought by the putative class in determining whether the $75,000 amount is satisfied. Again, the success of this argument depends upon whether, under the particular facts and governing law, it is reasonable to contend that the equitable relief, in combination with damages, is "worth" $75,000 per class member.

Third, *Zahn* itself also identifies an exception to its general rule, known as the "common fund" exception. That exception applies when several plaintiffs are enforcing a common or undivided interest. In that event, the amounts sought by each plaintiff may be aggregated for purposes of determining jurisdictional amount. Circumstances in which the common fund exception applies, however, are relatively rare. They generally involve a single piece of property or a single insurance policy. In that situation, the rights of a particular plaintiff cannot be determined without implicating the rights of others, and it is therefore appropriate to assess the value of the entire fund or piece of property in determining jurisdictional amount.

Finally, another argument pursued in the wake of *Zahn* is that, if at least one named plaintiff can meet the jurisdictional amount requirement, the other class members need not do so. This argument is based on the "supplemental jurisdiction" statute (enacted in 1990), 28 U.S.C. § 1367, which in certain circumstances allows a court as a matter of discretion to extend subject-matter jurisdiction over related parties, even when those parties cannot independently establish jurisdiction. This situation would apply if at least one class representative seeks relief worth greater than $75,000. (A few cases have also permitted courts to allocate attorneys' fees available to the putative class solely to the named representatives, thereby permitting supplemental jurisdiction even when the representatives had only small-value claims.) Before the U.S. Supreme Court's resolution of the issue in 2005, the courts were sharply divided on how to analyze the supplemental jurisdiction statute.

Courts holding that section 1367 overruled *Zahn* relied upon, among other things, section 1367(a), which states that a federal court "shall have supplemental jurisdiction" if the additional claims "form part of the same controversy" as the claims over which the district court has "original jurisdiction." These courts reasoned that there was original jurisdiction as long as the class representative and the defendant were from different states and the class representative's own claims exceeded $75,000. Thus, the court could exercise supplemental jurisdiction over the other class members' claims. These courts also relied on section 1367(b), which excludes from section 1367(a)'s reach "claims against persons made parties under Rule 14, 19, 20, or 24," but does not list Rule 23.

Courts holding that section 1367 did not overrule *Zahn* reasoned, among other things, that section 1367 was inapplicable when original jurisdiction over the action did not exist, and under *Zahn*, original jurisdiction did not exist unless *all* class members had claims exceeding $75,000. Those courts also relied on section 1367's legislative history, which indicates that section 1367 was not intended to affect jurisdictional requirements in class actions based solely on diversity.

The Supreme Court resolved this issue (at least in cases involving a single defendant) in *Exxon Mobil Corp. v. Allapattah*, 545 U.S. 546 (2005). In *Allapattah*, the Court held that "where the other elements of jurisdiction are present and at least one named plaintiff in the action satisfies the amount-in-controversy requirement, § 1367 [authorizes] supplemental jurisdiction over the claims of other plaintiffs in the same Article III case or controversy, even if those claims are for less than the jurisdictional amount specified in the statute setting forth the requirements for diversity jurisdiction." *Id.* at 2615. The Court based its decision on the plain language of section 1367(a), as well as on the fact that section 1367(b) did not include class actions among the exceptions to section 1367(a). (The Court adopted the same analysis for cases joined under Rule 20. *See* pp. 375–377, *infra.*) Because the Court deemed the language of section 1367 to be clear, it found no merit in contrary arguments based on the legislative history.

The Court noted that its ruling was not mooted by CAFA, which permits class members' claims to be aggregated under a new $5 million amount in controversy rule for certain class actions (*see infra* pp. 215–216). According to the Court, "many proposed exercises of supplemental jurisdictions, even in the class-action context, might not fall within CAFA's ambit." *Id.* at 2628. For example, the class may not satisfy the $5 million threshold, or it might fail to meet another separate requirement of CAFA.

By the same token, many cases will satisfy CAFA but not section 1367. Thus, as is common in many consumer cases, if every member of the class, including the representatives, has a claim below $75,000, then there would be no plaintiff who satisfied original jurisdiction, thereby foreclosing any theory of supplemental jurisdiction.

In short, when analyzing removal of class actions to federal court, both CAFA and section 1367 are potentially relevant, depending on the facts and circumstances of the particular case.

§ 8.3   The Class Action Fairness Act

A.   OVERVIEW

President George W. Bush signed CAFA into law on February 18, 2005. Pub. L. No. 109–2, 119 Stat. 4. The legislation resulted after years of complaints by certain members of Congress, as well as the business community, that state courts were not treating class action defendants fairly. Certain states—more precisely, certain counties within certain states—had become magnets for large multistate class actions, many of which sought hundreds of millions (or even billions) of dollars. Critics urged Congress to enact legislation that would shift large and important class actions from state court to federal court. Opponents of such legislation defended the role of state courts in adjudicating class actions and expressed concern that the proposals were nothing but disguised efforts to eliminate most class actions altogether. In addition, a number of federal and state judges expressed concern that such legislation would jeopardize important principles of federalism and would overload the federal courts. Despite these objections, however, CAFA passed overwhelmingly with strong bipartisan support.

CAFA did not focus solely on shifting class actions from state to federal court. It also addressed certain types of class action settlements—principally, so-called "coupon" settlements—that Congress perceived to benefit class counsel and defendants at the expense of class members. Jurisdictional issues under CAFA are discussed immediately below. Settlement issues under CAFA are discussed on pp. 266–272, *infra*.

B. SUMMARY OF CORE REQUIREMENTS FOR EXPANDED FEDERAL JURISDICTION OVER CLASS ACTIONS

Because cases involving federal questions are removable to federal court under 28 U.S.C. §§ 1331 and 1441, Congress focused its attention on class actions raising issues of state law. In particular, it focused on the requirements for diversity jurisdiction under 28 U.S.C. § 1332. Under CAFA, subject to various exceptions discussed below, Congress amended section 1332 to give federal courts diversity jurisdiction over a putative class action when:

(1) the case involves at least 100 class members (28 U.S.C. § 1332(d)(5)(B));

   (2) "minimal" (as opposed to "complete") diversity exists (28 U.S.C. § 1332(d)(2)); and

   (3) the aggregate amount in controversy for the putative class as a whole is greater then $5 million, exclusive of interest and costs (28 U.S.C. § 1332(d)(2)).

C.   ESTABLISHING "MINIMAL" DIVERSITY

Under CAFA, minimal diversity exists if (1) "any member of a class of plaintiffs is a citizen of a State different from any defendant"; (2) "any member of a class of plaintiffs is a foreign state or a citizen or subject of a foreign state and any defendant is a citizen of a State"; or (3) "any member of a class of plaintiffs is a citizen of a State and any defendant is a foreign state or a citizen or subject of a foreign state." 28 U.S.C. § 1332(d)(2).

Returning to an earlier example (p. 207, *supra*), in a products liability suit by a Missouri class representative against a Michigan automobile manufacturer, minimal diversity would exist even if the plaintiff also named a Missouri automobile dealership as a second defendant. Thus, under CAFA, assuming the other requirements of the statute are met, a plaintiff cannot defeat diversity simply by naming an in-state defendant. Notably, the statute looks to the citizenship of "any member" of the class in determining minimal diversity, not just to the citizenship of the class representatives.

D.   AGGREGATING CLAIMS

With respect to cases that meet the other requirements of the statute, CAFA overrules *Zahn* and permits the claims of individual class members to be aggregated to satisfy jurisdictional amount, provided that the total sought is greater than $5 million, exclusive of interest and costs. For most large, multi-state class actions, satisfying this jurisdiction amount will not be an issue because plaintiffs' counsel will not—and cannot—dispute, based on the class definition and prayer for relief, that the amount in controversy greatly exceeds $5 million. In those cases in which plaintiffs' counsel contemplate smaller recoveries, they can attempt to avoid federal jurisdiction by simply capping the relief requested in the complaint at a maximum of $5 million. This same practice was used frequently before CAFA to cap individual class member claims at or below $75,000.

If the class has not capped the recovery at or under $5 million, and the amount in controversy is not otherwise clear on the face of the complaint, courts under CAFA have considered evidence relevant to jurisdictional amount. Courts have resolved uncertainty regarding jurisdictional amount in favor of remand to state court. *E.g., Miedema v. Maytag Corp.,* 450 F.3d 1322 (11th Cir. 2006).

CAFA's approach to jurisdictional amount provides a solution to federal jurisdiction that is not encompassed by the supplemental jurisdiction statute, as construed in *Allapattah*: To exercise supplemental jurisdiction, at least one class representative must satisfy the $75,000 amount-in-controversy requirement. For many types of class actions, such as those involving economic damages for consumer products, class counsel might have difficulty identifying any member of the class with damages greater than $75,000, let alone someone who has signed up (or is willing to sign up) as the class representative.

E.   MASS ACTIONS

CAFA applies not only to class actions but also to so-called "mass actions," which are defined as "any civil action ... in which monetary relief claims of 100 or more persons are proposed to be tried jointly on the grounds that the plaintiffs' claims involve common questions of law or fact." Pub. L. No. 109–2, 119 Stat. 4, 11 (2005). This expansion beyond class actions to cover non-class joinder cases was based on Congress' concern that mass actions, like class actions, were being abused. Indeed, one of the states that concerned Congress was Mississippi, which permits mass actions but does not authorize class actions. Congress, however, did not give the mass action section the same teeth that it gave to class actions. Under CAFA, although a mass action need only satisfy minimal diversity, the $75,000 amount-in-controversy requirement still exists for each plaintiff; aggregation is not allowed as a way of satisfying jurisdictional amount.

F. EXCEPTIONS TO CAFA'S NEW JURISDICTIONAL RULES

CAFA contains several exceptions to its new, expanded jurisdiction. The exceptions, some of which are discretionary, are complicated and contain numerous ambiguities. It remains to be seen whether a significant number of larger and more important types of class actions targeted by Congress will qualify for one or more exceptions.

Home State and Local Controversy Exceptions. First, a federal court has *discretion* to decline jurisdiction when (1) more than one third, but fewer than two thirds, of the putative class members are citizens of the forum state; and (2) the "primary defendants" are likewise forum-state citizens. 28 U.S.C. § 1332(d)(3). The statute contains six criteria that the court is instructed to consider: (1) whether the claims "involve matters of national or interstate interest"; (2) whether the claims will be governed by the forum state's laws; (3) whether the action was "pleaded in a manner that seeks to avoid Federal jurisdiction"; (4) whether the forum has "a distinct nexus with the class members, the alleged harm, or the defendants"; and (5) whether the number of forum-state citizens in the putative class is "substantially larger than the number of citizens from any other State, and the citizenship of [other putative class members] is dispersed among a substantial number of States[.]" 28 U.S.C. § 1332(d)(3).

Second, under 28 U.S.C. § 1332(d)(4)(B), the district court *must* decline jurisdiction if two-thirds or more of the putative class members and the "primary defendants" are citizens of the forum state. 28 U.S.C § 1332(d)(4)(B).

Third, under 28 U.S.C. § 1332(d)(4)(A), even if 28 U.S.C. § 1332(d)(4)(B)'s requirements are not met, the court *must* decline jurisdiction if a series of requirements are met:

(1) more then two-thirds of the putative class members are citizens of the forum state;

(2) at least one defendant is a defendant: (a) from whom the putative class seeks "significant relief"; (b) whose conduct allegedly constitutes a "significant basis" of the putative class members' claims; and (c) who is a citizen of the forum;

(3) the "principal injuries" resulting from the conduct at issue occurred in the forum state; and

(4) no similar class action involving any of the same defendants was filed during the three-year period preceding the filing of the complaint at issue.

These exceptions leave many unanswered questions, including: (1) How will courts define various terms that are not defined in the statute, such as "primary defendants," "significant relief," and "principal injuries"? (2) Will courts apply the discretionary exception broadly to exclude federal jurisdiction or narrowly to uphold it? (3) To what extent will class counsel deliberately structure the class definition, selection of parties, and configuration of the case to take advantage of one or more of these discretionary or mandatory exceptions? Because CAFA was enacted in 2005, it is too early to predict how significant CAFA's home state and local controversy exceptions will be in practice.

Other Exceptions for State Officials, Securities and Corporate Governance Cases, and Small Class Actions. CAFA also excludes class and mass actions in which the "primary defendants" are "States, State Officials, or other government entities against whom the district court may be foreclosed from ordering relief[.]" 28 U.S.C. § 1332(d)(5)(A). This exception avoids removals in which the defendants argue that federal courts are barred by the Eleventh Amendment from ordering relief. Courts construing this exception have held that, because the exception is phrased in the plural, *all* of the primary defendants must be states for the exception to apply. *E.g., Frazier v. Pioneer Americas LLC,* 455 F.3d 542 (5th Cir. 2006).

In addition, CAFA excludes actions under the securities laws or involving "internal affairs or governance of a corporation or other form of business enterprise and that arise[] under or by virtue of the laws of the state in which such corporation or business enterprise is incorporated or organized[.]" 28 U.S.C. § 1332(d)(9). These latter exceptions are designed to maintain the current federal/state boundaries in securities and corporate governance cases.

Finally, as noted (p. 214, *supra*), CAFA is inapplicable to putative classes with fewer than 100 members, 28 U.S.C. § 1332(d)(5)(B), or when the aggregate amount in controversy is $5 million or less. 28 U.S.C. § 1332(d)(2).

G.   LIBERALIZED REMOVAL UNDER CAFA

Although CAFA creates original federal jurisdiction for cases meeting its requirements, Congress anticipated that many cases falling within CAFA would continue to be filed in state court. Plaintiffs' counsel might believe that, in some instances, they can fall within a CAFA exception, and that in other instances the defendants may decide, for whatever reason, to remain in state court. As a result, CAFA makes clear that if a qualified case is filed in state court, the defendant(s) may remove the case to federal court pursuant to the requirements of 28 U.S.C. § 1446. Congress, however, did not simply adopt the removal requirements verbatim. Instead, in addition to allowing removal without the need to satisfy complete diversity or the $75,000 per class member amount (provided that the other requirements of CAFA are met), CAFA liberalizes removal requirements in a number of important ways.

First, although 28 U.S.C. § 1446(b) bars removal on diversity grounds after one year following the commencement of the suit, cases under CAFA are not subject to the one-year limitation.

Second, pre-CAFA case law makes clear that *all* properly joined and served defendants (except those allegedly joined fraudulently) must join in removal. *E.g., Emrich v. Touché Ross & Co.*, 846 F.2d 1190 (9th Cir. 1988). Under CAFA, any defendant may remove a case without the need for consent by other defendants. 28 U.S.C. § 1453(b).

Third, under the "forum defendant" rule, a diversity case may not be removed if any of the defendants is a citizen of the forum state. 28 U.S.C. § 1441(b). Under CAFA, removal is permissible even if one or more defendants is a citizen of the forum state. 28 U.S.C. § 1453(b).

H. APPELLATE REVIEW

In the ordinary (non-CAFA) case, a party cannot seek appellate review of an order remanding a removed case to state court. Put another way, subject only to limited exceptions, a federal district court has complete, unreviewable authority to remand a case to federal court. (By contrast, a ruling declining to remand a case to state court is reviewable by the federal appellate court at the end of the case upon final judgment.) Congress, in enacting CAFA, wanted to avoid the situation in which a single federal judge could avoid CAFA simply by engaging in an unreviewable act of remanding a case to state court. Accordingly, it provided in CAFA for discretionary immediate appellate review of remand decisions (both granting and denying remand). Specifically, 28 U.S.C. § 1453(c)(1) gives federal courts of appeal discretion to grant immediate review of an order granting or denying a remand motion. The appeal, if granted, must be completed "not later than 60 days after the date on which such appeal was filed," subject to one extension of 10 days for good cause (upon agreement of all parties). 28 U.S.C. § 1453(c)(2), (3).

Despite the statute's reference to when the appeal was "filed," courts construing CAFA have held that the 60–day period for completing the appeal begins when the appeal is *accepted* by the appellate court, not when the appeal is *filed*. *E.g., Amalgamated Transit Union Local 1309, AFL–CIO v. Laidlaw Transit Servs., Inc.,* 435 F.3d 1140 (9th Cir. 2006). Given the time necessary for the appellate court to consider the application for appeal, focusing on the filing date would have made it impossible in many cases for the appellate court to comply with the 60–day (or even 70–day) period. CAFA provides that if the appeal is not resolved by the end of the 60–day (or 70–day) period, the appeal shall be deemed denied. 28 U.S.C. § 1453(c)(4).

Under CAFA, the application for appeal must be filed in the appellate court "not less than 7 days after entry of the order" granting or denying a remand motion. As written, this language would have led to absurd results: a party could not file an appeal until the seventh day but could do so any time thereafter. Courts addressing this issue have unanimously concluded, however, that "less than" was a typographical error and that Congress meant to allow appeals filed "within" or "not more than" seven days after entry of the order. *E.g., Miedema v. Maytag Corp.,* 450 F.3d 1322, 1326 (11th Cir. 2006).

I.   ISSUES LITIGATED DURING THE INITIAL MONTHS OF CAFA

Commencement of an Action. CAFA applies "to any civil action commenced on or after the date of enactment of this Act." Pub. L. No. 109–2, 119 Stat. 4, 14 (2005). CAFA was enacted on February 18, 2005. In numerous cases, defendants have attempted to argue that various cases filed before CAFA nonetheless "commenced" on or after its effective date. A few courts have taken the view that an action can commence only once, and that if the suit was initially brought before February 18, 2005, no amendment can constitute a new commencement. Most courts reject that bright line approach but nonetheless view amendments with skepticism for purposes of triggering CAFA removal. One line of cases holds that, to decide whether a case has commenced based on an amendment, the inquiry is whether, under the law of the forum state, the amendment "relates back" to the original filing for statute of limitations purposes. Under this approach, immaterial tinkering with the claims, factual allegations, or class definition does not qualify to recommence an action, because such amendments invariably relate back to the original complaint. On the other hand, a major change in the class definition or configuration of the case might not relate back, and thus might qualify as the commencement of a new action for purposes of CAFA. And the addition of a new defendant ordinarily would not relate back to the original filing (unless the new defendant knew before the amendment that it would have been joined but for a mistake by plaintiff in naming the correct party). Another line of cases applies the "relation back" doctrine for all amendments except those adding new parties. With respect to adding new parties, those courts find that adding new parties constitutes the commencement of a new case. These competing views are summarized in *Prime Care of Northeast Kansas, LLC v. Humana Ins. Co.,* 447 F.3d 1284 (10th Cir. 2006). (It should also be noted that, in some states, an action commences when the complaint is served. Thus, a few courts have found that a suit filed before CAFA but served afterwards is subject to CAFA.)

Another question that courts have addressed under CAFA is whether the act of removal to federal court itself constitutes the commencement of a new action. Here, courts are unanimous in holding that removal does not "commence" a new action for purposes of CAFA. *E.g., Pritchett v. Office Depot, Inc.,* 420 F.3d 1090 (10th Cir. 2005).

Burden of Proof. Courts are split over whether the plaintiff or the defendant has the burden of proof with respect to the requirements for obtaining jurisdiction under CAFA. Some district courts, relying on CAFA's legislative history, have held that the burden is on the plaintiff to demonstrate that federal jurisdiction does not exist. Thus far, however, all of the circuit courts that have considered the question have held that the burden is on the removing defendant to show that federal jurisdiction exists under CAFA. *E.g., Brill v. Countrywide Home Loans, Inc.* 427 F.3d 446 (7th Cir. 2005). Even these courts, however, hold that the burden of showing an *exception* to CAFA jurisdiction (such as the local controversy exception) is on plaintiffs. *E.g., Evans v. Walter Indus.*, 449 F.3d 1159 (11th Cir. 2006).

J. POTENTIAL IMPACT OF CAFA'S EXPANDED JURISDICTION

Commentators are split in their predictions on the impact of CAFA. Some believe that, because federal courts have been more restrictive than state courts in certifying class actions, CAFA will result in an end to most class actions. Other commentators predict that, because of various CAFA exceptions, along with the willingness of many federal courts to certify major class actions, CAFA will not have the seismic impact contemplated by its drafters and supporters.

Certainly, one possible impact of CAFA is that the class action plaintiffs' bar may become more consolidated. The time and expense simply to litigate the myriad interpretative issues under CAFA may discourage many smaller, non-repeat players from getting involved.

Another potential impact of CAFA is that plaintiff lawyers, in deciding where to bring multi-state class actions, may select those locations in which federal courts have been most receptive to class actions. Put another way, one might expect a fair degree of forum shopping among federal court venues, as class counsel search for federal judges who are sympathetic to major class action litigation.

III. *RES JUDICATA*, COLLATERAL ESTOPPEL, AND PARALLEL FEDERAL AND STATE–COURT PROCEEDINGS

Class actions are designed to adjudicate, in a single action, the claims of numerous parties with similar claims. One objective of a class action judgment is to prevent future litigation of *claims* that were, or could have been, litigated in the class action (*res judicata* or claim preclusion). Another goal is to prevent further litigation of *issues* that were determined in, and were necessary to, the class action (collateral estoppel or issue preclusion). This section examines the doctrines of *res judicata* and collateral estoppel in the context of class actions. It also examines the related questions of whether (and when) a federal court can enjoin ongoing state court proceedings, and when a federal court ruling denying class certification is binding on the class. Finally, this section discusses federal attempts to enjoin competing state court class actions.

§ 8.4 Claim Preclusion (*Res Judicata*) in the Class–Action Context

A. OVERVIEW

Rule 23(c)(3) requires a court rendering a class action judgment to identify the members of the class. This requirement is necessary to determine who is bound by the judgment for *res judicata* purposes.

The doctrine of *res judicata* in a class action arises when a court enters judgment on the merits, and one or more of the parties identified in that judgment (individual class members, the class as a whole, or the opposing party) pursues a claim in a separate court based upon the cause of action adjudicated in the prior judgment. *Res judicata* not only bars claims that were actually litigated during the class action, but also those that could have been litigated.

The difficulty in applying *res judicata* in the class action context is determining who is bound by the earlier judgment. Subject to certain exceptions discussed on pp. 229–231, *infra*, in class actions brought under Rule 23, the *res judicata* effect of a judgment extends to the entire certified class. As discussed in the following section, it may also extend to certain nonparties. *Res judicata* does not, however, bar an individual from pursuing his or her own claims when class certification is denied.

B. NONPARTIES WHO MAY BE BOUND BY THE PRIOR DETERMINATION

Courts have recognized that a judgment is binding not only on the parties but also on those in "privity" with them. Various courts recognize several categories of nonparties who are deemed to be in privity with a party to a proceeding: "(1) a nonparty who controls the original action; (2) a nonparty whose interests are represented by a party in the original action; and (3) a successor-in-interest to a party." *Sondel v. Northwest Airlines, Inc.,* 56 F.3d 934, 938 (8th Cir. 1995). Mere coincidental interests and the opportunity to participate in and contribute to the prior action are not enough to establish privity. Some courts have warned, however, that concepts of privity or "virtual representation" should be applied cautiously to avoid due process concerns. *See, e.g., Tice v. American Airlines, Inc.,* 162 F.3d 966, 972 (7th Cir. 1998) ("[T]he fact that virtual representation looks like a class action but avoids compliance with Rule 23 is a weakness, not a strength, of the doctrine."), *cert. denied,* 527 U.S. 1036 (1999).

C. CLASS MEMBERS WHO MAY NOT BE BOUND BY A PRIOR ADJUDICATION

There are two important exceptions to the general rule that the *res judicata* effect of a judgment extends to the entire certified class.

The first exception is when the absent class members are not provided with the required notice and opportunity to opt out of the class. The determination of whether absent class members are provided the requisite notice depends upon the type of Rule 23 class action at issue. In Rule 23(b)(3) class actions, best practicable notice and the opportunity to opt out are necessary to bind absent class members (although several lower courts have excused actual notice when notice was attempted but not achieved, such as when an apartment number was inadvertently omitted from an address (*see* p. 164, *supra*)). Lower courts are divided over whether, in "mandatory" class actions under Rules 23(b)(1)(A), 23(b)(1)(B) and 23(b)(2), in which monetary relief is sought, due process requires that absent class members be given an opportunity to opt out before they will be bound by a judgment in the class action. The Supreme Court has not decided the issue. *See* pp. 172–173, *supra*.

The second exception is when the appointed class representative and counsel fail to provide fair and adequate representation in the original suit. This factor requires a court to examine the qualifications and performance of both the named representatives and their attorneys. *See* pp. 51–66, *supra*. The adequacy analysis for *res judicata* differs from that by the original court in the sense that the original court may have ruled on adequacy at the outset but may not have revisited the issue in light of the actual performance at trial or during pretrial proceedings. For purposes of *res judicata*, a reviewing court may examine, for instance, whether the representatives were inadequate because they did not appeal an adverse ruling. As discussed on pp. 235–236, *infra*, however, some courts have found significant procedural limitations on a court's authority to review, on collateral attack, the adequacy findings of the certifying court. Other courts, by contrast, have permitted collateral attacks on the adequacy of representation, including the Second Circuit in the *Agent Orange* litigation. The Supreme Court granted certiorari in *Agent Orange* to address issues involving collateral attacks on adequacy. Ultimately, however, the Court split four to four (Justice Stevens not participating) and thus did not issue any precedent-setting rulings. *Dow Chem. Co. v. Stephenson*, 539 U.S. 111 (2003).

For a discussion of *res judicata* in the context of an employment discrimination class action in which the district court found no pattern or practice of discrimination, *see* pp. 316–317, *infra*.

D.   LIMITATIONS UPON THE *RES JUDICATA* EFFECT OF CLASS ACTIONS SEEKING ONLY DECLARATORY OR INJUNCTIVE RELIEF

Courts agree that notice and opt-out rights are not required to bind a class seeking *solely* declaratory or injunctive relief. Courts have also held, however, that a class action seeking solely equitable relief will not bar subsequent individual suits for damages.

§ 8.5 Issue Preclusion (Collateral Estoppel) in the Class Action Context

Issue preclusion, or collateral estoppel, differs from claim preclusion in a basic way: Rather than precluding a subsequent cause of action entirely, it bars a party from asserting a position or raising an issue that was adjudicated in an earlier proceeding. Collateral estoppel can be "mutual" or "non-mutual." When the plaintiff and defendant in the subsequent action were both involved in the initial action, collateral estoppel is called "mutual." When only one of the parties in the subsequent action was involved in the initial action, collateral estoppel may still apply, in which case it is "non-mutual." *Parklane Hosiery Co., Inc. v. Shore*, 439 U.S. 322 (1979). Issues involving both mutual and non-mutual collateral estoppel arise in class actions.

One issue is whether a defendant who prevails in an earlier class action can assert collateral estoppel against those class members who opted out of the earlier litigation. Courts have rejected such an attempt on the ground that "[a]n opt-out plaintiff is not a party to the class action and ... collateral estoppel cannot bind a person who was neither a party nor privy to a prior suit." *In re Corrugated Container Antitrust Litig.*, 756 F.2d 411, 418–19 (5th Cir. 1985).

Another situation involving an opt-out class member and collateral estoppel arises when the class prevails in the initial class action, and the opt-out class member in a subsequent lawsuit attempts to assert non-mutual collateral estoppel against the defendant. Courts have rejected such attempts. In *Premier Electrical Construction Co. v. National Electrical Contractors Ass'n, Inc.,* 814 F.2d 358 (7th Cir. 1987), the Seventh Circuit refused to permit plaintiffs who opted out of a prior class action to use offensive issue preclusion in their subsequent individual suit against the defendant. To hold otherwise, the court reasoned, would unfairly give the opt outs the best of all worlds: They would not be bound if the plaintiff class lost, but they could reap the benefits if the class won. According to the court, this sort of "one-way intervention" is precisely what Congress sought to eliminate when it did away with "spurious" classes in 1966. *Id.* at 362. *See* pp. 17–20, *supra.*

§ 8.6 Federal Control Over State Courts

Class actions frequently proceed on parallel tracks in federal and state court. At times, the same plaintiffs' lawyers may be pressing ahead on both tracks. At other times, two groups of plaintiffs' lawyers may be competing in a race to judgment. Such parallel litigation leads to several important issues, including: (i) what, if any, preclusive effect a state-court ruling has on a parallel federal proceeding; (ii) whether collateral attacks may be mounted based on inadequate representation; (iii) what effect a denial of class certification in federal court has on a subsequent state court class action; and (iv) what authority, if any, a federal court has to enjoin an ongoing state court class action. These issues are addressed below.

A. BINDING EFFECT OF STATE COURT SETTLEMENTS OF EXCLUSIVELY FEDERAL CLAIMS

When a state court class action has been settled, and the settlement releases not only state law claims but also claims that are within the exclusive jurisdiction of the federal courts, the question arises as to whether a member of the class is free to pursue those federal claims in federal court. Various aspects of this question were addressed by the Supreme Court in *Matsushita Elec. Indus. Co. v. Epstein,* 516 U.S. 367 (1996), and by the Ninth Circuit on remand in *Epstein v. MCA, Inc.,* 179 F.3d 641 (9th Cir.), *cert. denied,* 528 U.S. 1004 (1999). In that litigation, there had previously been two class actions against the same defendants, one in federal court (with exclusively federal claims) and one in state court (with exclusively state claims). The state-court plaintiffs settled on a classwide basis with the defendants, releasing all state and federal claims. Notice of the settlement was sent to the class, including the class representatives in the federal action, who did not exercise their right to opt out and did not appear at the settlement hearing. The state court subsequently conducted a hearing and approved the settlement. The defendants in the federal action then argued that the state court settlement was entitled to "full faith and credit" and precluded plaintiffs' federal claims. Defendants relied on the Full Faith and Credit Act, 28 U.S.C. § 1738, which requires federal courts to give state court judgments the same force and effect that they would receive in a state court in the rendering jurisdiction. The class members who sought to pursue their claims notwithstanding the settlement responded that the federal court should not grant full faith and credit to the state court settlement, since it was entered into in violation of the absent class members' right to adequate representation.

The Supreme Court held in *Matsushita* that a federal court is required to give full faith and credit to a state-court settlement that releases claims within the exclusive jurisdiction of the federal courts. It reasoned that, because the state court had jurisdiction over the subject matter of the dispute, the fact that the federal claims could not have been litigated in state court did not bar the parties from settling those claims in the state action. The court did not decide whether the claims could nonetheless go forward in federal court because of the plaintiffs' contention that the state court settlement resulted from inadequate representation.

B. COLLATERAL ATTACKS BASED ON ADEQUACY OF REPRESENTATION

On remand from the Supreme Court in *Matsushita*, the Ninth Circuit initially held that the claims could go forward despite *Matsushita* because the representation of the class in the state court case had been inadequate. That decision was arguably in accord with the traditional rule permitting collateral attack for inadequate representation. The court subsequently reversed itself, however, and held in a split decision that, under the Full Faith and Credit Act, federal courts are precluded from passing judgment on the adequacy of representation in state court if the issue has been fully and fairly litigated—and decided by the state court—in the context of the class settlement.

By contrast, the Second Circuit, in a decision affirmed by an equally divided Supreme Court (and thus without precedential value), permitted a collateral attack on adequacy. *Stephenson v. Dow Chem. Co.*, 273 F.3d 249 (2d Cir. 2001), *aff'd by an equally divided Court*, 539 U.S. 111 (2003). *In Stephenson*, the Second Circuit held that two veterans suing for health effects from exposure to Agent Orange could collaterally attack a prior classwide settlement of Agent Orange claims on the ground that the representation of the class had been inadequate. The court so held, even though the representation had been found adequate at the time of the original certification. In particular, the court found that the cutoff for claiming cash benefits contained in the settlement agreement disadvantaged veterans whose injuries manifested themselves after the cutoff date and that such veterans, by being put in this situation, had not been adequately represented. According to the court, "Because these plaintiffs were inadequately represented in the prior litigation, they were not proper parties and cannot be bound by the settlement." 273 F.3d at 261.

Most recently, in *In re Diet Drugs Prods. Liab. Litig.* 431 F.3d 141 (3d Cir. 2005), the Third Circuit expressly disagreed with the Second Circuit's *Ste-*

phenson decision, noting that "where the class action court has jurisdiction over an absent member of a plaintiff class and it litigates and determines the adequacy of the representation of that member, the member is foreclosed from later relitigating that issue." *Id.* at 146. Even more recently, the Second Circuit (in a partial retreat from *Stephenson*) has recognized that collateral attack on adequacy grounds is *not* permitted if the precise argument was "considered and rejected by the class action court," but that collateral attack *is* appropriate "if the class action court ruled only in general terms that representation was adequate...." *Wolfert v. Transamerica Home First, Inc.*, 439 F.3d 165 (2d Cir.), *cert. denied*, 127 S.Ct. 192 (2006). Ultimately, the Supreme Court will need to provide guidance on this important issue.

C. BINDING EFFECT OF PRIOR FEDERAL COURT DENIAL OF CLASS CERTIFICATION UPON A LATER STATE COURT CLASS ACTION

When a federal court denies class certification, an issue that may arise is whether a state court may grant class certification based upon similar claims. This question has not been decided by the Supreme Court, but it has been addressed by several lower courts.

In *J.R. Clearwater, Inc. v. Ashland Chemical Co.*, 93 F.3d 176 (5th Cir. 1996), an action was commenced in state court and then removed to federal court, where class certification was sought and ultimately denied. Later, the attorney for the class plaintiffs commenced another suit in state court against the same defendants, asserting essentially the same claims, and defining the class in the same terms as in the federal action. The defendants in the federal action requested that the district court enjoin certification of the state class on the ground that the federal court had already denied certification involving the same class. The district court refused to enjoin the state court from certifying a class, reasoning that the order denying class certification was not a final order. The Fifth Circuit affirmed, holding that the denial of certification was a discretionary ruling under Federal Rule of Civil Procedure 23, and that the Texas trial court might exercise its discretion differently under Texas' class action rules. Accordingly, the denial of certification could not be given preclusive effect, and thus the district court could not enjoin the state-court proceedings. The Third Circuit has generally endorsed the *Clearwater* approach in *In re General Motors Corp. Products Liability Litigation*, 134 F.3d 133 (3d Cir. 1998).

The Seventh Circuit took a different approach in *In re Bridgestone/Firestone, Inc., Tires Products Liability Litigation*, 333 F.3d 763 (7th Cir. 2003). As noted on p. 192, *supra,* the Seventh Circuit had held, in an earlier decision, that a nationwide class could not be certified because of the manageability problems raised by the need to apply the laws of all 50 states, the District of Columbia, and various U.S.

territories. After that ruling, plaintiffs' counsel filed suits in a number of state courts seeking certification of nationwide classes that were the same as, or similar to, the one that the Seventh Circuit had disapproved. Ford and Firestone sought to enjoin those actions, but the district court denied relief. On review, the Seventh Circuit held that, under collateral estoppel, its earlier ruling rejecting class certification was binding on both the named representatives and the unnamed class members. The court recognized that the unnamed class members were treated as parties for various other purposes, and that here it was proper to bind them because they received adequate representation in the federal case. The court reasoned that an injunction was appropriate because, absent an injunction, plaintiffs' counsel would continue to litigate in state courts until they found a court willing to certify a nationwide class. The result would be "an asymmetric system in which class counsel can win but never lose." *Id.* at 767.

It should also be noted that at least one state court has held that, when class allegations are stricken as a matter of law, such a ruling precludes other class members on *res judicata* grounds from seeking certification of the same class, in another proceeding, in the same state court system. *Duffy v. Si–Sifh Corp.,* 726 So.2d 438 (La.App. 4th Cir. 1999). In contrast to *Duffy,* which arose under Louisiana law, federal decisions on this issue have not relied on *res judicata.*

D.   FEDERAL COURT ATTEMPTS TO ENJOIN COMPETING STATE COURT CLASS ACTIONS

The Anti–Injunction Act, 28 U.S.C. § 2283, prohibits a federal court from enjoining state court proceedings, "except where expressly authorized by Act of Congress, or where necessary in aid of its jurisdiction, or to protect or effectuate its judgments." Anti–Injunction Act issues sometimes arise in class actions when a federal court certifies a mandatory class (under Rule 23(b)(1) or (b)(2)) that includes class members who are involved in a parallel state court class action. Some federal courts have held that the Anti–Injunction Act does not prohibit such an injunction of state court proceedings, particularly when the federal case is close to being settled.

For example, in *In re Joint Eastern and Southern District Asbestos Litigation*, 134 F.R.D. 32 (E. & S.D.N.Y. 1990), the court certified a mandatory class action and enjoined all pending state court claims. The court found that doing so was permitted under the "in aid of jurisdiction" exception to the Anti–Injunction Act. The court reasoned that the "in aid of jurisdiction" exception applied when a federal court is involved in settling a complex matter and state court proceedings could undermine that objective. The court also noted that it was in the process of evaluating the assets of the defendant for settlement purposes, and could only continue that task if the defendant's assets remained intact. According to the court, permitting other proceedings to continue against the defendant would jeopardize the fair and equitable distribution of the defendant's assets. (Another example of a court endorsing an injunction against state court proceedings is the *Bridgestone/Firestone* case, discussed on pp. 238–239, *supra*.)

Other courts, however, have viewed the Anti–Injunction Act as a far more serious roadblock. These courts have typically relied on *In re Federal Skywalk Cases,* 680 F.2d 1175 (8th Cir.), *cert. denied,* 459 U.S. 988 (1982), which suggested in *dicta* that certification of a limited-fund class action would have the practical effect of enjoining all other class actions and thus would violate the Anti–Injunction Act. (The court ultimately held that certification was inappropriate because no limited fund existed.)

IV.   CONSTITUTIONAL ISSUES

§ 8.7   Seventh Amendment

A.   OVERVIEW

The Seventh Amendment to the U.S. Constitution went largely unmentioned in class action litigation for many years after the 1966 amendments to Rule 23. In recent years, however, the Seventh Amendment has become a major issue, and a few appellate court rulings have called into question whether large, bifurcated class actions can be litigated consistent with Seventh Amendment protections.

The Seventh Amendment provides:

In Suits at common law, where the value in controversy shall exceed twenty dollars, the right of trial by jury shall be preserved, *and no fact tried by a jury shall be otherwise re-examined in any Court of the United States, than according to the rules of the common law.* (Emphasis added)

The section of the Seventh Amendment highlighted above is known as the Reexamination Clause. The Reexamination Clause was included in the Seventh Amendment out of concern that jury verdicts from local trial courts would be overturned by appellate courts that would not confine themselves to issues of law but would undertake a *de novo* review of the facts.

B. BIFURCATED TRIALS AND THE REEXAMINATION CLAUSE

As discussed on pp. 149–151, *supra*, some courts have utilized bifurcated trials to adjudicate common, classwide issues first, leaving the individual issues to be resolved in subsequent trials. For example, assume a negligence action against a pharmaceutical company for the production of an allegedly defective drug consumed by thousands of potential class members. A common issues trial might in some cases be warranted to determine whether the drug causes a particular illness or whether the company misrepresented the side effects of the medication. On the other hand, even if those issues were decided in favor of the class, individual trials would still be required to determine such issues as whether the particular class member in fact used the drug; whether he followed the instructions on the package; whether his illness was caused by some other source; and so forth.

In the type of bifurcated case described above, a series of juries are frequently used. Indeed, when large numbers of class members are involved, it is simply not feasible to assign a single jury to sit through months—or potentially years—of separate trials. In recent years, defendants have begun to express concern that this procedure requires multiple juries to reexamine the same issues in violation of the Seventh Amendment. Although the Supreme Court has not addressed this precise issue in the context of a class action, a number of appellate courts have done so, and several have questioned the constitutionality of various bifurcated jury trials in class actions.

An early opinion raising Seventh Amendment concerns in a class action case was in *State of Alabama v. Blue Bird Body Co., Inc.*, 573 F.2d 309 (5th Cir. 1978). In *Blue Bird*, the Fifth Circuit suggested that a trial that bifurcated liability and damages might require examination of overlapping issues by two juries in violation of the Seventh Amendment. Following *Blue Bird*, the Reexamination Clause was rarely invoked in class-action litigation for close to two decades.

Beginning in 1995, however, a number of class-action appellate decisions addressed the issue. The first, *In the Matter of Rhone–Poulenc Rorer Inc.,* 51 F.3d 1293 (7th Cir. 1995), brought the Reexamination Clause into the forefront of class action litigation. *Rhone-Poulenc* involved a nationwide class of hemophiliacs who contracted AIDS from contaminated blood transfusions in the early 1980s. Under the district court's proposed trial plan, an initial jury trial would determine certain common issues, such as whether defendants were negligent. If any defendants were found negligent, individual class members would then be permitted to file their own suits around the country, with the later juries being instructed on the first jury's findings. The Seventh Circuit held that this plan violated the Reexamination Clause. The court reasoned that issues to be decided by subsequent juries (such as comparative negligence and proximate causation) would overlap with issues decided by the first jury. For example, comparative negligence involves comparing the plaintiff's negligence to the negligence of the defendant, something the first jury would have already determined. The court found that these Seventh Amendment problems (in conjunction with other problems identified by the court (*see* pp. 286, 300–301, *infra*)) warranted the issuance of a writ of mandamus.

Subsequently, the Fifth Circuit in *Castano v. American Tobacco Co.*, 84 F.3d 734 (5th Cir. 1996), found similar Seventh Amendment problems in a proposed bifurcated class action. The case was a nationwide class action (involving potentially millions of individuals) against the nation's largest tobacco companies. The plaintiffs alleged, among other things, that the defendant tobacco companies negligently failed to inform consumers that nicotine is addictive and that the defendants had manipulated nicotine levels. The district court certified the class and found that manageability concerns—raised by the existence of myriad individualized comparative negligence issues—could be addressed through bifurcated proceedings. Although most of the Fifth Circuit's opinion reversing the district court addressed the deficiencies of the proposed class action under Rule 23(b)(3), the court also addressed the Seventh Amendment. Relying on both *Blue Bird* and *Rhone-Poulenc*, the court stated that, contrary to the Seventh Amendment, a second jury's consideration of comparative negligence with respect to individual class members would permit that jury to revisit the first jury's core finding as to negligence.

C. CRITICISM OF THE *RHONE-POULENC* AND *CASTANO* APPROACH

Rhone-Poulenc, *Castano*, and other similar cases have raised fundamental questions about the viability of many large, bifurcated class actions involving multiple juries. (Although the Seventh Amendment does not apply to state courts, many states have comparable right-to-jury-trial protections.) Not all courts, however, have agreed with the Seventh Amendment analysis in *Rhone-Poulenc* and *Castano*.

In *In re Copley Pharmaceutical, Inc.*, 161 F.R.D. 456 (D.Wyo. 1995), the district court certified a nationwide class action against a pharmaceutical company. Under the court's bifurcated trial plan, the first trial would focus solely on common issues, such as the defendant's negligence, while the second phase, if necessary, would focus on individual issues, such as causation and damages. The *Copley Pharmaceutical* court sharply criticized the *Rhone-Poulenc* decision, reasoning that its approach would essentially bar bifurcated trials in class actions. The court pointed out that the Advisory Committee expressly endorsed the use of bifurcated trials in its notes accompanying Rule 23(c)(4).

In *Robinson v. Metro–North Commuter Railroad Co.*, 267 F.3d 147 (2d Cir. 2001), *cert. denied,* 535 U.S. 951 (2002), the Second Circuit, while not expressly criticizing the *Rhone-Poulenc* approach to the Seventh Amendment, suggested that Seventh Amendment reexamination concerns in a bifurcated class action could be avoided by ensuring that the first jury makes precise, detailed findings that can be applied by later juries.

Several circuits have yet to address the issue. Ultimately, Supreme Court guidance will be necessary.

D.   OTHER SEVENTH AMENDMENT ISSUES

Although most attention has focused on the Seventh Amendment's Reexamination Clause, the basic guarantee of a jury trial for suits at common law may also be implicated in the class-action context. In *Cimino v. Raymark Industries, Inc.*, 151 F.3d 297 (5th Cir. 1998), for example, the Fifth Circuit disapproved of a district court's plan to decide over two-thousand asbestos-related tort cases using extrapolated data from a much smaller number of cases tried by a jury. The Fifth Circuit held that the use of extrapolated data denied the defendants their Seventh Amendment right to have a jury determine issues of causation separately for each claimant.

In *Ortiz v. Fibreboard Corp.*, 527 U.S. 815 (1999), the Supreme Court, without deciding the issue, expressed concerns that a mandatory settlement-only class action violated absent class members' Seventh Amendment rights by resolving their claims regardless of their consent.

§ 8.8 Due Process Issues

This text has discussed a variety of due process issues implicated in class actions, including notice, opt-out rights, and nationwide class actions. Due process issues have also arisen on occasion when class action cases have gone to trial (which itself is very rare). For instance, in *Broussard v. Meineke Discount Muffler Shops, Inc.*, 155 F.3d 331 (4th Cir. 1998), the Fourth Circuit reversed a $390 million judgment in a nationwide class action trial by current and former Meineke Discount Muffler franchisees against their franchiser and other parties. In addition to citing violations of Rule 23, the court also found that the defendant's fundamental rights were violated. Among other things, the court held that the class action allowed plaintiffs to falsely portray the class as a "unified group that suffered a uniform, collective injury," when in fact the class consisted of franchisees whose claims were factually and legally dissimilar. *Id.* at 345. Although the case is very fact-specific, it does point out that both the trial court and the parties must be attentive to potential jury confusion and other problems that could lead to reversal of a class-action trial.

CHAPTER 9

SETTLEMENTS, REMEDIES, AND ATTORNEYS' FEES

This chapter addresses various issues that arise when a class action lawsuit results in a class settlement. It further discusses related issue of class remedies and attorneys' fees.

§ 9.1 Class Action Settlements

In non-class litigation, court approval of settlements is generally not required. Different rules apply, however, when a class action is settled. Rule 23(e)(1)(A) states that "[t]he court must approve any settlement, voluntary dismissal, or compromise of the claims, issues, or defenses of a certified class." Rule 23(e)(1)(B) provides that "[t]he court must direct notice in a reasonable manner to all class members who would be bound by a proposed settlement, voluntary dismissal, or compromise." These requirements, along with additional provisions of Rule 23 adopted in 2003, raise a host of important issues.

A. OVERVIEW: INTERESTED PARTICIPANTS

Settlement negotiations in class actions are necessarily more complex than those involving traditional, non-class litigation. Numerous players have important roles, including the class representatives, class counsel, the unnamed class members, the defendant, defense counsel, objectors to the proposed settlement, insurers (who may be responsible for providing coverage for the claims), and the court. Surprising alliances frequently occur. For instance, it is not uncommon for class counsel and defense counsel to join forces in support of a settlement in the face of strong objections by intervening class members. Issues of collusion and conflicts of interest often arise in the settlement context. The various participants in the settlement process should be kept in mind when considering the issues raised in the following sections.

B. PRE–CERTIFICATION SETTLEMENT WITH ONLY NAMED PLAINTIFFS

Before discussing settlements that seek to bind the class as a whole, this section first examines pre-certification settlements that seek to bind only the named plaintiffs. At first blush, it might seem that such a settlement would not raise any concerns requiring judicial oversight. Some courts, however, have held that the 1966 version of Rule 23(e), which barred "dismiss[al] or compromise[] without the approval of the court," applied even prior to certification. Those courts have recognized that, prior to certification, there is a serious threat that the defendant will offer the named plaintiffs and plaintiffs' counsel an overly generous settlement, thereby resolving the claims of the class representatives and, hopefully, eliminating the threat of a class action. Put another way, the concern is that the named plaintiffs will leverage their status as representatives to enhance their bargaining power and achieve a lucrative settlement. Thus, some courts reason that, having filed a putative class claim, the representatives and class counsel cannot walk away from the case and settle only the representatives' claims without court approval. Such courts reason that they must ensure that the settlement amount (including attorneys' fees) is reasonable. An unusually large individual settlement for a dubious claim could indicate that the representatives and counsel discontinued the class claims for personal gain.

Other courts, however, have held that court approval is only required when a *certified* class is settled. The rationale of those cases is that, because only the named plaintiffs are bound by a pre-certification settlement, the putative class does not need the protection of court approval.

The 2003 amendments resolved the issue in favor of the latter approach. Rule 23(e)(1)(A) requires court approval only for settlement of "a certified class." The Advisory Committee Notes expressly mention the prior conflict in the case law and the amended rule's intent *not* to "require court approval of settlements with putative class representatives that resolve[] only individual claims."

The *Manual for Complex Litigation (4th)* notes that, despite Rule 23(e)(1)(A), courts "should inquire into the circumstances behind [a precertification dismissal]" when "a voluntary dismissal might represent an abuse of the class action process[.]" § 21.26 n.948. This might be the case, for example, when the named representatives receive an unusually large individual settlement that could be viewed as a payoff for agreeing not to prosecute the case as a class action.

C. NOTICE OF A PRE–CERTIFICATION SETTLEMENT OF INDIVIDUAL CLAIMS

Because the 2003 amendments do not require court approval of a pre-certification settlement, notice of such settlement to the putative class is also not required. Rule 23(e)(1)(B) requires notice only to "class members who would be bound by a proposed settlement, voluntary dismissal or compromise." Unnamed class members, of course, would not be bound by a settlement solely between named plaintiffs and defendants. And the Advisory Committee Notes state categorically that "notice is not required when the settlement binds only the individual class representatives."

The *Manual for Complex Litigation (4th)* points out, however, that notice to the putative class may be necessary in "unusual" cases involving possible "abuse of the class action procedure," § 21.312, such as concern about a representative reaping an unusually large individual settlement for agreeing not to prosecute the case as a class action. Such notice would be pursuant to Rule 23(d)(2) (*see* p. 174, *supra*).

D. CERTIFICATION FOR SETTLEMENT PURPOSES

A growing trend during the 1980s and 1990s has been the certification of class actions for settlement purposes only. At the same time, some courts and commentators have grown increasingly concerned about the fairness of such settlements, and have debated whether certification for settlement only should be granted under a more lenient standard than certification for trial. These issues reached the Supreme Court in *Amchem Prods., Inc. v. Windsor*, 521 U.S. 591 (1997).

In *Amchem*, the issue was whether a class had been legitimately certified for purposes of a global settlement of current and future asbestos-related claims. During negotiations, defendants had insisted that they would not settle the pending claims unless they received some kind of protection from future claims. Thus, settlement talks focused on creating an administrative scheme that would dispose of asbestos claims not yet in litigation. Class counsel, who represented the litigants in the thousands of asbestos cases already pending, also undertook to represent the interests of the anticipated future claimants. Objectors challenged the adequacy of class counsel and the named representatives, complaining of conflicts of interest between the pending and future claims. The district court found that the settlement was fair and certified the class for settlement purposes only.

The objectors appealed, arguing that the class of exposed asbestos claimants who had not already sued had not been properly certified under Rule 23. To resolve this issue, the appellate courts had to determine whether the standards for certification of a Rule 23(b)(3) class action for settlement purposes were less demanding than those mandated by Rule 23(b)(3) when a class is certified for trial. The argument for a lower standard was that, since the case was not going to trial, the Rule 23(a) and (b) criteria focusing on predominance, manageability, superiority, and commonality in the context of a class action trial were irrelevant. The Third Circuit ruled that settlement was not a proper consideration in applying the Rule 23 criteria and held that the certified class of future claimants did not satisfy the mandatory requirements of Rule 23(a) and (b)(3).

Although the Supreme Court affirmed in a 7–2 decision, its reasoning differed somewhat from that of the Third Circuit. Most importantly, the Court indicated that settlement *was* relevant to one aspect of class certification. In a settlement class, "a district court need not inquire whether the case, if tried, would present intractable management problems, see Fed. R. Civ. Proc. 23(b)(3)(D), for the proposal is that there be no trial." *Id.* at 620. The other requirements of Rule 23, however—"those designed to protect absentees by blocking unwarranted or overbroad class definitions—demand undiluted, even heightened, attention in the settlement context." *Id.*

The Court rejected the argument that, in the settlement context, satisfying Rule 23(a) and (b) was unnecessary because of the requirements of Rule 23(e) for a fairness determination and class notice. The Court noted that the Rule 23(e) requirements were in *addition* to the other standards under Rule 23 and did not supersede the normal certification inquiry. Applying the Rule 23 criteria, the Court agreed with the Third Circuit's holding that the Rule 23 requirements had not been satisfied by the sprawling settlement class certified by the district court.

Subsequently, in *Ortiz v. Fibreboard Corp.*, 527 U.S. 815 (1999), the Supreme Court, in striking down a proposed limited fund settlement class under Rule 23(b)(1)(B), reiterated that district courts must pay close attention to the requirements of Rule 23(a) and (b) in the settlement context. The Court stated that "a settlement's fairness under Rule 23(e) does not dispense with the requirements of Rule 23(a) and (b)."

Both *Amchem* and *Ortiz* involved settlements designed to deal with the unique and difficult problems of asbestos litigation. But those opinions have also assisted the lower courts in evaluating other settlement classes.

E. BINDING EFFECT IN LATER LITIGATION OF CONCESSION THAT SETTLEMENT CLASS IS APPROPRIATE FOR CERTIFICATION

Amchem makes clear that, apart from manageability, the requirements for certification under Rule 23(b)(3) apply not only to litigation classes but to settlement classes as well. Assume that the parties to a settlement present the proposal to a court, arguing that the case is properly certifiable as a settlement class. If the settlement does not go forward, is the defendant bound by such arguments in opposing certification of a class for litigation purposes? In *Carnegie v. Household Int'l, Inc.*, 376 F.3d 656 (7th Cir. 2004), the court ruled that, under the doctrine of judicial estoppel, a party that urged certification of a settlement class was barred, after the settlement was disapproved, from later arguing against certification of a litigation class. As the court reasoned, "[i]n the previous round of this protracted litigation, the defendants had urged the district court to accept the giant class as appropriate for a global settlement, had prevailed in their urging, and so are now precluded by the doctrine of judicial estoppel ... from challenging its adequacy, at least as a settlement class ...." *Id.* at 659–60. The *Carnegie* decision has been criticized by some commentators as misapplying the judicial estoppel doctrine.

F.   CONSIDERATIONS 1N APPROVING SETTLEMENTS

Criteria. Rule 23(e)(1)(C) provides that a court may approve a settlement binding on a class only after conducting a hearing and finding that the settlement is "fair, reasonable, and adequate." The rule contains no specific guidance on how courts should assess the fairness of class action settlements. Moreover, the Advisory Committee Notes simply refer to *In re Prudential Ins. Co. America Sales Practices Litigation Agent Actions,* 148 F.3d 283, 316–24 (3d Cir. 1998), and to the *Manual for Complex Litigation.* These and other authorities provide several factors that should be considered, including: (1) the nature of the claims and possible defenses; (2) whether the proposed settlement was fairly and honestly negotiated; (3) whether serious questions of law and fact exist, placing the ultimate outcome of the litigation in doubt; (4) whether the value of an immediate recovery outweighs the mere possibility of future relief after protracted and expensive litigation; (5) whether the parties believe that the settlement is fair and reasonable; (6) the defendant's financial viability; (7) the number and objective merit of any objections received from the class members; (8) the risks in establishing damages; (9) the complexity, length, and expense of continued litigation; and (10) the stage of the proceedings. Courts have generally applied a presumption that a settlement negotiated at arm's length is fair and reasonable. In applying such a presumption, courts have noted the strong policy considerations favoring settlement. *E.g., Wal–Mart Stores, Inc. v. VISA U.S.A., Inc.,* 396 F.3d 96 (2d Cir. 2005).

On the other hand, some appellate courts have rejected settlements when the record reflects a lack of careful consideration by the district court. For instance, in *Reynolds v. Beneficial Nat'l Bank,* 288 F.3d 277 (7th Cir. 2002), the Seventh Circuit, in an opinion by Judge Posner, reversed and remanded a class settlement. The court concluded that the trial court "should have made a greater effort (he made none) to quantify the net expected value of continued litigation to the class, since a settlement for less than that value would not be adequate. Determining that value would require estimating the range of possible outcomes and ascribing a probability to each point on the range [discounted to present value]." *Id.* at 284–85. The court was also troubled that "[t]wo classes were absorbed into the settlement even though their claims were sharply different from those of the classes represented by the settlement counsel." *Id.* at 285.

Side Agreements. In connection with the settlement approval process, amended Rule 23(e)(2) requires parties seeking settlement approval to "file a statement identifying any agreement made in connection with the proposed settlement, voluntary dismissal, or compromise." The Advisory Committee Notes point out that, even prior to the amendment, the parties were required to "disclose all terms of the settlement or compromise that the court must approve under Rule 23(e)(1)." The amendment is "aim[ed] instead at related undertakings that, although seemingly separate, may have influenced the terms of the settlement by trading away possible advantages for the class in return for advantages to others." The Notes point out that, while the court may request the actual agreements (or summaries thereof), the amendment "should not become the occasion for discovery by the parties or objectors."

Simultaneous Certification and Settlement. Some cases are settled after initially being certified as class actions. Other cases (such as *Amchem*) seek certification and approval of a settlement simultaneously. As the *Manual for Complex Litigation (4th)* points out, "[c]lass actions certified solely for settlement, particularly early in the case, sometimes make meaningful judicial review more difficult and more important." § 21.612. Indeed, some courts have held that more exacting scrutiny should be given to cases certified and settled simultaneously than to cases settled after initially being certified.

In-Kind Settlements. A major factor impacting a court's assessment of fairness is the use of in-kind payments. Class-action settlements have increasingly made use of in-kind payments, which are non-cash compensation paid by the defendant to the plaintiff class. These in-kind payments often take the form of a discount coupon that the class members can redeem when purchasing the defendant's products. Courts have had the opportunity to consider class-action settlements involving discounts on air travel, video games, kitchen appliances, automobiles, and even bar review courses. Some courts and commentators have expressed concern that such settlements, rather than punishing the defendant, offer the defendant a disguised promotional opportunity. As a result, some courts have rejected such settlements, although other courts have approved them. Some coupon settlements have been structured to include an additional cash component or to require minimum payments in the event of low coupon redemption. Significantly, CAFA places major new restrictions on coupon settlements. *See* pp. 266–267, *infra*.

Hearing Requirement. Another settlement-related issue is whether a fairness hearing must be held, even if no one lodges an objection to the proposed settlement. As a result of the 2003 amendments, Rule 23(e)(1)(C) now makes clear (consistent with the prevailing practice) that a hearing is required before court approval of *any* settlement binding on the class.

Lack of Court Authority to Alter Terms. Although a court may play a role in encouraging settlements, it does not have the power under Rule 23(e) to rewrite a proposed settlement on its own initiative or as requested by the objectors. Specifically, the court cannot force the parties to accept a settlement to which they have not agreed. The court is only authorized to: (1) accept the proposed settlement; (2) reject the settlement and postpone the trial to see if a different settlement can be reached; or (3) try the case. *Evans v. Jeff D.*, 475 U.S. 717 (1986). The parties who negotiated the settlement are free to modify it before they present it to the court for approval. Nonetheless, after the settlement has been presented to the court and the notice has been sent, substantial modification of the proposal may prejudice the rights of absent class members who relied on the original terms in deciding not to object. Courts vary as to whether they will permit modification at this late stage, but they are more likely to permit amendments that are merely technical in nature.

G.   NOTICE OF POST–CERTIFICATION SETTLEMENT

Rule 23(e)(1)(B) states that "[t]he court must direct notice in a reasonable manner to all class members who would be bound" by the settlement. In contrast to the explicit language of Rule 23(c)(2), however, Rule 23(e) does not dictate the method or content of the required notice. Thus, courts have substantial discretion, subject only to due process requirements.

In *Mullane v. Central Hanover Bank & Trust Co.*, 339 U.S. 306 (1950), the Supreme Court stated that, to meet due process standards, notice must be "reasonably calculated, under all the circumstances, to apprise interested parties of the pendency of the action. . . ." *Id.* at 314. Although the case was not a class action, its due process standards were incorporated into Rule 23 when the rule was amended in 1966.

Rule 23 establishes varying notice requirements, depending on the nature of the class action and the purpose of the notice. For example, explicit notice requirements are mandated by Rule 23(c)(2)(B) for a Rule 23(b)(3) type class action, whereas Rule 23(d)(2) provides more flexibility.

Under *Eisen v. Carlisle & Jacquelin*, 417 U.S. 156 (1974), first-class mail to identifiable individuals combined with publication fully satisfies the notice requirements of both Rule 23 and the Due Process Clause. *See* pp. 162–163, *supra*. Because this method satisfies the higher notice standard of Rule 23(c)(2), it clearly satisfies the lesser standards imposed under Rule 23(e).

The more difficult issue is whether—and when—notice short of that required under (c)(2) satisfies the lesser standard of Rule 23(e). Because the matter is largely left to the discretion of the trial court, there is no clear answer. Some courts have found that simple publication, or even posting, may suffice, reasoning that the form of notice need not reach every class member. Other courts have taken a more rigorous approach and have required greater efforts to ensure that notice is received by class members who can be reasonably identified. The Advisory Committee Notes to the 2003 amendments point out that in some circumstances, individual notice in the settlement context may be required "in the manner required by Rule 23(c)(2)(B) for certification notice to a Rule 23(b)(3) class." The Notes explain that "[i]ndividual notice is appropriate, for example, if class members are required to take action—such as filing claims—to participate in the judgment, or if the court orders a settlement opt-out opportunity under Rule 23(e)(3)" (*see* discussion in the following section). Of course, if the case is certified under (b)(3) at the same time that the settlement is approved, then the notice requirements of Rule 23(c)(2)(B) would apply.

As explained on p. 261, *supra*, although Rule 23(e) does not specify all of the information that must be included in a notice, certain items—including the settlement's terms and information about the fairness hearing—should normally be included.

H.   OPPORTUNITY TO OPT OUT OF A PROPOSED SETTLEMENT AFTER EXPIRATION OF ORIGINAL OPT–OUT PERIOD

A noteworthy provision added to Rule 23 in 2003 is Rule 23(e)(3), which provides that in a case previously certified under Rule 23(b)(3), "the court may refuse to approve a settlement unless it affords a new opportunity to request exclusion to individual class members who had an earlier opportunity to request exclusion but did not do so." This provision deals with the situation in which the time to opt out has expired before a proposed settlement is reached. Without another opt out opportunity, class members would be forced to accept the settlement or try to derail it through objection. They could not opt out. Now the court has discretion to condition approval of the settlement on allowing class members another opportunity to opt out. This judicial option to afford another opt-out right is limited to (b)(3) class actions.

Thus far, few courts have actually ordered a second opt-out period, and the Second Circuit has indicated that appellate courts will apply a deferential standard when a court refuses to grant a second opt-out right. *Denney v. Deutsche Bank AG*, 443 F.3d 253 (2d Cir. 2006).

I. OBJECTIONS TO SETTLEMENT

Any class member may lodge objections to a proposed settlement. Rule 23(e)(4)(A). These objections may result in agreed modifications favorable to the class or they may lead the court to reject the settlement. In some circumstances, however, as the *Manual for Complex Litigation (4th)* notes, objections may be made "for improper purposes" that would "benefit only the objectors and their attorneys (*e.g.,* by seeking additional compensation to withdraw even ill-founded objections)." § 21.643. As the *Manual* points out, even baseless objections "can be costly and significantly delay implementation of a class settlement." *Id.*

Objectors can gain access to information necessary to challenge a proposed settlement by asking the district court to allow them to take discovery. In rare circumstances, such discovery may even include depositions of counsel involved in settlement negotiations.

As amended in 2003, Rule 23(e)(4)(B) provides that objections to settlement pursuant to Rule 23(e)(4)(A) "may be withdrawn only with the court's approval." The Advisory Committee Notes state that judicial review is "required if the objector formally withdraws the objections," and that "the court may inquire into the circumstances" if "the objector simply abandons pursuit of the objection[.]"

One issue that previously divided courts was whether a class member who timely objected to a class settlement at the fairness hearing had the power to bring an appeal without first intervening. The Supreme Court resolved this issue in *Devlin v. Scardelletti,* 536 U.S. 1 (2002). In *Devlin*, an unnamed class member, Devlin, sought to intervene but his motion was denied. Later, Devlin objected to the settlement at the fairness hearing, but the settlement was approved despite his objections. The Fourth Circuit held that since Devlin was not a named representative and had correctly been denied intervention, he lacked standing to challenge the settlement on appeal. The Supreme Court reversed, reasoning that the right to appeal was not restricted to named parties to the litigation. The Court held that "nonnamed class members are parties to the proceedings in the sense of being bound by settlement." *Id.* at 10. As a result, so long as they objected to the settlement in a timely fashion at the district court level, they are allowed to challenge the settlement on appeal without being required to intervene in the case. One open issue under *Devlin* is whether the decision applies only to mandatory classes (*Devlin* itself involved a mandatory class). Some courts have concluded that *Devlin* does not apply to opt-out classes, reasoning that the objectors could have avoided their problem by exiting from the class. Other courts, however, have declined to so limit *Devlin*.

§ 9.2 CAFA Settlement Provisions

CAFA addresses a variety of settlement issues. The overriding concern expressed by Congress was that courts (particularly state courts) had been approving settlements that rewarded plaintiffs' counsel handsomely but offered little, if any, meaningful recovery to the class. To address this concern, Congress focused on four areas: coupon settlements, net-loss settlements, settlements that favor some class members over others based on geographic location, and notification of appropriate federal and state officials.

A. COUPON SETTLEMENTS

CAFA regulates fee awards in coupon settlements. Under 28 U.S.C § 1712(a), if a class settlement provides for recovery of coupons to the class, "the portion of any attorney's fee award to class counsel that is attributable to the award of the coupons shall be based on the value to class members of the coupons that are redeemed." This provision is designed to discourage coupon settlements that afford little real value to class members but provide the basis for large attorneys' fees for class counsel. For instance, a coupon good for $500 off the price of a $30,000 automobile almost certainly does not yield $500 in value to each class member.

Most class members would never use such a coupon, particularly to buy the very brand of vehicle about which they complained. A secondary market for such coupons (such as through eBay) would undoubtedly yield a cash price of far less than $500. Yet, in the past, class counsel have used the face value of coupons in claiming a percentage of the "fund" as attorneys' fees.

The statute does not define "coupon," and thus myriad open questions remain. For instance, it is unclear whether an in-kind award—for example, a free tape or DVD—would constitute a coupon settlement. Moreover, CAFA does not explain how the actual value of coupons should be calculated, or when the calculation should be made (at the time of settlement, only after the expiration of the redemption period, or at some intermediate point). Presumably, Congress anticipated that courts would rely on expert testimony to determine value; CAFA explicitly permits a court to "receive expert testimony from a witness qualified to provide information on the actual value to class members of the coupons that are redeemed." 28 U.S.C § 1712(d).

B.   NET LOSS SETTLEMENTS

Under 28 U.S.C § 1713, a court may approve a settlement in which a class member receives a "net loss" only upon finding in writing "that nonmonetary benefits to the class member substantially outweigh the monetary loss." Congress passed this provision in response to isolated but highly publicized cases in which class members actually suffered a net loss under a class settlement (after deductions for attorneys' fees). In practice, net loss settlements were extremely rare even prior to CAFA. Moreover, even prior to CAFA, Rule 23(e) provided a tool for addressing such settlements by requiring a court to find, as a condition to approval, that a class settlement is "fair, reasonable, and adequate." Fed. R. Civ. P. 23(e)(1)(C).

C. PROHIBITION AGAINST GEOGRAPH-IC–BASED DISCRIMINATION IN SET-TLEMENTS

Under 28 U.S.C § 1714, "[t]he court may not approve a proposed settlement that provides for the payment of greater sums to some class members than to others solely on the basis that the class members to whom the greater sums are to be paid are located in closer geographic proximity to the court." The source of concern that led Congress to enact this provision is unclear; the legislative history cited no instances of disparate payments based solely on geographic location. In all events, Rule 23(e)(1)(C) already provided a vehicle for courts to invalidate such a settlement by requiring a court to find that a class settlement is "fair, reasonable, and adequate" before approving it.

D.   NOTICE TO GOVERNMENT OFFICIALS

Under 28 U.S.C § 1715(b), within 10 days after a proposed settlement is filed with the court, "each defendant that is participating in the proposed settlement shall serve upon the appropriate State official of each State in which a class member resides and the appropriate Federal official, a notice of the proposed settlement ...." The notice must contain numerous items including, *inter alia,* the complaint, notice, settlement terms, names of class members (or, if not feasible, an estimate by state of the number of class members), and any applicable agreements of counsel and opinions by the court. 28 U.S.C § 1715(b)(1), (8). The purpose of the notice is to allow interested officials to weigh in—in a timely fashion—on the fairness of the proposed settlement. Usually, the appropriate federal official to notify is the U.S. Attorney General. The appropriate state official, however, is not always clear. CAFA requires notification of "the person in the State who has primary regulatory or supervisory responsibility with respect to the defendant; or who licenses or otherwise authorizes the defendant to conduct business in the State, if some or all of the matters alleged in the class action are subject to regulation by that person." 28 U.S.C § 1715(a)(2). Often, multiple officials arguably fit this description, raising a dilemma for defense counsel.

The penalty for noncompliance with the notice requirement is severe: a class member, at his or her option, may choose not to be bound by the settlement. 28 U.S.C § 1715(e)(1). For that reason, commentators have urged defense counsel to err in favor of notice to officials who may (but are not necessarily) within the statutory mandate.

It is too early to ascertain whether the notification provision will impact the settlement approval process. The amount of material required to be disclosed under this part of CAFA may, in many cases, be voluminous. Whether the targeted officials will scrutinize such materials and participate in the settlement process to voice concerns when appropriate remains to be seen.

E.   GAPS IN CAFA'S SETTLEMENT PROVISIONS

CAFA's settlement provisions contain several limitations and gaps. Two serious ones are worth noting.

First, the settlement provisions apply only to federal court class actions. Thus, the parties to a settlement—even of a federal case—can settle the case in state court, thereby avoiding CAFA's limitations. If both sides are comfortable, for example, with a coupon settlement that would determine fees based on the face value of coupons, the parties can refile in state court, and present the coupon settlement in state court. Because the defendant will not want to remove the case to federal court, CAFA's settlement provisions will not apply, 28 U.S.C. § 1771(2) (limiting term "class action" to cases filed in or removed to federal court), and the parties can settle without CAFA's restrictions. The existing federal case would then be dismissed as *res judicata*. Congress arguably did not anticipate such an easy route to circumvent CAFA, and it could potentially fix the problem by making state cases that would qualify under CAFA subject to the settlement provisions, even if the defendant chooses not to remove the particular case to federal court.

Second, the underlying principle of the coupon provisions—basing fees on actual "value" to the class—is not carried forth with respect to non-coupon settlements. For example, a common approach to settlement is for defendant to set up a "fund" from which payments claimed by class members are made, with any unclaimed funds reverting to defendant. To illustrate, if a settlement calls for a payment by a computer company of $10 for each defective computer monitor made during a particular period of time (1 million monitors in all), the parties might set up a fund for $10 million, with any unclaimed funds to revert to the defendant. Given the small amounts involved, it is likely that most class members will not go to the trouble of filing claims. If attorneys' fees are based on the total fund, not the amount actually claimed, then the situation is analytically very similar to fees based on the face amount—rather than the actual value—of coupons in a coupon settlement. Most courts have permitted fees to be based on the entire fund set up, even if the likelihood is that most of the fund will revert to the defendant. Although the policy of CAFA would appear contrary to such fee awards, CAFA (by its terms) does not forbid them.

§ 9.3   Class Action Remedies

Courts utilize a variety of approaches in allocating remedies among class members. In some instances, individual class members will be required to come forward and prove their damages separately, sometimes in full-blown jury proceedings. In many instances, particularly when a settlement fund is involved, courts are able to utilize more efficient procedures, such as summary proceedings before a special master or the submission of proof-of-claim forms or other documentation establishing injuries. Certain kinds of cases, such as securities fraud cases, are particularly suitable for simplified administrative procedures. Others, such as discrimination and mass tort cases, are less suitable for summary procedures, and may sometimes require mini-trials or arbitrations.

In many cases, individual adjudication of damages is not feasible, either because of difficulty identifying individual class members or because the damages that would be allocated to each class member are so small that they would be outweighed by the administrative costs of distributing the awards. One device that some courts have used (mainly in settlements) is the fluid recovery or *cy pres* ("as near as possible") approach. Fluid recovery permits the calculation of damages on an aggregate basis and the distribution of funds to benefit the entire class. Two common approaches are used: (1) requiring a defendant to reduce the market price of a good or service (such as taxicab fares) for a period of time to compensate for alleged overcharges; and (2) using the recovery to provide funding for a public interest organization or a project that will benefit the class as a whole (*e.g.*, a contribution to a public interest organization for health research or to a water pollution cleanup fund). Courts using the fluid recovery mechanism often point out that it prevents wrongdoers from being unjustly enriched when damages are too small to be distributed to individual class members in a cost-effective way.

Several federal courts have rejected the use of fluid recovery as a means of resolving manageability difficulties associated with proving individual claims. As the Ninth Circuit has stated, "allowing gross damages by treating unsubstantiated claims of class members collectively significantly alters substantive rights under the [statute in question]...." *In re Hotel Telephone Charges*, 500 F.2d 86, 90 (9th Cir. 1974). Other courts, however, such as the Seventh Circuit in *Simer v. Rios*, 661 F.2d 655 (7th Cir. 1981), indicate that the propriety of using fluid recovery to award damages should be evaluated on a case-by-case basis.

When damages are awarded pursuant to a statutory scheme and are not dependent upon individualized proof, the concerns about circumventing manageability issues by avoiding individualized damages assessments do not arise. Nonetheless, some courts have still expressed concern that the funds are not going directly to the class members.

The use of fluid recovery is less controversial when a court uses it solely for the purpose of distributing *unclaimed* damages, rather than as a tool for distributing the damages as a whole. *See Six (6) Mexican Workers v. Ariz. Citrus Growers*, 904 F.2d 1301 (9th Cir. 1990). Because the fluid recovery affects the interests of only those class members who have not presented claims, courts are more receptive to a fluid-recovery approach when only unclaimed damages are involved.

In addition to fluid recovery, other options exist for distributing unclaimed damages. One is to allow the funds to revert or "escheat" to the government. Another, as noted above, is to allow the unclaimed funds to be returned to the defendant. Some courts do not favor the latter approach out of concern that it would result in a windfall to the defendant, thus undermining the goal of deterring future misconduct. In addition, some courts have used expert and statistical proof to extrapolate damages to the class. This controversial approach is discussed on pp. 307–310, *infra*.

§ 9.4 Attorneys' Fees

A. OVERVIEW OF NEW RULE 23(h)

Rule 23(h), adopted in 2003, specifically authorizes a court in a certified class action to "award reasonable attorney fees and nontaxable costs authorized by law or by agreement of the parties[.]'' A request for attorneys' fees must be made by motion, Rule 23(h)(1), and "[a] class member, or a party from whom payment is sought, may object to the motion." Rule 23(h)(2). The court is permitted, but not required, to hold a hearing, but it "must" make findings of fact and conclusions of law in support of a fee award. Rule 23(h)(3). The Rule also permits the court to refer any issues regarding the amount of fees to a magistrate or special master. Rule 23(h)(4). As discussed on pp. 278–279, *infra,* although Rule 23(h) does not address the criteria for awarding fees, the relevant considerations are set forth in the Advisory Committee Notes.

B. METHODS FOR SETTING THE AMOUNT OF FEES

Under the "American Rule," each party bears its own costs and attorneys' fees. This rule raises issues in class actions because, if any fee agreement exists at all, it is generally only between class counsel and the class representatives, and such an agreement is usually a contingent-fee agreement. Absent class members almost never have fee agreements with class counsel and thus have no contractual obligation to pay the fees and costs incurred in bringing a class action. Some courts resolve this dilemma by holding that the fee agreements between class counsel and the class representatives may be enforced against the absent class members (without discussion of contract or due process issues). Other courts hold that the absent class members are equitably liable for their *pro rata* share of the attorneys' fees and costs because they derived benefits from the litigation. Typically, fees are paid out of a settlement fund, with the balance of the fund being used to pay class members.

Regardless of whether a fee agreement exists, the amount of attorneys' fees in class actions must ultimately be determined by the court. This is true whether the case goes to trial or results in a settlement. Courts have generally used two methods to set the amount of fees to be awarded to class counsel: the percentage-of-the-fund method and the "lodestar" approach. Neither Rule 23(h) nor the Advisory Committee Notes take a position on which of the two approaches a court should utilize.

The Percentage Method. The percentage method is traditionally used in common-fund cases, *i.e.*, those in which an attorney creates, preserves, or increases the value of a common fund for the benefit of the class members. Such a fund may be created as a result of a trial verdict or a settlement. The Supreme Court in *dictum* has expressed approval of the percentage method. *Blum v. Stenson*, 465 U.S. 886 (1984). The underlying theory of that method is that the beneficiaries of the fund will be unjustly enriched unless the plaintiffs' attorneys are allowed to recover for their efforts. Under that method, the court's principal focus is on the size of the fund. Other factors that may also be considered include the skills of counsel, the complexity of the case, attorney time devoted to the case, awards in comparable cases, and the existence of objections by class members to a potential award. In most class actions, fee awards fall between twenty-five and thirty percent of the total fund. Courts generally hold that fifty percent is the upper limit of a reasonable award, although there are exceptions for unusually complicated or protracted cases.

Some courts have criticized the percentage method on the ground that the resulting awards are too high. These courts are particularly troubled by situations in which large attorneys' fees are awarded even though the case settled promptly and before the attorneys had invested a significant amount of time.

The Lodestar Method. The lodestar method, devised in 1973 by the United States Court of Appeals for the Third Circuit, *Lindy Bros. Builders v. American Radiator & Standard Sanitation Corp.,* 540 F.2d 102 (3d Cir. 1976), uses a formula to calculate attorneys' fee awards, multiplying the number of hours reasonably spent by the class attorneys times a reasonable hourly rate for the work. The multiplication of the number of hours and the hourly rate is known as the "lodestar" of the fee determination. The lodestar may then be increased or decreased through so-called "multipliers" based upon the particular circumstances. Class attorneys often request upward multipliers because of the risk they took in bringing a contingent-fee case (a "risk" multiplier), the quality of work performed, the complexity of legal and factual issues, and the result obtained.

Most courts utilize some form of the lodestar method in fee-shifting cases, *i.e.*, cases in which a statute provides for an award of "reasonable" attorneys' fees for the prevailing party. In fee-shifting cases, however, courts are not permitted to use risk multipliers to increase the award above the lodestar amount. *City of Burlington v. Dague*, 505 U.S. 557 (1992).

The lodestar method has been criticized by some courts on the ground that, by focusing on hours expended, it encourages lawyer inefficiency and provides a disincentive for early settlement. In addition, some courts have noted that the lodestar method gives insufficient consideration to the amount of the award and requires substantial court effort to review attorney time sheets to determine the reasonableness of the work performed. In light of these concerns, a majority of courts in common fund cases have opted for the percentage method over the lodestar method. Some courts utilizing the percentage method, however, permit the use of the lodestar method as a cross-check.

Criteria Set Forth in the Advisory Committee Notes. In contrast to the text of Rule 23(h), the Advisory Committee Notes provide extensive comments on the criteria for determining fees. For instance, the Notes state that the court should look closely to determine the value of the results achieved for the class; that the court may wish to defer a fee determination until the actual payout is known; that courts should scrutinize non-monetary settlements with extra care to ensure that the awards give actual value to the class; and that the court must scrutinize fees closely even if there are no objections to a requested fee.

Applicability of Benchmarks. Although many courts have utilized a benchmark figure as a guide in awarding fees, some recent authority has rejected the notion of a benchmark for attorneys' fees. For instance, in *Goldberger v. Integrated Resources, Inc.,* 209 F.3d 43 (2d Cir. 2000), the Second Circuit declined to adopt a benchmark of 25 percent of a settlement fund. The court noted that "even a theoretical construct as flexible as a 'benchmark' seems to offer an all too tempting substitute for the searching assessment that should properly be performed in each case." *Id.* at 52.

CHAPTER 10

APPELLATE REVIEW

As noted throughout this text, the class-certification decision is often the single most important issue in a class action case. As such, litigants frequently desire to obtain immediate appeal of issues relating to class certification. Absent immediate review, defendants frequently feel compelled to settle when certification is granted, and class representatives (and other class members) frequently give up the litigation altogether when certification is denied. And those plaintiffs and defendants who are willing to continue with the litigation after a certification ruling face potentially serious inefficiencies by having to wait until the end of the case to appeal the certification ruling. If certification is granted, the lack of an immediate appeal means that the parties must go through an entire class action trial before the appellate court decides whether a class action should have been certified in the first place. If the appellate court decides that certification was inappropriate, the entire trial will have been wasted. By the same token, if certification is denied, the parties must wait until the conclusion of the named plaintiff's case before seeking review of the certification ruling. If the appellate court rules that certification should have been granted, then the trial court will have wasted time trying an individual case when it could have been trying a class action.

Because of the foregoing considerations, litigants have attempted—with mixed success—to use various mechanisms, discussed below, for obtaining immediate review of class certification rulings. In 1998, Rule 23 was amended to permit appellate courts to allow interlocutory review of decisions granting or denying class status. This amendment is addressed in detail below. Rule 23(f) renders those various other mechanisms much less significant. Nonetheless, because Rule 23(f) is discretionary and contains strict time limits, these other potential mechanisms should still be understood by a lawyer considering an interlocutory appeal of a class certification ruling. Moreover, these mechanisms provide the historical context for Rule 23(f). Finally, because Rule 23(f) applies only to orders "granting or denying class certification" under Rule 23, these other mechanisms may need to be considered for interlocutory appeals of other class action rulings, such as orders involving class notice.

This chapter concludes by discussing a variety of miscellaneous appellate issues that sometimes arise in the class action context.

§ 10.1 Whether an Order Denying Class Certification Is a Final Decision Under 28 U.S.C. § 1291

Under 28 U.S.C. § 1291, federal courts of appeals have jurisdiction over appeals from all "final decisions" of federal district courts. In *Coopers & Lyb-*

rand v. Livesay, 437 U.S. 463 (1978), the Supreme Court held that a trial court's order denying class certification or decertifying a class is not a "final decision" within the meaning of 28 U.S.C. § 1291 and, therefore, is not appealable as a matter of right. The Court rejected appellants' arguments that the certification order was appealable under two previously recognized exceptions to the final-judgment rule.

First, appellants argued that the order was appealable as a "collateral order" pursuant to *Cohen v. Beneficial Industrial Loan Corp.*, 337 U.S. 541 (1949). Under that exception, review of a non-final order may be allowed if it (1) conclusively determines disputed questions; (2) resolves an important issue completely separate from the merits of the action; and (3) cannot be effectively reviewed on appeal from a final judgment. The Court found that, in the case of a class certification ruling, these criteria are not satisfied because certification is subject to revision by the trial court; the class issues are intertwined with the merits; and the certification ruling can be reviewed on appeal from a final judgment.

Appellants' second argument in *Coopers & Lybrand* relied upon the "death knell" exception that had been judicially adopted in several circuits. That doctrine assumed that a lawsuit was effectively over when the district court denied class certification in cases in which the individual plaintiffs would not find it economically prudent to pursue their claims in the absence of a class. In *Coopers & Lybrand,* the

Court discredited the "death knell" exception, finding that it was based on policy considerations more appropriately left for Congress and that it unfairly facilitated early appeals only by plaintiffs and not by defendants.

§ 10.2 Appeal From a Denial of Class Certification When Class Representative Fails to Prosecute Individual Claim

The circuits are split on a question—which the Supreme Court has not addressed—of whether a litigant may directly appeal the denial of class status if the putative class member is willing to waive his or her individual claims (effectively creating a final judgment). Some courts have held that appellants may not evade the policy against piecemeal review by failing to prosecute their individual claims. Other courts, however, have held that an order denying a motion for class certification merges into the final judgment that results from the class representative's failure to prosecute his or her individual claims. Because those potentially meritorious individual claims are forfeited, these courts reason that reviewing the merits of the class certification order will not substantially undermine the policy against piecemeal review.

§ 10.3 Appeal of Denial of Certification Under Federal Rule 54(b)

Rule 54(b) of the Federal Rules of Civil Procedure provides for "the entry of a final judgment as to one or more but fewer than all of the claims or parties" in a lawsuit when the court determines that "there

is no just reason for delay...." Although class
action allegations are not "claims," a few courts
hold that the denial of class certification may be
designated by a district court as a "final judgment"
pursuant to Rule 54(b). Such courts reason that the
trial court is in the best position to determine
whether there is any "just reason" for refusing to
sever the certification decision from the merits of
the individual claims. Most courts, however, hold
that Rule 54(b) is unavailable for the appeal of
orders denying class certification because such orders are interlocutory and subject to change before
final disposition of the case. The Supreme Court has
not addressed the question.

§ 10.4 Appeal of Denial of Certification Under 28 U.S.C. § 1292(a)(1)

Section 1292(a)(1) grants appellate courts jurisdiction over interlocutory orders of the district
courts "granting, continuing, modifying, refusing or
dissolving injunctions, or refusing to dissolve or
modify injunctions...." In *Gardner v. Westing-
house Broadcasting Co.,* 437 U.S. 478 (1978), the
Supreme Court narrowly interpreted this jurisdictional statute with respect to review of orders denying class certification. Even though plaintiff's complaint sought equitable relief for the entire class,
the Court reasoned that the order denying class
certification did not entirely dispose of the relief
sought, but merely limited its scope. Accordingly,
the order was not appealable under section
1292(a)(1).

§ 10.5 Appeal of Class Certification Ruling Under 28 U.S.C. § 1292(b)

Section 1292(b) permits a district court to certify an otherwise nonappealable order for appellate review when three criteria are met: (1) the order involves a controlling question of law; (2) there is substantial ground for difference of opinion regarding the order; and (3) an immediate appeal from the order may materially advance the ultimate termination of the litigation. The district court must state in writing that these criteria are satisfied and application for an appeal must then be made within ten days after entry of the certification order. If the district court refuses to certify the case for appeal, the court of appeals cannot hear the case unless another legal basis exists for interlocutory review. Even if the district court certifies an order for appeal under section 1292(b), the court of appeals has unreviewable discretion to decline the appeal for any reason (including docket congestion). *Coopers & Lybrand v. Livesay*, 437 U.S. 463 (1978). For the most part, district courts and appellate courts alike have been reluctant to certify class-action rulings for section 1292(b) appeal.

§ 10.6 Mandamus Review of Certification Ruling

The All Writs Act, 28 U.S.C. § 1651, permits an appellate court to grant a petition for mandamus in extraordinary circumstances. Under the mandamus power, the courts of appeals may take jurisdiction and intervene to prevent or correct fundamental injustices by a district court. The mandamus power, however, is rarely warranted. A writ of mandamus is justified only when there is irreparable harm and a clear usurpation of judicial power by the district court.

Litigants have petitioned the appellate courts to exercise this power to intervene when district courts have granted or refused to grant class certification. Although most efforts have not been successful, mandamus has occasionally been granted to undo class certifications. For example, in *In Matter of Rhone–Poulenc Rorer, Inc.*, 51 F.3d 1293 (7th Cir. 1995), the Seventh Circuit granted a writ of mandamus and ordered the district court to decertify the plaintiff class of HIV-hemophiliacs. The court reasoned that the class certification order would probably never be reviewed following final judgment because the defendants would likely be forced to settle with the class members rather than expose themselves to the enormous risk of classwide liability. The court was particularly troubled by this pressure to settle because the defendants had previously won twelve of the thirteen individual claims that had been brought. The court also found that mandamus was warranted because of choice-of-law and Seventh Amendment concerns raised by the district court's certification order.

Likewise, the Sixth Circuit granted mandamus and reversed a class certification ruling in *In re American Medical Systems, Inc.*, 75 F.3d 1069 (6th Cir. 1996), a nationwide class action involving alleged injuries from penile prostheses. The court found mandamus was warranted because of the district court's failure to look beyond the pleadings and conduct a rigorous analysis into whether Rule 23's requirements were met. The court emphasized that many different models of prostheses were involved, that class members claimed different kinds of malfunctions, that complicated choice-of-law issues existed, and that the district court failed to make factual findings regarding adequacy of representation.

Notwithstanding *Rhone-Poulenc* and *American Medical Systems,* however, most courts have refused to grant mandamus in the context of class certification rulings.

§ 10.7 Appeal Under Rule 23(f)

Overview of Criteria. As discussed above, the patchwork of potential appellate vehicles has posed difficulties for parties seeking immediate appeal of certification rulings. As a result, a class certification ruling often operated, as a practical matter, as a final decision in the case. Plaintiffs whose individual claims could not justify the costs of litigation were effectively barred from continuing their case if they could not obtain immediate review of an order denying class certification. On the other hand, if a class was certified, defendants often felt compelled to settle because the risks of an adverse class verdict were too substantial to justify going forward.

To address some of these concerns, Rule 23(f) was added in 1998. That rule provides:

A court of appeals may in its discretion permit an appeal from an order of a district court granting or denying class action certification under this rule if application is made to it within ten days after entry of the order. An appeal does not stay proceedings in the district court unless the district judge or the court of appeals so orders.

There are no specific criteria or limitations in the text of Rule 23(f), and the Advisory Committee Notes state that the courts of appeals have "unfettered discretion whether to permit the appeal, akin to the discretion exercised by the Supreme Court in acting on a petition for certiorari." The Notes suggest that "[p]ermission is most likely to be granted when the certification decision turns on a novel or unsettled question of law, or when, as a practical matter, the decision on certification is likely dispositive of the litigation."

In summarizing the reach of Rule 23(f), the Seventh Circuit has stated that "the more fundamental the question and the greater the likelihood that it will escape effective disposition at the end of the case, the more appropriate is an appeal under Rule 23(f)." *Blair v. Equifax Check Services, Inc.*, 181 F.3d 832, 835 (7th Cir. 1999). The court noted that "it would be a mistake for us to draw up a list that determines how the power under Rule 23(f) will be exercised." *Id.* at 834.

Rule 23(f) has already resulted in a significant number of appellate decisions. The circuit courts have devoted considerable attention to the criteria for granting Rule 23(f) review. These decisions differ somewhat in nuance, and a litigant faced with a Rule 23(f) issue should consult the law of the applicable federal circuit.

By way of illustration, one federal circuit has identified five guideposts for deciding whether to grant Rule 23(f) review: (1) "whether the district court's ruling is likely dispositive of the litigation by creating a 'death knell' for either plaintiff or defendant"; (2) whether the district court ruling contains "a *substantial* weakness"; (3) "whether the appeal will permit the resolution of an unsettled legal issue that is 'important to the particular litigation as well as important in itself'"; (4) "the nature and status of the litigation," such as "the status of discovery, the pendency of relevant motions, and the length of time the matter already has been pending"; (5) "the likelihood that future events"—such as the possibility of settlement, bankruptcy of one of the parties, or modification of class certification ruling—"may make immediate appellate review more or less appropriate." *Prado-Steiman v. Bush,* 221 F.3d 1266, 1274–76 (11th Cir. 2000) (emphasis in original).

One issue that has divided the federal circuits is the weight to be given to the validity of the decision. Some circuits have held that Rule 23(f) review may be proper to correct a manifestly erroneous decision. Other circuits, however, have held that even a seriously erroneous decision is not subject to Rule 23(f) review unless the decision would likely be the death knell of the litigation or resolve an important class action legal issue that otherwise would evade review.

A thorough discussion of the various circuit court approaches to Rule 23(f) is contained in the Ninth Circuit's decision in *Chamberlan v. Ford Motor Co.*, 402 F.3d 952 (9th Cir. 2005).

Scope. Rule 23(f) applies only to a district court order "granting or denying class action certification under this rule...." As the Advisory Committee Notes make clear, "[n]o other type of Rule 23 order is covered by this provision." Thus, for example, an order relating to the scope or content of a class notice, an order restricting communications with class members, or an order allowing or barring certain class discovery would not be reviewable under Rule 23(f) unless such an order was somehow intertwined with an order granting or denying class certification. In addition, one court has held that Rule 23(f) does not apply to collective actions under Section 216(b) of the Fair Labor Standards Act. *Baldridge v. SBC Communications, Inc.*, 404 F.3d 930 (5th Cir. 2005). Collective actions are discussed on pp. 318–322, *infra*.

Views of District Court. Unlike review under 28 U.S.C. § 1292(b), review under Rule 23(f) does not require the approval of the district court. Nonetheless, the Advisory Committee Notes point out that the district court "often will be able to provide cogent advice on the factors that bear on the decision whether to permit appeal." According to the Notes, "[t]his advice can be particularly valuable if the certification decision is tentative," but it can be helpful "[e]ven as to a firm certification decision" by "focus[ing] the court of appeals" on the critical issues and possibly "persuad[ing] the disappointed party" not to seek Rule 23(f) review.

Timing of Filing and Responding. Rule 23(f) requires that the application for review be "made within ten days after entry of the order." Courts addressing the issue have held that the 10–day period does not include weekends or holidays.

Although Rule 23(f) does not set a time period for responding to a Rule 23(f) petition, Federal Rule of Appellate Procedure 5, which governs appeals by permission, addresses the issue: "A party may file any answer in opposition or a cross-petition within 7 days after the petition is served." Fed. R. App. P. 5(b)(2). The Federal Rules of Appellate Procedure exclude weekends and holidays from this 7–day period. Fed. R. App. P. 26(a)(2).

When a motion for reconsideration of the district court's certification decision has been filed within 10 days of that decision, courts have held that the Rule 23(f) clock does not begin to run until the district court has ruled on the motion for reconsideration.

Rule 23(f) Petitions in Defendant Class Actions. Rule 23(f) is not limited by its terms to plaintiff class actions. Courts have thus applied it to cases brought *against* a class of defendants. *See* pp. 335–344, *infra* (discussing defendant class actions). In *Tilley v. TJX Cos., Inc.*, 345 F.3d 34 (1st Cir. 2003), the First Circuit addressed the Rule 23(f) criteria in the context of a defendant class action. The court held that Rule 23(f) review is warranted in defendant class actions "when one of three circumstances exists: (i) denial of certification effectively disposes of the litigation because the plaintiff's claim would only be worth pursuing as against a full class of defendants; or (ii) an interlocutory appeal would clarify an important and unsettled legal issue that would likely escape effective end-of-case review; or (iii) an interlocutory appeal is a desirable vehicle either for addressing special circumstances or avoiding manifest injustice." *Id.* at 39.

§ 10.8 Intervention for Purposes of Appeal

When a trial court denies class certification and judgment is later entered in favor of the named plaintiffs on their individual claims, the successful plaintiffs have no need to appeal the denial of certification. Under those circumstances, the issue arises whether a putative class member may intervene in the district court pursuant to Fed.R.Civ.P. 24 for purposes of appealing the denial of certification.

The Supreme Court answered in the affirmative in *United Airlines, Inc. v. McDonald*, 432 U.S. 385 (1977). In allowing a class member to appeal after intervening in the case, the Court held that the intervention was timely even though the intervenor did not move to intervene until shortly after final judgment had been entered for the named plaintiffs. The Court reasoned that the intervenor moved promptly after ascertaining that the named plaintiffs would no longer be protecting the interests of the class.

A related issue is whether, when class certification is granted and the case proceeds to judgment, an unnamed class member—or a former class member who opts out—may appeal a final judgment in favor of the defendants, such as an order granting defendants' motion for summary judgment. As illustrated by *In re Brand Name Prescription Drugs Antitrust Litigation*, 115 F.3d 456 (7th Cir. 1997), most courts have held that, in such a situation, neither opt outs nor unnamed class members may appeal unless they attempted to intervene in the district court.

As discussed above (pp. 265–266, *supra*), the Supreme Court has made clear that an unnamed class member who makes a timely objection to a class settlement at the district court level is not required to intervene to appeal the settlement. *Devlin v. Scardelletti*, 536 U.S. 1 (2002). Some courts have limited *Devlin* to mandatory classes. *See* pp. 265–266, *supra*. It remains unclear whether *Devlin* will affect case law outside the settlement context.

§ 10.9   Whether Tender to Named Plaintiffs Over Their Objection Can Terminate Appellate Rights

A named plaintiff's right to appeal an adverse class certification decision cannot normally be rendered moot by defendant's tender of judgment on the individual claim and the dismissal of the claim.

Deposit Guar. Nat'l Bank v. Roper, 445 U.S. 326 (1980). In *Roper,* although the named plaintiffs no longer had any personal stake in the substantive claim, the Court found that they had a continuing individual interest in the resolution of the class certification question because of their desire to shift part of the costs of litigation to the class. Critical to the holding was the fact that the named plaintiffs rejected the tender and objected to the district court's entry of judgment dismissing the action.

§ 10.10   Standard of Review

A final issue involves the standard of review that applies when an appellate court reviews decisions granting or denying class certification. It is well settled that district court class certification decisions are reviewed under an abuse of discretion standard. In applying the criteria for class certification under Rule 23, however, purely legal questions sometimes arise, such as whether a specific federal statute prohibits the maintenance of class action suits in particular kinds of cases or whether a "predominance" inquiry should be conducted under Rule 23(b)(2). In those circumstances, a *de novo* standard of review is appropriate.

CHAPTER 11

SPECIAL FOCUS ON MASS TORT, EMPLOYMENT DISCRIMINATION, AND SECURITIES FRAUD CLASS ACTIONS

Although this text cannot focus on every type of suit that may be brought as a class action, this chapter focuses on three types of cases that have raised some of the most significant and controversial issues: mass tort, employment discrimination, and securities fraud class actions.

§ 11.1 Mass Torts

No area of class-action law has generated more judicial and scholarly debate than mass tort class actions. A key element of that controversy arises from the 1966 Advisory Committee Notes, which state:

> A "mass accident" resulting in injuries to numerous persons is ordinarily not appropriate for a class action because of the likelihood that significant questions, not only of damages but of liability and defenses of liability, would be present, affecting the individuals in different ways. In these circumstances an action conducted nominal-

ly as a class action would degenerate in practice into multiple lawsuits separately tried.

This Note caused a number of early courts to refuse to certify mass tort cases. Later, several courts sought ways to certify mass tort class actions notwithstanding the concerns expressed by the Advisory Committee. In recent years, however, a number of courts have again begun to view mass tort class actions with skepticism. This subchapter provides a brief historical overview of mass tort class actions and surveys some of the key issues facing courts today.

Preliminarily, it is important to define the term "mass tort." At its broadest, the term can apply to any multi-party lawsuit involving tort claims. In general, the term is used to describe either (1) a mass accident (a single event, such as an airplane crash, involving injuries to many people) or (2) personal injuries on a widespread basis, typically involving allegedly defective products (such as breast implants or other medical devices). Most of these claims arise under state law rather than federal law. Mass tort cases may also involve widespread damage to property or other economic loss. The *Manual for Complex Litigation (4th)* identifies various examples of "single incident mass torts": "a hotel fire, the collapse of a structure, the crash of a commercial airliner, a major chemical discharge or explosion, or an oil spill." § 22.1. It also addresses "dispersed mass torts," which usually involve use of or exposure to allegedly dangerous substances (*e.g.*, "asbestos, Dalkon Shield intrauterine devices, silicone gel breast implants, and diet drugs"). *Id.* In some instances, the exposed victims know of their exposure and have suffered injury. In other instances, exposed class members may know of their exposure but have not developed any injuries. These latter claimants are commonly referred to as "future claimants."

As the *Manual* notes, the line between single incident and dispersed mass torts is sometimes difficult to draw. This is because "[e]ven single event torts with a strong local nexus, such as plant emission or a spill of toxic materials, may include latent exposure effects or be affected by individual variables, such as smoking." *Id.*

Nonetheless, some generalization is possible. As a rule, despite the cautionary language in the Advisory Committee Notes with respect to "mass accidents," courts have been more willing to certify "single incident mass torts" than they have been to certify "dispersed mass torts."

A. JUDICIAL TRENDS IN MASS TORTS CLASS ACTIONS

(1) Mass Torts in the 1960s and 1970s

Many courts in the 1960s and 1970s relied upon the Advisory Committee Notes in rejecting efforts to certify mass tort cases. In the late 1970s, a number of federal trial courts began permitting plaintiffs to bring mass tort class actions. Most of these efforts, however, were reversed on appeal.

Two highly publicized examples of cases that were certified and reversed on appeal were (1) the class action involving the collapse of two skywalks at the Kansas City Hyatt Regency, killing 114 people (certified in 1982 and reversed the same year); and (2) a nationwide class of persons claiming injuries from the Dalkon Shield birth control device (certified in 1981 and reversed in 1982).

(2) Mass Torts in the Mid–1980s

In the mid–1980s, the explosion of asbestos suits, as well as the highly publicized Agent Orange litigation, led to a major shift in attitude among many federal courts in favor of certifying mass tort cases. One landmark ruling was *Jenkins v. Raymark Industries*, 782 F.2d 468 (5th Cir. 1986). In that case, the Fifth Circuit upheld the certification under Rule 23(b)(3) of hundreds of claims involving asbestos-related personal injuries. The court noted the prior reluctance of courts to certify mass tort cases, but stated that, in light of the 5,000 pending asbestos cases in that circuit, "[n]ecessity moves us to change and invent." *Id.* at 473.

In certifying the class under Rule 23(b)(3), the district court had found that the "state of the art" defense—that the dangerous nature of asbestos could not reasonably have been known at the time asbestos was placed on the market—predominated over any individual issues. As a result, the district court had permitted the consolidation of approximately 900 cases pending in its district into a class of plaintiffs under Rule 23(b)(3). The Fifth Circuit approved this certification, finding that the predominance and superiority requirements were satisfied. The Fifth Circuit noted that the district court's "plan is clearly superior to the alternative of repeating, hundreds of times over, the litigation of the state of the art issues with, as [the] experienced [district court] judge says, 'days of the same witnesses, exhibits and issues from trial to trial.' " *Id.* at 473.

Other significant appellate court rulings upholding class certification during the mid–1980s included the *Agent Orange* and *School Asbestos* cases. *In re School Asbestos Litig.*, 789 F.2d 996 (3d Cir.), *cert. denied*, 479 U.S. 852 (1986); *In re "Agent Orange" Prods. Liab. Litig.*, 818 F.2d 145 (2d Cir. 1987), *cert. denied*, 484 U.S. 1004 (1988). In *School Asbestos*, the Third Circuit upheld Rule 23(b)(3) certification of an action by school districts in several states seeking recovery of the costs of testing and removing asbestos from school buildings. In so doing, the court noted that "the trend has been for courts to be more receptive to use of the class action in mass tort litigation." 789 F.2d at 1009. In *Agent Orange*, the Second Circuit upheld the certification of a class of former military members and their families seeking damages for injuries caused by exposure to the herbicide Agent Orange.

This receptiveness by appellate courts led plaintiffs throughout the country to bring a variety of mass tort class actions: cases involving toxic spills, pharmaceutical products, and medical devices, among others. In 1989, for example, certification of a class action in the Dalkon Shield litigation was approved by a federal appellate court (albeit in the settlement context). *In re A.H. Robins Co.,* 880 F.2d 709 (4th Cir. 1989). This case was significant because, as noted above, a different appellate court had overturned an order certifying a class in the Dalkon Shield litigation seven years earlier.

During this shift in favor of certifying mass tort cases, a number of prominent federal district court judges took leading roles in resolving thousands of Agent Orange, asbestos, and Dalkon Shield cases.

(3) Recent Judicial Skepticism

Critics of the trend in favor of certifying mass tort cases argued that the mere threat of class certification is so devastating that defendants routinely choose to settle rather than risk bankruptcy on the results of a single trial. This view gained momentum in the mid–1990s, when various federal appellate courts issued a series of significant rulings.

An important ruling (discussed in various places in this text) was the Seventh Circuit's decision in *In the Matter of Rhone–Poulenc Rorer Inc.,* 51 F.3d 1293 (7th Cir. 1995). That case involved a nationwide class of hemophiliacs infected by the AIDS virus against drug companies that manufactured blood solids. The district court certified a class action, but the Seventh Circuit granted mandamus and reversed. The court was concerned that defendants were being coerced to settle out of fear of a potential classwide adverse verdict; that difficult choice-of-law questions were presented; and that the bifurcated trial approach envisioned by the trial court would violate defendant's Seventh Amendment jury-trial rights. The court distinguished *Jenkins* as involving a judicial crisis unique to asbestos.

Another significant ruling (also discussed in various places in this text) occurred in *Castano v. American Tobacco Co.*, 84 F.3d 734 (5th Cir. 1996). In that case, the district court certified a class under Rule 23(b)(3) of all nicotine-dependent persons in the United States who have purchased and smoked cigarettes manufactured by defendants (along with the estates, spouses, children, relatives, and "significant others" of these nicotine-dependent smokers). The claims went back to 1943. The Fifth Circuit reversed, finding that individual issues of reliance and choice-of-law, among others, would predominate over common issues. The court echoed *Rhone-Poulenc's* concern regarding the rush to settle class actions and about the Seventh Amendment problems in bifurcated jury trials.

The Supreme Court, in the late 1990s, issued two important mass tort class action cases. Both cases involved settlement classes involving exposure to asbestos.

In the first decision, *Amchem Prods., Inc. v. Windsor*, 521 U.S. 591 (1997), discussed on pp. 253–255, *supra*, the Supreme Court rejected a Rule 23(b)(3) settlement class consisting of all persons who had been exposed occupationally to asbestos manufactured by one or more of the 20 defendants in the case and who had not yet filed an asbestos-related lawsuit against one of the defendants (along with the spouses, parents, children, and other relatives of those class members). The Supreme Court held that the proposed class did not satisfy the predominance requirement because it was too sprawling, involving individuals exposed to different asbestos-containing products, for different amounts of time, in different ways, and over different periods. Furthermore, the class members had developed different symptoms because of their exposures, with some having no symptoms at all. Moreover, choice-of-law problems counseled against predominance, as did conflicts between present and future (exposure only) claimants.

Two years later, the Court decided *Ortiz v. Fibreboard Corp.*, 527 U.S. 815 (1999). *Ortiz*, which is discussed in detail on pp. 76–79, *supra*, involved a mandatory "limited fund" settlement class that had been certified under Rule 23(b)(1)(B). The defendant, Fibreboard Corporation, having a net worth of approximately $235 million, was litigating with its insurance companies over disputed coverage for what promised to be billions of dollars of asbestos liability. Fibreboard was able to agree with its insurance carriers to establish a settlement fund of approximately $1.5 billion, which then became the "limited fund" against which a mandatory class of asbestos claimants claimed entitlement under various tort theories. Unlike the defendants in *Amchem*, the defendant in *Ortiz*, by virtue of the mandatory class action, stood to gain a definitive cap on its asbestos liability by forcing all claimants to recover from a fund consisting almost entirely of insurance proceeds, thereby permitting the corporation to continue with virtually all of its net worth intact.

The Supreme Court held that the class did not qualify for certification under (b)(1)(B). Although the Court stopped short of holding that limited-fund settlement classes could never be certified under (b)(1)(B) in mass tort settlement cases, it stated that "the applicability of Rule 23(b)(1)(B) to a fund and plan purporting to liquidate actual and potential tort claims is subject to question...." *Id.* at 864.

(4) Responses to Judicial Skepticism

It would be a serious mistake to view such decisions as *Rhone-Poulenc*, *Castano*, *Amchem*, and *Ortiz*, as the end of aggregate mass tort lawsuits. Mass tort class actions—and lawsuits that function similarly to class actions—have continued to be filed, and some of those cases have been successful.

First, some federal courts have not shut the door altogether on mass tort class actions. One such example is a nationwide class action against a pharmaceutical company. *In re Copley Pharm., Inc.*, 161 F.R.D. 456 (D.Wyo. 1995). Furthermore, a number of federal circuits have not yet weighed in on whether they will endorse the approaches taken by the Fifth and Seventh Circuits in *Castano* and *Rhone-Poulenc*.

Second, federal setbacks have stimulated a focus on state court alternatives. Although some state courts have looked with skepticism upon mass tort class actions, plaintiffs have generally found more receptive audiences in state courts than in federal courts. Of course, the Class Action Fairness Act will make it more difficult for plaintiffs to keep substantial, multi-state class actions in state court. *See* pp. 214–227, *supra*.

Third, theories have been advanced in both state and federal court that purport to resolve some of the manageability problems in mass tort cases. One prime example accepted by some courts is the so-called "medical monitoring" claim, under which plaintiffs exposed to a toxic substance allege that they should receive periodic medical observation at the defendant's expense, even though they have exhibited no physical symptoms. *See* p. 72, *supra*. Plaintiffs asserting medical monitoring claims have argued that such claims eliminate the need to prove individualized injuries and damages. As a related matter, litigants have asserted tort theories premised not upon current injuries but upon fear of future disease or increased risk of future damages. Other litigants have attempted to overcome issues of individual proof by arguing for the elimination of certain traditional tort elements, such as the reliance requirement in certain fraud cases. In addition, plaintiffs have argued that individualized damages issues can be minimized through statistical proof. *See* pp. 307–310, *infra*.

Litigants have also devised a variety of surrogates for class treatment. One highly publicized example involves cost-recoupment suits filed against the tobacco and firearms industries by government entities (or, in the case of tobacco, by private entities, such as health insurers) for medical costs allegedly resulting from tobacco-and firearm-related injuries.

These efforts, taken together, reveal that large mass tort cases are not going to disappear any time soon. Indeed, plaintiff lawyers have continued to devote substantial resources to cases involving tobacco, lead paint, cell phones, fast foods, and firearms. (In 2005, Congress eliminated suits against firearms manufacturers based on the misuse of a firearm by a third person. Protection of Lawful Commerce in Arms Act, Pub. L. 109–92, 119 Stat. 2095.)

B.   OTHER ISSUES IN MASS TORT CASES

The recent trend in mass tort class actions discussed above is only one of many important topics in the mass tort context. This section identifies several other important issues.

(1) Exposure–Only Claimants

One important issue in mass tort class actions that deserves attention is whether a "future claimant," *i.e.,* a person who has been exposed to a harmful substance but has shown no ill effects, can nonetheless sue for damages. In the context of asbestos, a number of courts have allowed such claims to go forward, reasoning that, even prior to the display of any symptoms, exposed individuals have suffered injury at the cellular level. Some courts have applied this reasoning in other kinds of exposure-only cases as well, such as those involving exposure to lead paint and those involving Dalkon Shields.

Other courts have refused to certify classes alleging only exposure but no physical injury, finding that the proposed class did not meet the prerequisites of Rule 23. Some courts have found that individualized issues, such as the extent and nature of any injuries and the degree and length of exposure, predominated over common questions. Other courts have pointed to the difficulty in giving notice to exposure-only plaintiffs, who may not know they were exposed and who may lack adequate information to opt out of the class.

In *Ortiz v. Fibreboard*, 527 U.S. 815 (1999), the Supreme Court raised, but did not decide, whether "exposure-only" plaintiffs lacked "injury in fact," and thus did not have standing to sue. *Id.* at 831.

(2) "Mature" Versus "Immature" Mass Torts

An important inquiry that courts have utilized in evaluating the appropriateness of certifying a mass tort case is whether the case involves a "mature" tort or an "immature" tort. Courts in recent years have been particularly reluctant to certify immature tort cases—those in which there have been few individual trials and verdicts. As the *Manual for*

Complex Litigation (4th) explains, "[a] court should be cautious before aggregating claims or cases, particularly for trial, learning first about the nature of the litigation and whether the issues are appropriate even for pretrial aggregation or consolidation." § 22.2.

The concept of mature versus immature torts was important to the Fifth Circuit's decision in *Castano*, which involved a putative nationwide class of nicotine-dependent cigarette smokers. The court stated that, because these types of "addiction as injury" cases had never been tried before, there was no "prior track record of trials" from which the district court could assess Rule 23(b)(3)'s predominance and superiority requirements. 84 F.3d at 747. Other courts, however, have rejected "maturity" as a consideration in whether to certify a class.

(3) Problems of Classwide Proof in Mass Tort Cases

A major issue in mass tort cases (and sometimes in other types of class actions) is whether plaintiffs can offer proof of damages on a classwide basis through the use of expert and statistical evidence. Most circuits have not squarely addressed the issue. The courts that have done so have reached conflicting results.

In *In re Fibreboard Corp.*, 893 F.2d 706 (5th Cir. 1990), the Fifth Circuit rejected that approach in the context of thousands of asbestos cases. Under the trial plan proposed by the district court, plaintiffs and defendants were each to choose 15 illustrative plaintiffs, whose individual claims would be tried along with those of the 11 class representatives. Then, based upon the 41 cases plus expert testimony, the jury would determine total damages suffered by the remaining 2,990 class members. The Fifth Circuit—the same court that had upheld class certification by the same district judge in *Jenkins*—invalidated the trial plan and, in so doing, indicated that such aggregated proof raised due process and Seventh Amendment concerns. The court rejected plaintiffs' theory that "statistical measures of representativeness and commonality [would] be sufficient for the jury to make informed judgments concerning damages." *Id.* at 710. It also rejected the very argument that resonated with the same court of appeals in *Jenkins*: that this approach was "the only realistic way of trying these cases," and that "the difficulties faced by the courts as well as the rights of the class members to have their cases tried [cried] powerfully for innovation and judicial creativity." *Id.* at 712. The court noted that such arguments were "compelling," but that "they are better addressed to the representative branches—Congress and the state legislature." *Id.* The court also stressed that the trial plan would have altered the substantive law of Texas, in violation of *Erie R.R. v. Tompkins*, 304 U.S. 64 (1938), by eliminating the need for each claimant to prove causation and damages.

The Fifth Circuit took a similar approach in a subsequent post-trial phase of *In re Fibreboard Corp.*, in which the same district court again tried to determine classwide damages through the use of a sample of class members. *Cimino v. Raymark Indus.*, 151 F.3d 297 (5th Cir. 1998). The *Cimino* appellate court specifically found that the district court's trial plan violated the defendant's Seventh Amendment right to a jury trial on each plaintiff's claim. The court also reiterated the state-law problems cited in *Fibreboard*.

By contrast, in *Hilao v. Estate of Marcos*, 103 F.3d 767 (9th Cir. 1996), the Ninth Circuit upheld proof of damages on an aggregated basis. The case was a class action suit under the Alien Tort Claims Act by victims of Ferdinand Marcos's regime in the Philippines. The complaint alleged that the class members and their deceased relatives had been tortured or executed or had simply "disappeared" as a result of actions by Philippine military or paramilitary groups. The case was certified as a class and went to trial. On the issue of damages, the district court determined damages for more than 9,000 claims based on approximately 130 randomly selected claims. An expert witness then determined an average award for each type of claim (torture, execution, disappearance) and multiplied the amount by the number of class members in each category. On appeal, the Ninth Circuit rejected defendant's due process and related challenges to the calculation of aggregated damages for the class. The court noted that the approach was "justified by the extraordinarily unusual nature of [the] case." *Id.* at 786. It pointed out that "the time and judicial resources required to try the nearly 10,000 claims in this case would alone make resolution of [the] claims impossible," *id.*, and the "similarity in the injuries suffered by many of the class members would make such an effort, even if it could be undertaken, especially wasteful...." *Id. Hilao*, unlike *Cimino* and *Fibreboard*, was brought under federal law (the Alien Tort Claims Act), so it did not raise *Erie* issues. Furthermore, the defendant in *Hilao* did not raise a Seventh Amendment challenge. Nonetheless, despite these distinctions, the basic approach of the Ninth Circuit is difficult to reconcile with the Fifth Circuit's approach.

§ 11.2   Employment Discrimination Class Actions

This section discusses several important issues that have arisen in employment discrimination class action cases. Class actions are widely used in cases claiming that an act of discrimination is part of a larger pattern of similar conduct. For example, an African–American who claims that he was terminated during a reduction-in-force because of his race and that less qualified white employees were retained may also claim that other similarly-situated African–Americans were the victims of discrimination. If the requirements of Rule 23 are satisfied, such claims may be pursued on a classwide basis.

Multiparty race, color, religion, sex, and national origin claims have been brought as class actions under Title VII, 42 U.S.C. §§ 2000e *et seq.*, and multi-party race claims have been brought under 42 U.S.C. § 1981. Likewise, multi-party disability discrimination claims have been brought as class actions under the Americans With Disabilities Act ("ADA"), 42 U.S.C. § 12101 *et seq.* By contrast, cases alleging age discrimination under the Age Discrimination in Employment Act of 1967 ("ADEA"), 29 U.S.C. §§ 621–34, are not subject to Rule 23 but are subject instead to different procedures under a separate statutory scheme applicable to "collective" actions. This chapter examines both Rule 23 discrimination suits and ADEA collective actions.

A.   RULE 23 CASES

(1) Applicability of Rule 23 Requirements in Discrimination Cases

Prior to the Supreme Court's decision in *East Texas Motor Freight System, Inc. v. Rodriguez*, 431 U.S. 395 (1977), a number of lower courts took the view that the requirements for class certification should be liberally construed in Title VII cases, and that the requirements of Rule 23 did not need to be applied strictly. *Rodriguez* made clear that, while "suits alleging racial or ethnic discrimination are often by their very nature class suits, involving classwide wrongs, . . . careful attention to the requirements of Fed. R. Civ. P. 23 remains nonetheless indispensable." *Id.* at 405. The Court reiterated the point five years later in *General Telephone Co. of Sw. v. Falcon,* 457 U.S. 147 (1982), noting that "a Title VII class action, like any other class action, may only be certified if the trial court is satisfied, after a rigorous analysis, that the prerequisites of

Rule 23(a) have been satisfied." *Id.* at 161. In light of *Rodriguez* and *Falcon,* courts must apply the Rule 23 requirements as stringently in Title VII cases as they do in other kinds of cases.

One context that has been greatly impacted by *Rodriguez* and *Falcon* is the so-called "across-the-board" claim of discrimination. Such a claim involves all persons allegedly affected by a particular type of discrimination. For instance, in an "across-the-board" class action, a female claiming discrimination in hiring might seek to represent females who claimed discrimination in promotion opportunities, females who claimed that they were terminated based on their sex, and females who claimed discrimination in pay. Relying on Rule 23(a)'s typicality requirement, the Supreme Court in *Falcon* raised serious doubts on the general viability of "across-the-board" class actions.

In *Falcon,* a plaintiff who alleged that he was not *promoted* by the defendant because he was Mexican–American attempted to represent a class that included Mexican–Americans who alleged that they were not *hired* because they were Mexican–American. Reversing the trial court and the court of appeals, the Supreme Court held that plaintiff could not represent such a class. The Court reasoned that "it was error for the District Court to presume that respondent's claim was typical of other claims against [the defendant] by Mexican–American employees . . . ." 457 U.S. at 158–59. According to the Court, "[i]f one allegation of specific discriminatory treatment were sufficient to support an across-the-board attack, every Title VII case would be a potential companywide class action." *Id.* at 159. The Court could "find nothing [in Title VII] to indicate that Congress intended to authorize such a wholesale expansion of class-action litigation." *Id.* In an important footnote, however, the Court stated that "[s]ignificant proof that an employer operated under a general policy of discrimination conceivably could justify a class of both applicants and employees if the discrimination manifested itself in hiring and promotion practices in the same general fashion...." *Id.* The Court gave as an example the use of "entirely subjective decision making processes" and the use of a "biased testing procedure to evaluate both applicants for employment and incumbent employees...." *Id.*

Following *Falcon*, many courts have refused to certify across-the-board classes. Other courts have certified such classes, relying on the *Falcon* footnote and identifying a single practice that allegedly was applied in a variety of contexts, such as in both hiring and termination decisions.

(2) Distinction Between Disparate Impact and Disparate Treatment Claims

An important distinction is made in employment law between "disparate treatment" claims and "disparate impact" claims. In the former, the plaintiff must prove a discriminatory motive or intent on the part of the employer; in the latter, the plaintiff need only show that an employment practice had a discriminatory impact on a protected group, regardless of motive. An example of the latter would be an aptitude test that, while not designed to discriminate against African–Americans, had the effect of disproportionately excluding them from the better jobs. Courts have generally held that disparate impact cases should be more liberally certified as class actions because they are usually based on objective standards applied evenly to the employees in question. By contrast, as the Fourth Circuit has noted, "the disparate treatment pattern or practice must be one based upon a specific intent to discriminate against an entire group, to treat it as a group less favorably simply because of [discriminatory animus]. The greater intrinsic difficulty of establishing the existence and common reach of such a subjectively based practice is obvious." *Stastny v. Southern Bell Tel. & Tel. Co.*, 628 F.2d 267, 274 (4th Cir. 1980).

(3) Rule 23(b) Requirements

Most employment class actions are certified, if at all, under either Rule 23(b)(2) or Rule 23(b)(3). As explained on p. 84, *supra*, Rule 23(b)(2) was adopted specifically for civil rights cases, and numerous civil rights suits seeking injunctive relief in the employment context have been certified under (b)(2). Most courts have historically allowed certification even if damages are also sought, as long as equitable relief is the principal relief sought.

In *Allison v. Citgo Petroleum Corp.*, 151 F.3d 402 (5th Cir. 1998), however, the Fifth Circuit held that when the damages sought are not merely "incidental," certification under Rule 23(b)(2) is inappropriate. The court defined "incidental" damages as those to which class members who establish liability "automatically would be entitled...." *Id.* at 415. A case seeking damages that would "require additional hearings to resolve the disparate merits of each individual's case" would not be suitable for (b)(2) certification. *Id.* This issue is extremely important because, under the Civil Rights Act of 1991, compensatory and punitive damages may be recoverable in Title VII cases against employers who engaged in unlawful intentional discrimination. *Allison* is discussed more fully on pp. 88–92, *supra*.

Rule 23(b)(3) has been used as a vehicle for employment class actions seeking primarily damages. Although some courts have been liberal in certifying (b)(3) employment cases, others have been more restrictive. Courts granting certification have often relied upon allegations of a pervasive discriminatory practice. Courts denying certification have frequently emphasized the existence of individualized issues, such as whether the employer in fact discriminated against each class member or instead treated individual class members unfavorably because of legitimate, non-discriminatory reasons, including poor performance, excessive absenteeism, or misconduct.

(4) Pattern-and-Practice Cases

Some courts have been receptive to certifying cases alleging a "pattern and practice" of discrimination. These courts frequently divide such cases into two phases—liability and remedy—and certify solely the question of whether defendant engaged in a pattern and practice of discrimination. A finding of a pattern and practice permits an award of injunctive relief and establishes a rebuttable presumption that individual class members were victims of discrimination. Courts adopting this approach reason that, at the first phase, the class members need not establish that they were individually discriminated against. As a result, disparities from employee to employee are irrelevant. Accordingly, these courts conclude that a pattern-and-practice trial achieves efficiencies by adjudicating common issues without becoming sidetracked by individual employee-specific issues. Other courts, however, refuse to certify discrimination cases even when a pattern and practice is alleged. For instance, some courts reason that since a pattern and practice finding establishes only a rebuttable presumption, individualized issues will still exist in the remedial phase in deciding whether a particular class member was a victim of the pattern and practice of discrimination.

(5) Whether a Finding of No Pattern or Practice Precludes Subsequent Individual Actions

In *Cooper v. Federal Reserve Bank of Richmond*, 467 U.S. 867 (1984), the Supreme Court addressed whether, in light of a class-action determination that no pattern and practice of discrimination existed, members of the class could bring individual discrimination claims. In a unanimous opinion, the

Court held that such suits *could* be brought. As the Court explained, "a class plaintiff's attempt to prove the existence of a companywide policy, or even a consistent practice within a given department, may fail even though discrimination against one or two individuals has been proved." *Id.* at 878. As a result, "the rejection of a claim of classwide discrimination does not warrant the conclusion that no member of the class could have a valid individual claim...." *Id.* Thus, under *Cooper*, even if a pattern and practice is not found, individual class members are entitled to bring separate discrimination claims.

(6) Seventh Amendment Issues

Under the Civil Rights Act of 1991, jury trials are now authorized in Title VII cases. As a result, potential Seventh Amendment issues are implicated in trying such cases. In particular, certification of bifurcated employment discrimination class actions—in which, for example, common issues are decided by one jury in the first phase and individual issues are decided by a different jury in the second phase—may be more difficult, at least in some circuits, in light of recent case law construing the Seventh Amendment right to jury trial. As discussed on pp. 242–246, *supra*, some courts have invalidated bifurcated class action jury trials on Seventh Amendment grounds, particularly in the mass torts area. These courts have relied on the principle that the Seventh Amendment is violated when an issue decided by one jury is reexamined by a subsequent jury. Other courts, however, have not endorsed this analysis.

B.   COLLECTIVE ACTIONS

(1) Overview of Age Discrimination Suits

The ADEA prohibits discrimination in employment on the basis of age against individuals age 40 and over. As noted at the outset of this chapter, age discrimination suits under the ADEA are *not* subject to Rule 23. Instead, those actions follow the procedures of a labor-specific statute, the Fair Labor Standards Act, 29 U.S.C. § 216(b). The differences between the Rule 23 approach and the ADEA approach are substantial.

First, under the ADEA, the sole inquiry for a collective action is whether the individuals alleging discrimination are "similarly situated" to one another. The "similarly situated" inquiry is a fact-specific one focusing on whether the individuals were subject to a single discriminatory decision, policy, or plan. Although a few courts have held that the Rule 23 criteria apply in ADEA cases, most courts have held otherwise. Under the latter approach, no specific inquiry into numerosity, adequacy, typicality, and commonality is required, and the plaintiffs need not satisfy any of the Rule 23(b) criteria. Some courts have stated that the "similarly situated" standard is more easily satisfied than Rule 23.

Second, suits under Rule 23 are either "opt out" actions ((b)(3)) or mandatory class actions in which opt outs generally are not allowed ((b)(1), (b)(2)). By contrast, ADEA actions are "opt-in" actions: A plaintiff is *not* part of the collective action unless he or she affirmatively opts into the class by filing a written consent to join the action. Although all of these types of actions are commenced by representative plaintiffs, the size of an ADEA collective action depends upon how many other individuals take affirmative steps to become part of the suit.

Third, plaintiffs who opt into an ADEA collective action have full party status, unlike unnamed class members in Rule 23 actions. Thus, each ADEA plaintiff is a party in court to advance his or her own individual case. To be sure, the court has wide latitude in structuring the trial: It may, for example, try all of the opt-in plaintiffs at one time, rendering a judgment as to each, or it may have a liability phase, focusing solely on whether there is a pattern and practice of discrimination, and a subsequent remedial phase to determine the remedy for each opt-in plaintiff who proves that he or she was part of the pattern and practice. Because few ADEA collective actions have gone to trial, there is little case law on trial structure for ADEA collective actions.

As discussed in the following sections, the differences between a Rule 23 class action and an ADEA collective action have generated some important legal issues.

(2) Notice to Plaintiffs in ADEA Cases

Because the notice requirements of Rule 23 do not apply to ADEA cases, courts have faced legal issues regarding the propriety of notice in ADEA cases. The contexts of Rule 23 and ADEA are very different for purposes of notice. In a Rule 23 case, notices are sent to putative class members who will be bound unless they are entitled to opt out. In ADEA cases, by contrast, notices (when authorized) are sent to people who will not be part of the case unless they affirmatively opt in.

In *Hoffmann-La Roche Inc. v. Sperling*, 493 U.S. 165 (1989), the Supreme Court addressed whether the district court could authorize notice to potential members of the collective action on whose behalf an ADEA case has been brought. The Court held that a district court has discretion to send out notices to potential plaintiffs advising them of the suit and giving them a cutoff date for filing written requests to opt into the case. The Court recognized that "once an ADEA action is filed, the court has a managerial responsibility to oversee the joinder of additional parties to assure that the task is accomplished in an efficient and proper way." *Id.* at 170–71. The Court rejected the argument—based on the differences between Rule 23 and ADEA actions—that the district court should not be allowed to send notices to people who have not yet opted into the case.

(3) Certification of an ADEA Case as a Collective Action

As discussed on p. 120, *supra*, courts in Rule 23 cases have discretion in certain cases to grant or deny class certification without discovery. Moreover, in cases in which discovery is allowed, there is no clear pattern as to whether courts will certify or refuse to certify the classes.

The ADEA rules are very different. Most courts adopt a two-part approach. At the first stage, the court decides whether to give notice of the action to potential plaintiffs. Applying a very lenient standard, courts generally grant conditional certification of an ADEA case as a collective action. Then, courts usually allow a period of discovery to address whether the claims of the plaintiffs who opt in are similarly situated to each other. At the conclusion of discovery, courts apply a much higher standard with respect to whether the certification decision should remain intact. District courts have routinely decertified the class at the second stage on the ground that the opt-in plaintiffs are not similarly situated. *E.g., Mooney v. Aramco Servs. Co.*, 54 F.3d 1207 (5th Cir. 1995) (discussing case law). The reasons for decertification at the second stage are, among others, that the opt-in plaintiffs differ in age, job status, and job locations, and suffered adverse employment actions by different supervisors at different times for different asserted reasons. Thus, courts in ADEA collective actions generally allow discovery relating to certification issues, but they usually find after such discovery that certification is unwarranted.

One recent exception is *Thiessen v. General Electric Capital Corp.*, 267 F.3d 1095 (10th Cir. 2001), *cert. denied*, 536 U.S. 934 (2002). There, the court held that the district court had erred in decertifying a collective ADEA action at stage two. The court reasoned that, although individualized issues may exist at the second phase of trial, the first phase—the pattern-and-practice phase—involved common issues and common defenses. Because of the common pattern-and-practice issues, the opt-in plaintiffs were similarly situated for purpose of 29 U.S.C. § 216(b).

§ 11.3   Securities Fraud Class Actions

A.   OVERVIEW

In its most basic form, a securities fraud class action arises when a group of people lose money in the stock market as a result of an allegedly fraudulent misstatement or omission by a corporation. For example, if a pharmaceutical company promotes a new drug as a risk-free cure for a particular ailment and fails to note (as reflected in its in-house research) that the drug has severe—and potentially fatal—side effects, a subsequent announcement regarding those side effects may cause the company's stock price to plummet. Shareholders whose portfolios dropped in value when the true facts were disclosed may wish to sue for damages. Frequently, however, the losses suffered by individual shareholders are too small to warrant separate lawsuits. Moreover, litigating separately for each shareholder the identical question of whether the company committed fraud would be extremely inefficient. Thus, courts and commentators have often cited securities fraud suits as being particularly well-suited for class treatment. That is not to say, however, that all securities suits are suitable as class actions. The facts of a particular case may dictate that certification of a securities class action would be inefficient or unfair.

This section addresses some of the major procedural issues that have arisen in securities fraud class actions. The particular focus is on class actions under § 10(b) of the Securities Exchange Act of 1934, 15 U.S.C. § 78a ("Section 10(b)"), and Securities and Exchange Commission Rule 10b–5, 17 CFR § 240.10b–5 ("Rule 10b–5").

B.   ELEMENTS OF A RULE 10b–5 CLAIM

Most securities fraud class actions seek damages based upon Section 10(b) and Rule 10b–5 and are brought under Fed.R.Civ.P. 23(b)(3). Rule 10b–5 makes it unlawful for any person to "make any untrue statement of a material fact or to omit to state a material fact necessary in order to make the statements made, in light of the circumstances under which they were made, not misleading." To make out a claim under section 10(b) and Rule 10b–5, a plaintiff must allege and prove that the defendant made a representation or omission of material fact, upon which the plaintiff justifiably relied, and which caused the plaintiff to suffer damages.

(1)   The Reliance Element

The securities law issue that has generated the most analysis for class action purposes is the element of reliance. As noted above, reliance is required in claims under section 10(b) and Rule 10b–5 (although certain other securities statutes do not require reliance). As discussed on pp. 99–100, *supra*, the need to show individual reliance upon a misrepresentation or omission is frequently a reason why fraud claims are not certified as class actions. Because reliance is specific to each individual, courts often find that individual issues predominate over common issues, thereby rendering a class unsuitable under Rule 23(b)(3). In the securities area, reliance is a required element in a section 10(b)/ Rule 10b–5 claim. Reliance provides the crucial link between a defendant's misrepresentation or omission and a plaintiff's decision to buy or sell a stock.

Courts have developed at least three potential ways in which a plaintiff can avoid having to show individual reliance: (1) the "fraud-on-the-market" theory; (2) the *Affiliated Ute* presumption; and (3) the "fraud-created-the-market" theory. If a particular case falls within one of these categories, a major impediment to class certification disappears. If not, then a court is likely to find that the need to prove reliance separately for each class member renders the case unsuitable as a class action.

(2) Fraud-on-the-Market Approach to Reliance

The fraud-on-the-market doctrine assumes that shareholders rely not so much on what a company says or omits but on the fact that the market price of the stock takes into account all publicly available information and thus reflects a fair value for the stock. The theory is that when the corporation does not disclose material information, the stock price is an artificial one. For instance, in the above pharmaceutical example, the stock price was artificially inflated during the period when the true facts about the drug's side effects were withheld. When the true facts were revealed, the stock price dropped to reflect the stock's true value.

The fraud-on-the-market approach was endorsed by the Supreme Court in the seminal case of *Basic Inc. v. Levinson*, 485 U.S. 224 (1988). *Basic* involved a class of shareholders who sued under Rule 10b–5, claiming that they sold their shares at artificially depressed prices because the company falsely denied that it was engaged in merger discussions. After the class members sold their stock, the company announced an offer by another company to buy all outstanding shares of its stock. In analyzing the claims, the Supreme Court noted that ''[r]equiring proof of individualized reliance from each member of the proposed class effectively would have prevented [the class members] from proceeding with a class action, since the individual issues then would have overwhelmed the common ones.'' *Id.* at 242. The Court then addressed fraud on the market as a way of avoiding the need for individual reliance. Under that doctrine, a person who trades in stock is presumed to have done so in reliance on the validity of the price set by the market, even where the price in fact is artificially high or low because of the company's misstatements or omissions. This presumption only arises, however, if certain requirements are met.

Most importantly, the market must be an "efficient" one—*i.e.*, one in which the market price of a security accurately reflects all publicly disclosed information. A heavily-traded stock on a major stock exchange, such as the New York Stock Exchange or the American Stock Exchange, almost certainly would qualify. A stock that sells only in low volumes and does not trade on a major stock exchange generally would not qualify. In *Basic*, the Court upheld the lower court determinations that the company's stock, which traded on the New York Exchange, traded in an efficient market.

Under *Basic*, however, the presumption of reliance resulting from an efficiently traded stock is rebuttable. As the Court noted, "[a]ny showing that severs the link between the alleged misrepresentation and either the price received (or paid) by the plaintiff, or his decision to trade at a fair market price, will be sufficient to rebut the presumption of reliance." *Id.* at 248. The Court gave the following examples of how the presumption could be rebutted: (1) if "market makers" (dealers who buy and sell the particular security on their own account) knew the truth about the company's merger plans; (2) if news of the merger discussions was in fact public at the time of the alleged fraud (a situation sometimes referred to as "truth-on-the-market");

and (3) if someone sold shares because of issues unrelated to the merger talks, despite knowing or believing that the company was presenting false information about the status of merger discussions. In each of these circumstances, the shareholder cannot be said to have relied on the false statements.

Courts have looked at a variety of factors in evaluating whether a stock is traded in an efficient market. These include: average weekly trading volume; number of analysts following the stock; market capitalization of the company; evidence of a relationship between the announcement of major news and effect on stock price; and several others. Courts have indicated that the assessment of whether a stock trades in an efficient market must be made based not on mere allegations but on a careful analysis of the evidence, under a standard of proof similar to that required for obtaining a preliminary injunction or resolving jurisdictional disputes. *E.g., Unger v. Amedisys, Inc.,* 401 F.3d 316 (5th Cir. 2005).

(3) The *Affiliated Ute* Presumption of Reliance

A second way in which plaintiffs can avoid individualized proof of reliance in securities cases is when defendants are alleged to have failed to disclose a material fact, as opposed to affirmatively misrepresenting a fact. When an omission is involved, individualized proof of reliance is not required. This principle was established by the Supreme Court in *Affiliated Ute Citizens v. United States*, 406 U.S. 128 (1972). In allowing an exception to the need for proving reliance on an individualized basis, the Court in *Affiliated Ute* recognized the practical difficulty in showing affirmative reliance on an omission, as opposed to showing reliance on a misrepresentation.

Although a case involving solely alleged omissions is clearly governed by *Affiliated Ute*, the courts are split on whether *Affiliated Ute* should apply when both omissions and misrepresentations are involved. Some courts apply *Affiliated Ute* only if a 10b–5 case is based *solely* on omissions. Others apply the doctrine even when misrepresentations are involved as well, provided that the case is "primarily" one involving omissions.

(4) Fraud-Created-the-Market Theory

A third exception to the need for proving reliance on an individualized basis involves the situation in which defendants allegedly conspired to bring to the market securities that they knew were unmarketable. This doctrine, known as the "fraud-created-the-market" doctrine, applies only when the fraud is so extensive that the security should not be trading at all in an open and developed market. For example, the doctrine would apply to offering statements for stock issued by a startup company, when the company is part of a fraudulent scheme and has no value. A plaintiff relying on this exception must show that the underlying business is essentially worthless. Merely buying into what turns out to be a bad deal is not enough.

(5) Materiality of the Misrepresented or Omitted Fact

Basic also addressed the Rule 10b–5 element of materiality, offering a standard that can be assessed on a classwide basis. According to the Court, information that was misrepresented or withheld in a Rule 10b–5 case is material if there is "a substantial likelihood that the disclosure of the omitted fact would have been viewed by the reasonable investor as having significantly altered the 'total mix' of information made available." *Basic, Inc. v. Levinson*, 485 U.S. 224, 231–32 (1988). This inquiry is an objective one and thus need not be made separately for each class member.

Courts have also developed several doctrines that enable them to determine, on a classwide basis, whether alleged misstatements or omissions are *immaterial* as a matter of law. One example, known as "puffing," involves positive, upbeat statements that are so vague that no reasonable investor would have relied on them. Another example is the "bespeaks caution" doctrine, which involves cautionary statements that accompany a written or oral communication. The cautionary statements are deemed to render the alleged omission or misrepresentation immaterial as a matter of law. For example, rosy forecasts of future growth may be deemed immaterial if accompanied by cautionary statements that the future is uncertain and that a significant period of lower earnings is possible.

(6) Zero Price Change

Some courts have found statements immaterial as a matter of law when disclosure of the alleged fraud did not result in a change in stock price. *E.g., Oran v. Stafford,* 226 F.3d 275 (3d Cir. 2000). Other courts, however, have refused to endorse that approach. *E.g., No. 84 Employer–Teamster Joint Council Pension Trust Fund v. America West Holding Corp.,* 320 F.3d 920 (9th Cir. 2003).

C. REFORM LEGISLATION

(1) The Private Securities Litigation Reform Act of 1995

The ease with which securities class actions have been certified has led to a large number of securities fraud lawsuits. Critics contend that many of the lawsuits have been meritless, and that the threat of classwide verdicts has forced companies to settle such suits for significant sums of money, thereby injuring companies and their shareholders. Critics have also attacked the large fees that some plaintiff firms have received in such cases. On the other hand, defenders of such suits have argued that such suits have had a salutary effect on corporate conduct and have served to compensate shareholders injured by fraudulent conduct.

The criticisms leveled at securities fraud suits convinced Congress to take a hard look at the situation. After extensive hearings, Congress enacted the Private Securities Litigation Reform Act of 1995 ("Reform Act"). Pub. L. No. 104–67, 109 Stat.

737 (1995). The Reform Act contains a series of new requirements governing federal securities fraud actions, including numerous requirements—in addition to those in Rule 23—that must be satisfied in securities class actions. Some of the major features of the Reform Act include the following:

a.   Each named plaintiff who wishes to become a class representative must file a sworn certification stating that the plaintiff has read the complaint and authorized its filing, that the plaintiff did not purchase the security at issue at the direction of counsel or for purposes of participating in a securities fraud action, and that the plaintiff is willing to serve as a representative, including providing deposition and trial testimony. The sworn certification must also describe all transactions in the security made by the plaintiff during the class period; disclose any other federal securities fraud actions that the plaintiff has been involved in during the preceding three years; and confirm that the plaintiff will not accept any payment beyond his or her *pro rata* share of the recovery, except as authorized by the court (for such things as wage losses directly attributable to service as a class representative). 15 U.S.C. § 78u–4(a)(2); *see id.* § 78u–4(a)(4).

b.   The Reform Act requires that, within 20 days of the filing of a securities fraud class action, the plaintiffs' attorneys must publish a notice in a "widely circulated" newspaper, advising potential class members of the suit, the claims involved, and the potential class period. The notice must also state that, within 60 days of the notice, any plaintiff may move the court to serve as lead plaintiff. The court is then required to "appoint as lead plaintiff the member or members of the purported plaintiff class that the court determines to be most capable of adequately representing the interests of class members...." 15 U.S.C. § 78u–4(a)(3)(B)(i). In making this determination from among the persons who have submitted motions, the court is required to apply a rebuttable presumption that the person or group of persons having the "largest financial interest in the relief sought by the class" should be chosen "most adequate plaintiff," and should thus serve as class representative. 15 U.S.C. § 78u–4(a)(3)(B)(iii)(I). Some courts have permitted a group of unrelated investors to server collectively as lead plaintiff, but other courts have refused to endorse that approach.

Under the Reform Act, the individual selected as lead plaintiff shall have responsibility for selecting and retaining counsel, subject to court approval. 15 U.S.C. § 78u–4(a)(3).

c. Courts may not award attorneys' fees that exceed a "reasonable percentage of the amount of any damages and prejudgment interest actually paid to the class." 15 U.S.C. § 78u–4(a)(6).

d. Courts in securities fraud suits are required to make findings at the conclusion of the litigation as to whether any party or attorney violated Fed. R.Civ.P. 11(b) (a rule providing that attorneys who sign court papers thereby certify that the case is warranted under existing law or a good faith extension thereof). In making these findings, the court shall apply a presumption in favor of awarding attorneys' fees and costs if Rule 11 has been violated. 15 U.S.C. § 78u–4(c)(1).

e.   To prevent the perceived use of burdensome and intrusive discovery to coerce an early settlement, the Reform Act provides for an automatic stay of discovery during the pendency of any motion to dismiss, except for discovery required to preserve evidence or prevent undue prejudice to a party. 15 U.S.C. § 78u–4(b)(3)(B).

f.   The Reform Act requires that class action settlements generally cannot be placed under seal except for good cause shown, with good cause defined as "direct and substantial harm to any party." 15 U.S.C. § 78u–4(a)(5). Furthermore, any proposed settlement disseminated to a class must include, in addition to any other information required by the court, a statement of the amount of the settlement proposed to be distributed to the class (both in the aggregate and on a per share basis); a statement of the potential outcome of the case (if the parties agree on damages recoverable, then a statement of that amount; otherwise, a statement from each party concerning the issues on which there is disagreement); a statement of the attorneys' fees sought and an explanation in support of the request; the name and contact information of a representative of class counsel who is available to answer questions; and a brief statement of the reasons for proposing a settlement. 15 U.S.C. § 78u–4(a)(7).

g.   The Reform Act imposes heightened pleading standards regarding the defendant's state of mind in securities fraud suits covered by the Act. (5) U.S.C. § 78u–4(b)(2).

(2) Post–Reform Act Federal Removal Legislation

In the years following the Reform Act, the number of securities fraud cases filed nationwide actually increased. Much of this litigation has been in state court rather than federal court, reflecting a belief that, for the most part, state courts are more receptive to securities fraud suits than post-Reform Act federal courts.

In 1998, in response to this shift to state court, Congress passed the Securities Litigation Uniform Standards Act of 1998, 15 U.S.C. § 77p. That Act provides for exclusive federal-court jurisdiction in most securities fraud class actions and requires that federal law be applied. *See Merrill Lynch, Pierce, Fenner & Smith, Inc. v. Dabit,* 126 S.Ct. 1503 (2006). As stated in the legislative history, the Act's purpose is "to prevent plaintiffs from seeking to evade the protections that federal law provides against abusive litigation by filing suit in State, rather than federal court." H.R. Rep. No. 105–803 (1998) (Conf. Rep.). The result is that the Reform Act and Rule 23 will govern the vast majority of securities fraud class actions.

CHAPTER 12

DEFENDANT CLASS ACTIONS, DERIVATIVE SUITS, AND SUITS INVOLVING UNINCORPORATED ASSOCIATIONS

The traditional model of a class action is a suit by a class of plaintiffs against one or more individual defendants. This chapter discusses three types of class actions (or related proceedings) that do not fit within that model: defendant class actions, shareholder derivative suits, and suits involving unincorporated associations. Defendant class actions are authorized by the text of Rule 23 itself; derivative suits are governed by Rule 23.1; and actions by or against the members of an unincorporated association are governed by Rule 23.2.

§ 12.1 Defendant Class Actions

A. OVERVIEW

Most class-action lawsuits are brought *by* a class of plaintiffs. Rule 23, however, permits suits *against* a class a well. Rule 23(a) provides that "[o]ne or more members of a class may sue *or be sued* as representative parties ..." (emphasis added). In

335

fact, the Supreme Court recognized the concept of a defendant class action more than a century ago. *Smith v. Swormstedt*, 57 U.S. (16 How.) 288 (1853).

Relatively few class actions today are defendant class actions. As a result, the law is sparse, and a number of issues raised by commentators have not been settled—or even widely addressed—by the courts.

Some of the most frequent uses of defendant class actions are in securities litigation, patent infringement litigation, and civil rights litigation. In securities litigation, defendant classes often include claims brought by stock purchasers who allege fraud against a large number of brokerage houses involved in underwriting a stock offering. In patent infringement cases, defendant class actions often involve a party seeking to enforce a particular patent against a defendant class of infringers. In the civil rights area, plaintiffs often seek certification of defendant classes consisting of large numbers of state officials (for example, the sheriff in each county of a state that has numerous counties), thus enabling plaintiffs to enjoin all of the relevant public officials from enforcing state laws that violate the plaintiffs' statutory or constitutional rights.

Rule 23 provides no meaningful guidance for applying class-action principles to defendant classes. Indeed, many of the Rule 23 concepts were designed for plaintiff class actions and are not easily applied to defendant classes. The following sections address some of the most significant defendant-class issues.

B. RULE 23 CRITERIA AND
DEFENDANT CLASSES

(1) Overview

As with plaintiff classes, a plaintiff suing a class of defendants must satisfy all of the criteria of Rule 23(a)—numerosity, commonality, adequacy, and typicality. Although numerosity and commonality generally have not been difficult issues in defendant classes, the typicality and adequacy requirements have raised some unique questions. A defendant class, like a plaintiff class, must also satisfy one of the subdivisions of Rule 23(b) (namely, (b)(1)(A), (b)(1)(B), (b)(2), or (b)(3)). Like the Rule 23(a) requirements, the Rule 23(b) criteria have posed some difficult issues for courts in defendant classes. These topics are addressed below.

(2) Typicality

The Rule 23(a)(3) requirement that "the claims or defenses of the representative parties [be] typical of the claims or defenses of the class" generally raises no unique issue in the context of defendant class actions. If a representative defendant has a unique issue or circumstance, that representative may be deemed atypical and thus not qualified to serve.

The more complicated typicality issues arise in the context of "bilateral" class actions—in which a class of plaintiffs sues a class of defendants. Courts have held that a named plaintiff who has no claim against a particular defendant cannot be typical of those class members who do have claims against that defendant. Under that approach, the only plaintiff class representative who could satisfy typicality would be one who has a claim against every defendant, and in some circumstances, no such class member may exist. Thus, the fact that the suit is brought against a class of defendants complicates a named plaintiff's task in establishing typicality to represent a plaintiff class.

The exception to this rule of typicality is when the plaintiffs have alleged a conspiracy among the defendants or there is a "juridical link" among the defendants—namely, a legal relationship that unites defendants in a way that makes a single lawsuit more efficient than separate suits against the individual defendants. Examples of juridical links would be several underwriters who are each accused of having a role in a fraudulent prospectus, and state officials from various parts of the state who apply the same challenged regulation, even though only one official actually dealt with the particular plaintiff class representative.

(3) Adequacy of Representation

Rule 23(a)(4) requires, as a prerequisite to certification, the presence of adequate class representatives and class counsel. The adequacy requirement poses several unique issues in the case of defendant class actions.

First, because the plaintiff selects the class representative for the defendant class, the person named as the representative may not want to serve as the representative and may, in fact, vigorously oppose the very notion of a defendant class. In a plaintiff class, a representative's opposition to class certification would obviously be disqualifying. In a defendant class, however, courts may view a representative's objection to class certification as confirming that the representative will vigorously assert the interests of the defense. An enthusiastic defendant, by contrast, might be acting in collusion with the plaintiff.

Second, because the defenses asserted by various defendants may differ, courts must scrutinize whether a defendant class representative has a conflict of interest in representing other defendants. The handful of courts that have addressed the issue have generally found defendant class representatives adequate, notwithstanding a potential conflict.

Third, a defendant class representative may be inadequate if his or her claim is small relative to the class as a whole. Courts may view the representative as having so little at stake that he or she would prefer to admit liability than to spend the time and resources defending a class action. By contrast, courts are less likely to reject plaintiff class representatives merely because their personal stake in the controversy is small.

(4) Rule 23(b)(1)(A) Classes

Rule 23(b)(1)(A) encompasses defendant classes. It applies when "the prosecution of separate actions by *or against* individual members of the class would create a risk of … inconsistent or varying adjudications with respect to individual members of the class which would establish incompatible standards of conduct for those opposing the class'' (emphasis added). Nonetheless, despite the wording of (b)(1)(A), defendant classes are not frequently certified under that subdivision. A major reason is the difficulty in showing the risk of ''incompatible standards of conduct for the party opposing the class…..'' In a defendant class, the focus is on whether the *plaintiff* would be subject to incompatible standards. But a plaintiff who simply recovers against some, but not all, defendants is not thereby subjected to incompatible standards.

(5) Rule 23(b)(1)(B) Classes

Rule 23(b)(1)(B) also contemplates suits *against* defendant classes. It allows for class certification when separate actions ''by *or against* individual members of the class … would as a practical matter be dispositive of the interests of the other members not parties to the adjudications or substantially impair or impede their ability to protect their interest'' (emphasis added). Again, however, there is not a wide body of case law in the context of defendant class actions, but examples can certainly be found. For instance, some courts have certified defendant classes under (b)(1)(B) consisting of the partners of a general partnership with joint and several liability, reasoning that a finding of tort or contractual liability against one partner could substantially impair the other partners from mounting a defense.

(6) Rule 23(b)(2) Classes

Unlike Rule 23(b)(1)(A) and (b)(1)(B), the language of Rule 23(b)(2) does not expressly refer to defendant class actions. Rule 23(b)(2) authorizes a class action when "the party opposing the class has acted or refused to act on grounds generally applicable to the class, thereby making appropriate final injunctive relief or corresponding declaratory relief with respect to the class as a whole...." Courts are divided over whether defendant classes are allowed under Rule 23(b)(2). *See Henson v. East Lincoln Township,* 814 F.2d 410 (7th Cir. 1987) (discussing case law). Courts that have permitted such class actions generally have not attempted to justify that result based on the wording of Rule 23(b)(2). Nonetheless, some litigants seeking a (b)(2) defendant class have relied on the "sued or be sued" language of Rule 23(a) and argued that this wording supports defendant classes under all of Rule 23(b)'s subdivisions. Examples of (b)(2) defendant classes have included suits to enjoin classes of government officials from enforcing an unconstitutional statute.

Courts refusing to certify (b)(2) defendant classes point out that the defendant (the alleged wrongdoer), not the plaintiff, is always the one who will have "acted or refused to act on grounds generally applicable to the class." They also point out that the Advisory Committee Notes relating to (b)(2) refer solely to plaintiff classes.

(7) Rule 23(b)(3) Classes

Rule 23(b)(3) authorizes an opt-out class when common questions of law or fact "predominate" over individual questions and a class action is "superior" to other methods for resolving the disputes. The opt-out feature of Rule 23(b)(3)—as opposed to the mandatory nature of classes under (b)(1) and (b)(2)—raises special issues in the context of defendant class actions. Obviously, defendants usually have a much stronger interest in opting out of a class than do plaintiffs. Individual class members in a plaintiff class action generally will opt out only if (1) they believe they can do better through separate lawsuits or (2) for some personal reason they do not want to be involved, even as an unnamed class member. In most plaintiff class actions, the number of opt outs is small, since the class members like the convenience of taking a passive role but still being allowed to share in the recovery. In the context of a defendant class action, however, there may be strong incentives to opt out. Among other things, plaintiffs may not bother to sue those defendants who opt out. Courts are split on whether the possibility of massive opt outs prevents a defendant class action from being the superior device for adjudicating the claims. In some circumstances, courts have minimized opt-out concerns by noting that plaintiffs would simply join, as individual defendants, those defendants who choose to opt out.

C. OTHER ISSUES

In addition to issues under Rule 23(a) and (b), defendant classes have occasionally raised issues involving statutes of limitations, notice, and personal jurisdiction.

(1) Statutes of Limitation

As discussed on pp. 199–204, *supra*, the filing of a plaintiff class action generally tolls the statute of limitations with respect to all putative class members. The tolling doctrine raises complicated issues in defendant class actions. If applied to unnamed defendant class members, tolling could result in unfairness because those unnamed members may not be notified of a pending suit within the statute of limitations period and thus may not know, for example, that they need to preserve evidence to defend a claim. On the other hand, application of the tolling doctrine provides judicial economy. Without tolling, individual plaintiffs would be required to file a multiplicity of suits to protect themselves from a denial of class certification, resulting in a waste of judicial resources—the very problem that class actions are supposed to combat. Few courts have had the opportunity to consider tolling as it applies to a defendant class, and those that have done so are divided as to whether the filing of a defendant class action tolls the statute of limitations as to unnamed class members.

(2) Notice

Consistent with the law governing plaintiff classes, courts have required notice to members of defendant classes certified under Rule 23(b)(3). With respect to (b)(1) and (b)(2) classes, some courts have held that due process mandates notice to members of a defendant class, even if Rule 23 does not. Courts and commentators have noted the serious ramifications of an absent defendant class member being subjected to a judgment without notice, thus incurring an out-of-pocket loss, as opposed to the situation of an absent member of a plaintiff class, who stands to lose a claim but faces no out-of-pocket loss. A few courts have not mandated notice for defendant class members in (b)(2) classes, but these cases generally involve defendant classes consisting of governmental entities.

(3) Personal Jurisdiction

In *Phillips Petroleum v. Shutts*, 472 U.S. 797 (1985), discussed on pp. 186–190, *supra,* the Supreme Court left open the issue of whether a court must have personal jurisdiction over the members of a defendant class in order for those members to be bound by the court's decision. Few lower courts have addressed this issue, and those that have are divided. Some focus on facilitating the use of the class action device for defendant classes (which would be frustrated if personal jurisdiction requirements applied); others focus on the perceived unfairness of binding defendants over whom there are insufficient contacts.

§ 12.2   Shareholder Derivative Suits

A.   OVERVIEW

Rule 23.1 authorizes shareholders to file suit on behalf of the corporation when the corporation itself has failed to take appropriate action against its directors, controlling shareholders, or third parties. (The rule likewise entitles members to enforce the rights of an unincorporated association when the latter has failed to do so.) A shareholder derivative action is similar to a class action. In both, the named plaintiff is asserting both its own interests and those of others similarly situated. In addition, Rule 23.1 shares several procedural requirements with Rule 23: The named plaintiff must "fairly and adequately" represent the interests of other shareholders; a derivative action cannot be dismissed or settled without court approval; and "notice of the proposed dismissal or compromise shall be given to shareholders or members in such manner as the court directs."

Shareholder derivative suits differ from class actions in certain respects, however, most importantly in the nature of the alleged injury. In a shareholder derivative suit, the allegedly aggrieved party is the corporation—not the individual shareholders—and any recovery is for the benefit of the corporation. Another difference is that, unlike Rule 23(b)(3), Rule 23.1 contains no provision for opting out of the action.

Rule 23.1 became a separate rule as part of the 1966 revision to Rule 23. Prior to that time, provisions relating to shareholder derivative suits were part of Rule 23.

B.   REQUIREMENTS OF RULE 23.1

Rule 23.1 sets forth a number of requirements for maintaining a shareholder derivative suit. These include: (1) the claim asserted must belong to the corporation; (2) the plaintiff must have been a shareholder at the time of the alleged wrongdoing; (3) the plaintiff must demand that the corporation file suit on its own behalf or allege why such a demand would be futile; (4) the action must not be collusive, or designed to confer federal court jurisdiction; (5) the plaintiff must "fairly and adequately" represent the interests of other shareholders similarly situated; (6) court approval must be secured prior to settlement or dismissal; and (7) notice of a proposed settlement or dismissal must be given to the shareholders in "such manner as the court directs." These requirements are discussed below.

(1) Derivative Injury Requirement

Under Rule 23.1, the claim asserted must belong to the corporation and not any individual shareholder. In categorizing the claim, courts look to the type of injury suffered. If the injury is suffered by all shareholders jointly as a result of their status as such, then the claim belongs to the corporation. By contrast, if the injury suffered is unique to the plaintiff shareholder, then the suit may not be maintained as a derivative action. Examples of derivative claims include claims of mismanagement resulting in injury to the company; a claim that the corporation failed to pursue an antitrust action; and a claim of tortious interference with the corporation's contract. On the other hand, claims to prevent dilution of voting rights, claims of interference with a shareholder's right to vote, and claims for fraudulent sale of stock have been classified as distinct shareholder injuries that cannot support a derivative action. Courts are divided over whether insider trading claims are derivative (on the theory that a corporation is harmed by a drop in stock price and damage to its reputation) or direct (on the theory that individual shareholders are harmed when the value of their stock drops).

(2) Plaintiff Must be a Shareholder at the Time of the Alleged Wrongdoing

The person bringing a derivative suit must have been a shareholder at the time of the alleged wrongful conduct. The only exception is if the alleged wrongdoing began prior to plaintiff's stock ownership but continued after the stock was purchased *and* plaintiff had no knowledge of the alleged wrongful acts at the time of the stock purchase. The plaintiff must be a shareholder at the time suit is filed, and most courts also require that the plaintiff remain a shareholder while the suit is pending.

(3) Demand for Corporate Action

Before bringing a derivative suit, a plaintiff-shareholder must make a demand on the corporation to file the proposed lawsuit on the shareholder's behalf. A demand gives the board the opportunity to address the alleged wrong, encourages intracorporate problem-solving, and allows the board to control any resulting litigation.

In general, a demand should provide several pieces of information, including the nature of the potential claim, injury suffered, and relief sought. Courts usually require that the board be given adequate time to respond, which in complicated cases could mean several months. After receiving a demand, the board may either commence a suit on the corporation's behalf or reject the demand. If the board's decision not to commence a suit is reasonable and is made in good faith, courts usually will not second-guess it.

Rule 23.1 provides that a plaintiff need not make a demand on a corporation if such demand would be futile. To establish futility, plaintiff must demonstrate that the board was biased, acted in bad faith, or had a financial interest in the matter. Establishing futility is very difficult because courts usually defer to the board's decisions.

(4) Derivative Actions May Not be Collusive

A plaintiff must allege that the derivative action is "not a collusive one"—namely, that it is not designed to confer federal jurisdiction where none would otherwise exist. The purpose of this requirement is to prevent transfer of a small number of shares of stock to someone who is not the real party in interest but whose residence enables the suit to be based on federal diversity jurisdiction.

(5) Plaintiff Must Fairly and Adequately Represent the Interests of Other Shareholders Similarly Situated

As in Rule 23 class actions, a derivative plaintiff must "fairly and adequately" represent the interests of other shareholders similarly situated. Some courts hold that this requirement entails two inquiries: (i) the qualifications of the plaintiff's attorney, and (ii) whether plaintiff has any interests antagonistic to those of the class. Other courts focus on the vigor with which the plaintiff will pursue the corporate claim, the commonality of interests between the plaintiff and the other shareholders, and the representative's familiarity with the case.

(6) Notice of a Proposed Settlement to Shareholders

Like Rule 23(e), Rule 23.1 requires that notice of a proposed settlement be given to all shareholders in a manner directed by the court. The notice should provide the shareholders with sufficient information to decide whether to contest the settlement. Although the rule does not set out what the notice should contain, courts recognize that it normally should describe the pending action (including the types of claims asserted), set forth the basic terms of the proposed settlement, inform shareholders of their right to object, and tell them where they may obtain additional information.

(7) Court Approval of Settlement or Dismissal

Like Rule 23(e), which governs class action settlements, Rule 23.1 provides that a derivative action may not be dismissed or compromised without court approval. In evaluating the fairness of a proposed settlement, courts look at, among other things, the likelihood of success if the case proceeded to trial. Lower courts are divided over whether a nonparty shareholder must intervene at the trial level in order to contest the fairness of a settlement on appeal. The Supreme Court has not definitively resolved the issue, although its *Devlin* decision in the context of Rule 23 settlements (*see* pp. 265–266, *supra*) is likely to be considered by courts addressing this issue in the derivative suit context.

§ 12.3   Class Actions Involving Unincorporated Associations

A.   OVERVIEW

The Federal Rules of Civil Procedure contain a separate rule—Rule 23.2—addressing class actions by or against unincorporated associations. At common law, such entities (which include civil rights groups, religious organizations, and nonprofit public interest groups) were not legal entities and often could not be made parties to a lawsuit. The only way for an unincorporated association to sue or be sued, therefore, was to join all its members, a potentially insurmountable task. Even then, such a suit was not always economically viable, because the only damages recoverable were from the members' personal assets, not from the assets of the association.

Early on, some state legislatures enacted laws enabling unincorporated associations to sue and be sued as entities in their state courts. In 1922, the Supreme Court held in *United Mine Workers of America v. Coronado Coal Co.*, 259 U.S. 344 (1922), that an unincorporated association could be sued in federal court, even if state and common law said otherwise, if the purpose of the suit was to enforce a substantive federal right. In 1938, the holding of that case was codified by the passage of the original Federal Rule of Civil Procedure Rule 17(b), which in relevant respects remains unchanged today. Rule 17(b) states, in pertinent part:

> [A] partnership or other unincorporated association, which has no ... capacity [to sue or be sued] by the law of [the] state [where the district court is held] may sue or be sued in its common name for the purpose of enforcing for or against it a substantive right existing under the Constitution or laws of the United States....

Rule 17(b) thus permits an unincorporated association to sue and be sued as an entity when the purpose of the suit is to enforce a substantive federal right.

Of course, not all litigation in federal courts is federal question litigation. Many litigants rely on the diversity statute, 28 U.S.C. § 1332, to bring state-law claims in federal court. Rule 17(b) established that, with respect to diversity actions, the federal court should look to the law of the state in which it is sitting to determine the capacity of an unincorporated association to sue or be sued. But even after the enactment of Rule 17(b), many states adhered to the common law rule that denied unincorporated associations the capacity to sue or be sued. As a result, the ability to sue an unincorporated association in a diversity case still depended upon the laws of the individual states.

Moreover, Rule 17(b) did not address the problem that, even if state law permitted an unincorporated association to sue or be sued, such an association would often be unable to satisfy the requirements of diversity jurisdiction. The reason is that federal courts look to each member's citizenship to determine diversity, and unincorporated associations whose members reside in multiple states would frequently have one or more members with the same citizenship as the opposing party.

B.   ENACTMENT OF FEDERAL RULE 23.2

(1) Diversity Jurisdiction Issues

Rule 23.2, adopted in 1966, facilitates suits based on diversity by allowing representative actions by (or against) members of an unincorporated association. Rule 23.2 states:

> An action brought by or against members of an unincorporated association as a class by naming

certain members as representative parties may be maintained only if it appears that the representative parties will fairly and adequately protect the interests of the association and its members. In the conduct of the action the court may make appropriate orders corresponding with those described in Rule 23(d), and the procedure for dismissal or compromise of the action shall correspond with that provided in Rule 23(e).

In explaining Rule 23.2, the Advisory Committee Notes state:

Although an action by or against representatives of the membership of an unincorporated association has often been viewed as a class action, the real or main purpose of this characterization has been to give "entity treatment" to the association when for formal reasons it cannot sue or be sued as a jural person under Rule 17(b).

As the Note explains, Rule 23.1 gives entity treatment to an association that *cannot* be sued as an entity under state law. This explanation raises the issue of whether Rule 23.2 may be used if state law *permits* an unincorporated association to sue and be sued as an entity. If Rule 23.2 cannot be invoked when state law allows the association to sue or be sued as an entity, then securing diversity jurisdiction will be difficult because the citizenship of each member of the association will be considered, as opposed to simply the citizenship of the representative parties. Courts have taken two views on this question.

Most courts have adopted a restrictive view of Rule 23.2, finding such an approach compelled by the plain language and logical implication of the above-quoted Advisory Committee Notes. These courts conclude that Rule 23.2 applies only when state law does not give an unincorporated association capacity to sue or be sued as an entity.

Some courts, however, hold that Rule 23.2 may be invoked even if state law permits an association to sue and be sued. These courts reason that neither the language of Rule 23.2 nor the Advisory Committee Notes compel a contrary result, and that the issue of diversity jurisdiction should not turn on state-law treatment of unincorporated associations.

(2) Limitation on Qualifying Organizations

Courts have broadly construed the kinds of organizations that qualify as unincorporated associations under Rule 23.1. These include labor unions, fraternal organizations, athletic leagues, political parties, and student organizations. Rule 23.2 does not, however, apply to organizations that were formed only after the events at issue in the lawsuit, such as an organization formed specifically for the purpose of conducting a class-action suit.

(3) Incorporation of Rule 23 Requirements into Rule 23.2

An important issue under Rule 23.2 is whether the requirements of Rule 23 apply. Because Rule 23.2 explicitly references Rule 23(d) (concerning court orders in the conduct of class actions) and

Rule 23(e) (concerning court approval of dismissal or compromise), these parts of Rule 23 unquestionably apply. Furthermore, Rule 23.2, like Rule 23(a)(4), provides that "the representative parties will fairly and adequately protect the interests of the association and its members," and courts use the same basic criteria for determining adequacy under Rule 23.2 as under Rule 23(a)(4). But Rule 23.2 does not state whether the requirements of Rule 23(a)(1), (a)(2), and (a)(3), Rule 23(b), and Rule 23(c) apply.

The majority view is that, other than those provisions explicitly referenced in Rule 23.2, the requirements of Rule 23 do not apply. Courts taking that view reason that, because Rule 23.2 refers expressly to subdivisions (d) and (e) of Rule 23, the drafters knew how to incorporate portions of Rule 23 when they intended to do so.

By contrast, a minority of courts have held that *all* of the requirements of Rule 23 apply to class actions under Rule 23.2. These courts reason, among other things that while Rule 23.2 does not include a numerosity or commonality requirement, certifying a Rule 23.2 class that is not numerous or that lacks significant common issues would make no sense.

CHAPTER 13

ETHICAL AND POLICY ISSUES IN CLASS ACTIONS

This chapter surveys some of the principal ethical and policy issues that arise in class-action litigation. It also briefly discusses some of the proposals that have been advanced by legislators and others to reform class actions.

§ 13.1   Ethical Issues in Class Actions

A.   OVERVIEW

Class actions raise a host of potential ethical issues for both plaintiffs' counsel and defense counsel. Although the number of court decisions finding class counsel to have engaged in ethical violations is relatively small (particularly when compared with the overall number of class action cases litigated), there is an extensive body of commentary discussing the unique—and often very serious—ethical issues faced by lawyers in class action cases. Moreover, several courts have alluded to these issues as well in recent years. As a result, ethical issues are a significant topic in many courses on complex litigation, class actions, and mass torts.

Most state bar associations have enacted versions of either the ABA Model Rules of Professional Conduct ("Model Rules") or the ABA Model Code of Professional Responsibility. The Model Rules are used below to illustrate some of the ethical issues relating to class actions. A state's relevant ethical rules must, of course, be consulted for specific guidance on a case-by-case basis.

B. ATTORNEY COMMUNICATIONS WITH CLASS MEMBERS

(1) Pre–Certification Communications

Prior to certification, it is unlikely that unnamed class members will have had any communication with counsel for the class representative, let alone anything approaching an attorney-client relationship. As a result, some courts addressing the issue have held that unnamed class members are not deemed to be represented by class counsel prior to certification. This conclusion has important ramifications.

First, from the perspective of the plaintiffs' lawyer, this means that the lawyer cannot view the unnamed class members as "clients" and must follow restrictions on lawyer solicitation and advertising, such as those contained in Model Rules 7.1, 7.2, and 7.3.

From the defense standpoint, if unnamed class members are not represented by counsel, then the "represented person rule" does not apply. That rule provides that, "[i]n representing a client, a lawyer shall not communicate about the subject of the representation with a person the lawyer knows to be represented by another lawyer in the matter, unless the lawyer has the consent of the other lawyer or is authorized to do so." Model Rule 4.2. Because the unnamed class members are not deemed to be represented prior to certification, the represented person rule does not apply.

Nonetheless, some courts apply the represented person rule when a putative class action suit is *filed*, even before the court rules on class certification. These courts reason that, while unnamed class members are not yet clients, they are nonetheless players in litigation, and class counsel has a fiduciary duty to them even prior to certification. Adding to these points, some commentators have noted concerns about defense lawyers engaging in settlement discussions with, or taking formal statements from, unnamed class members at the pre-certification stage.

(2) Post–Certification Communications

After a class is certified, it is well accepted that the unnamed class members are treated as clients of class counsel unless and until they opt out of the class. This means that defense counsel are subject to the represented person rule, and generally may not communicate directly with unnamed class members without the consent of class counsel. Business communications not involving the suit are usually permitted, however. *See* p. 182, *supra.*

C. CONFLICTS OF INTEREST

(1) Collusion Between Plaintiffs' Counsel and Defense Counsel in Settlements

Courts and commentators have occasionally raised concerns that, in some cases, plaintiffs' counsel and defense counsel may have colluded to reach a settlement that is not in the class members' best interests. The concern is that, because defendants want to minimize their overall payment and plaintiffs' counsel want to maximize their fees, settlements end up offering little to the class members themselves.

This concern frequently arises in the context of so-called "coupon" settlements in lieu of cash payments to class members, *see* pp. 266–267, *supra*, although the thrust of the attack is generally on the fairness of the settlement itself rather than upon the ethical conduct of the lawyers. In one important case, the Third Circuit invalidated a coupon settlement in a nationwide class action and remanded the case for further findings. *In re General Motors Corp. Pick–Up Truck Fuel Tank Prods. Liab. Litig.*, 55 F.3d 768 (3d Cir.), *cert. denied* 516 U.S. 824 (1995). Although the court did not find the lawyers' conduct unethical, it did note that, when a court lacks sufficient information about a class, "the judge cannot as effectively monitor for collusion ... and other abuses." *Id.* at 787.

The Class Action Fairness Act singles out coupon settlements for special judicial scrutiny. *See* pp. 266–267, *supra*.

(2) Conflicts Among Class Members

Another potential ethical issue arises when the same lawyers represent both present and future claimants. In *Amchem Prods., Inc. v. Windsor*, 521 U.S. 591 (1997), for example, a proposed settlement covered both present claimants alleging exposure to asbestos and future claimants who also alleged exposure but who had not developed any physical injuries. The Supreme Court discussed the concerns about having the same lawyers represent both present and future claimants:

In significant respects, the interests of those within the single class are not aligned. Most saliently, for the currently injured, the critical goal is generous immediate payments. That goal tugs against the interest of exposure-only plaintiffs in ensuring an ample, inflation-protected fund for the future. *Id.* at 595.

The Supreme Count reiterated these concerns in *Ortiz v. Fibreboard Corp.*, 527 U.S. 815 (1999). In *Ortiz*, the Supreme Court struck down the certification of a single nationwide class consisting of both present and future claimants and stated that, to address conflicts of interest, district courts should divide such massive classes into homogeneous subclasses under Rule 23(c)(4)(B), with separate counsel for each subclass to eliminate conflicting interests of counsel. On a separate conflicts issue, the Court in *Ortiz* expressed concern that some of the counsel for the class had a conflict arising from their separate representation of certain non-class claimants, whose settlements were in part contingent upon a successful settlement of the class suit. *See* pp. 77–78, *supra*.

Other conflicts among clients may also make representation by a single lawyer inappropriate. For example, some class members may be more interested in recovering damages, while others may be more interested in securing injunctive relief. In a mass torts case, some class members may want to maximize the award to those with personal injuries, while others may seek to maximize the reward for property damage claims. Again, this problem may require the creation of subclasses and separate counsel.

(3) Conflicts Between Class Counsel and the Class Members

Courts generally do not allow attorneys to serve as both class representatives and counsel to the class. The concern is that an attorney cannot be objective if he or she has a stake in both the fees and the class-member proceeds. Courts have raised similar concerns when the class representative is the spouse, law partner, employee, or close relative of the class attorney. Serious conflicts may also arise if plaintiffs' counsel simultaneously represents a party opposing the class in other, unrelated matters.

(4) Contingent–Fee Agreements

Class counsel are frequently compensated based on a percentage of the recovery. *See* pp. 276–277, *supra*. Ethical issues sometimes arise because class counsel with a large financial stake in the litigation may have more incentive to settle than any individual class member, especially when the settlement includes a generous sum earmarked for attorneys' fees and insubstantial distributions to the individual class members. In addition, such attorneys may tend to focus solely on potential monetary recovery, and thus fail to pursue non-monetary relief that may be of more benefit to class members than a very small *pro rata* distribution of money. Although this type of conflict of interest potentially exists in non-class litigation, the client in traditional litigation is generally in a better position to ensure that the lawyer follows the client's directions. In a class action with a large number of class members, the class lawyer cannot, as a practical matter, follow the instructions of every class member. Although courts have alluded to the ethical issues of contingent fee agreements in class actions, the discussions generally occur in the context of a court's authority to review and approve settlements pursuant to Rule 23(e), not in the context of alleged ethical violations by counsel.

D.   OTHER ETHICAL ISSUES

(1) Advancing Costs of Litigation

Jurisdictions are split over whether a plaintiffs' lawyer may ethically advance costs in a class action with no expectation that such costs will be recouped. The approach depends in part on the particular ethical canons adopted in the jurisdiction. Under ABA Model Rule 1.8, a lawyer may pay for costs, without recovery from the client, even if the suit is unsuccessful. By contrast, under Disciplinary Rule 5–103(b) of the ABA Code of Professional Responsibility, a lawyer may advance costs only if the client remains "ultimately liable." But even in states adopting the latter canon, some courts have carved out an exception for class actions, holding that requiring class members to be ultimately liable for costs would violate Rule 23 and impose unfair hardships on the class representatives. Other courts have held that, while class representatives must reimburse counsel for costs, that obligation extends not to all costs incurred, but only to their *pro rata* share (which, in a class action involving numerous class members, would normally be relatively small).

(2) Restrictions on Right to Practice

The canons of ethics universally prohibit agreements restricting a lawyer's right to practice law. Under those canons, it is unethical for a lawyer to agree, as part of a classwide or individual settlement, not to bring additional claims against the defendant. The concern is that such agreements deprive similarly-situated people of the right to counsel of their choice. Although this concern is not unique in the class action context, some commentators have observed that it is especially likely to occur in such cases.

(3) Failure to Communicate With Class Members

Model Rule 1.4 provides that attorneys have a duty to keep their clients reasonably informed about the status of their matters. This rule poses unique challenges in class actions with large numbers of class members. Several commentators have argued that class action lawyers have a duty to communicate with individual clients under this rule, even when there are hundreds or thousands of class members, and have suggested the use of the Internet, toll-free telephone numbers, and television hook-ups for "town meetings" as ways to enable class members to keep in touch with their counsel.

§ 13.2   Policy and Reform Issues

In the past decade, legislators, judges, scholars, and practitioners have offered dozens of proposals for reforming federal class actions. Although a comprehensive survey is beyond the scope of this text, this section summarizes a few of the most prominent proposals—those introduced in Congress and those recommended by the Advisory Committee on Civil Rules. (The Class Action Fairness Act is discussed on pp. 213–227 and 266–272, *supra*.)

A.   REFORM PROPOSALS

A comprehensive discussion of class action reform proposals is beyond the scope of this text. Two sources of reform should be noted briefly, however.

First, the American Law Institute ("ALI") is currently addressing class actions and other multiparty litigation in its project, "Principles of the Law of Aggregate Litigation." A draft of the project was presented to the full body of the ALI in May 2006.

The draft, which focuses on both class and non-class aggregate litigation, is divided into three broad chapters: General Principles of Aggregation; Aggregate Treatment of Common Issues; and Settlement.

Second, the Advisory Committee on Civil Rules has repeatedly focused on Rule 23. The Committee's painstaking work led to Rule 23(f) in 1998 and a variety of other amendments to Rule 23 in 2003. The Committee considered several other interesting proposals in the 1990s that were not adopted but are still worthy of debate.

To begin with, proposed Rule 23(b)(4) would have created a special category of settlement classes. It would have partially overruled the Supreme Court's decision in *Amchem Products, Inc. v. Windsor,* 521 U.S. 591 (1997), by authorizing certification of settlement classes under Rule 23(b)(3) even if such classes did not satisfy the predominance and superiority requirements of (b)(3) for purposes of trial. A settlement class would still have been subject to the notice and opt-out rights that apply in all (b)(3) classes. Furthermore, adequacy of representation and all other subdivision (a) requirements would have needed to be satisfied. This proposal would have addressed concerns about the difficulty in securing a class settlement post-*Amchem*. Moreover, it would have avoided putting defense counsel in the potentially troublesome position of being unable to oppose class certification after unsuccessfully arguing in favor of a settlement class. *See* p. 256, *supra.*

Two other proposals of the Advisory Committee would have added factors for courts to consider in assessing the certification of (b)(3) classes. The first would have required the court to analyze other litigation that involves class members and the "maturity" of the related litigation. This provision would have given the trial court discretion to consider whether class adjudication would be appropriate in light of the existence of ongoing individual claims. The judge presumably would be more likely to rule in favor of class certification if the results of individual suits have been uniform, but less likely to certify if individual litigation has yielded inconsistent decisions.

The second proposal is sometimes referred to as the "it just ain't worth it" factor. It would have required the court to balance the possible relief to individual class members against the cost, burdens, and effects of litigation to determine if class litigation was justified. The rationale was that if the amount of expected individual relief was slight, the main justification of class enforcement disappeared. Opponents of this proposed amendment argued that removing the threat of class actions in cases involving small claims would eliminate a significant deterrent against corporate misconduct.

CHAPTER 14

NON-CLASS AGGREGATION DEVICES UNDER THE FEDERAL RULES OF CIVIL PROCEDURE

In many instances, a class action is not necessary to achieve the efficiencies of party aggregation. Indeed, as noted on pp. 103–104, *supra*, a court evaluating the superiority of a class action under Rule 23(b)(3) is required to address other devices for aggregating parties. Thus, it is important to understand the requirements not only of class actions, but of other devices for litigating claims on a multi-party basis.

This chapter addresses the various multi-party devices under the Federal Rules of Civil Procedure. These include permissive joinder (Fed.R.Civ.P. 20), compulsory joinder (Fed.R.Civ.P. 19), impleader (Fed.R.Civ.P. 14), interpleader (Fed.R.Civ.P. 22), intervention (Fed.R.Civ.P. 24), and consolidation (Fed.R.Civ.P. 42).

§ 14.1 Permissive Joinder of Parties

A. OVERVIEW

The Federal Rules of Civil Procedure distinguish between circumstances in which joinder is permissible and those in which it is required when feasible. This section addresses permissive joinder.

Federal Rule 20 governs permissive joinder of plaintiffs as well as defendants. In other words, Rule 20 governs the circumstances in which multiple plaintiffs can join together against a particular defendant (or defendants), and the circumstances in which a plaintiff (or plaintiffs) may sue multiple defendants.

The rule constitutes an expansion of the common law, which allowed joinder only when plaintiffs claimed a joint right or sued multiple defendants based on a theory of joint liability. Rule 20 contains no similar limitations.

Permissive joinder is designed to promote efficiency and avoid multiple, duplicative, and sometimes inconsistent suits involving similar issues. As a result, Rule 20 is construed liberally. *United Mine Workers of America v. Gibbs*, 383 U.S. 715 (1966). Despite its salutary purposes, however, joinder under Rule 20 is not mandatory. (Compulsory joinder is governed by Rule 19, discussed on pp. 377–385, *infra*.) A plaintiff is free to sue multiple defendants separately or to decline to join with other plaintiffs having similar claims.

Rule 20 is a procedural rule and thus governs joinder in all federal court actions, even those based on diversity. As a result, state-specific limitations on joinder are irrelevant in federal cases. On the other hand, because joinder is simply procedural, it does not create or alter substantive rights under either federal or state law. Thus, the mere fact that Rule 20 authorizes joinder in a particular circumstance says nothing about whether the particular claims have merit.

Rule 20 joinder should not be confused with impleader. The latter, which is governed by Rule 14, addresses the situations in which an existing defendant can bring *additional* parties into the case. Similarly, joinder should be distinguished from intervention under Rule 24 (discussed on pp. 398–407, *infra*), which allows *nonparties* to intervene in certain circumstances and become parties. Nonparties cannot "join" in a suit under Rule 20.

B.   JOINDER OF PLAINTIFFS

Federal Rule 20(a) allows for joinder of plaintiffs as parties if (1) "they assert any right to relief jointly, severally, or in the alternative in respect of or arising out of the same transaction, occurrence, or series of transactions or occurrences"; and (2) there is "any question of law or fact common to all these persons. . . ." Both requirements must be satisfied, based on the allegations in the complaint, before Rule 20 joinder will be allowed.

When joinder is authorized, each plaintiff becomes a party to the case. In contrast to a class action, no one plaintiff speaks for the group as a whole, and each plaintiff may be represented by separate counsel (although in most cases a small number of attorneys end up representing the entire group).

(1) Same Transaction or Occurrence

Courts have generally adopted a flexible, case-by-case approach in evaluating whether the plaintiffs allege the same transaction or occurrence or a series of similar transactions and occurrences. Some courts look for guidance to case law under Federal Rule of Civil Procedure 13, because that rule contains a "transaction or occurrence" requirement in connection with cross-claims and compulsory counterclaims. Courts typically examine whether there is a logical relationship between the plaintiffs' claims. This is a fact-based inquiry. For instance, the transaction or occurrence requirement is frequently satisfied if the plaintiffs are complaining about the same behavior of the same defendant in the same time frame, such as a stock broker's misrepresentations about a particular stock to several clients during a specific time period.

Other courts focus on whether, based on the factual similarities, joinder would be fair to the defendant. For example, courts have allowed joinder of plaintiffs who complain of similar harassment or beatings by the same police officers, even if the individual plaintiffs were victimized at different times over a period of months.

On the other hand, courts may refuse to allow joinder of multiple plaintiffs who complain about different kinds of conduct by the same defendant, such as when one plaintiff alleges sexual harassment by a supervisor and another alleges that the supervisor committed race discrimination in making promotion decisions. Likewise, courts have held that the "transaction or occurrence" test is not satisfied if plaintiffs all complain about an allegedly defective product, such as an automobile, but the plaintiffs used the product in different ways, at different times, and in different locations. In general, while prior court decisions are instructive, they are of only limited value in determining whether a specific set of facts involves the same transaction or occurrence.

(2) Common Question of Fact or Law

In addition to the transaction or occurrence element, Rule 20(a) requires the existence of a common question of law or fact. This "common question" requirement appears in many places in the Federal Rules, including class actions (Rule 23(a)(2)), permissive intervention (Rule 24(b)), and consolidation (Rule 42(a)). In all of these situations, only one common legal or factual question must exist (although, as noted on p. 39, *supra*, a few courts require more than one question under Rule 23(a)(2)). There is no requirement that all legal or factual issues be common or that common issues predominate over individual issues (except in the Rule 23(b)(3) type of class action).

In most instances, the common question requirement is easily satisfied. Indeed, if the "transaction or occurrence" requirement is satisfied, it is almost always possible to identify at least one common factual or legal question. Examples of potentially common issues are whether a product used by multiple plaintiffs is inherently defective; whether a pollutant to which multiple plaintiffs were exposed is toxic; and whether an airline crash involving numerous injured plaintiffs stemmed from pilot negligence. Nonetheless, courts have occasionally denied joinder for lack of a common legal or factual question—for example, when multiple plaintiffs sue the same defendant for discrimination but the employment decisions were made by different supervisors in different corporate divisions.

Because the transaction or occurrence requirement is separate from the common question requirement, it is possible that the latter requirement, but not the former one, will be satisfied. For instance, assume that an agency denies permits to different people at different times for the same reason. The question whether the reason is lawful is common, even though different transactions or occurrences are involved. In this situation, even though Rule 20 joinder is not appropriate, a court may allow the parties' claims to be consolidated for trial or pretrial proceedings under Fed.R.Civ.P. 42 (discussed on pp. 407–410, *infra*).

Even if the two requirements for permissive party joinder are satisfied, a court is not required to permit joinder. Rather, the decision whether to permit joinder is within the discretion of the trial court. Although joinder is generally encouraged when the requirements are met, a court may refuse to allow it when, under the particular facts, joinder would cause undue jury confusion that would not be remedied by a limiting instruction.

(3) Interest in Obtaining All Relief Granted

Rule 20 makes clear that joinder is appropriate even if the plaintiff is "not . . . interested in obtaining . . . all the relief demanded." Thus, joinder is not defeated simply because a particular plaintiff is not seeking all of the damages sought by other plaintiffs, or is litigating only certain of the causes of action set forth in the complaint.

C. JOINDER OF DEFENDANTS

As noted above, Rule 20 allows for joinder of defendants as well as joinder of plaintiffs. The requirements for joining defendants under Rule 20(a) are essentially the mirror-image of those governing plaintiffs: (i) a claim asserted against multiple defendants jointly, severally, or in the alternative involving the same transaction or occurrence, or series of similar transactions or occurrences; and (ii) one or more common legal or factual questions. The major difference is that, when Rule 20 is invoked by plaintiffs, the plaintiffs usually have *chosen* to sue collectively, whereas when defendants are joined under Rule 20, they generally are placed in that position involuntarily by the plaintiff.

Defendants have been joined in a variety of situations. Examples include: master-servant cases alleging negligence by the servant and invoking *respondent superior* against the master; defendants who are alleged to be jointly and severally liable for tortuous conduct; parties who are allegedly all guilty of patent infringement; and parties who share a common interest in the property or *res* involved in the case.

On the other hand, courts have sometimes refused to permit joinder of defendants who are alleged to have engaged in similar wrongful conduct (such as similar anti-competitive business practices) but who are not linked by a conspiracy, concerted action, or some other theory.

Under Rule 20(a), defendants may be joined even if they are not "interested in . . . defending against all the relief demanded." For example, a defendant who is sued on multiple claims can be joined with another defendant who is sued on only some of the claims.

D.   ORDERS TO AVOID PREJUDICE

Rule 20(b) allows a court in which parties are joined to issue orders necessary to prevent embarrassment, prejudice, or delay. The one specific type of order mentioned in Rule 20(b) is that the court "may order separate trials. . . ." For example, separate trials may be ordered for some or all of the joint plaintiffs out of concern that a jury would confuse the claims of the various plaintiffs or find defendants liable as to all plaintiffs simply because of the sheer number of plaintiffs raising the same claim. The court also has authority to order joint trials on common issues, followed by separate trials on individual issues. Regardless of whether the trials are separate or joint, the court has the authority to allow for joint discovery.

E.   MISJOINDER OF PARTIES

Rule 21 of the Federal Rules of Civil Procedure provides that "[m]isjoinder of parties is not ground for dismissal of an action." Rather, the court has broad discretion to add or drop parties—either at a party's request or *sua sponte*—"at any stage," including on appeal. Moreover, "[a]ny claim against a party may be severed and proceeded with separately." Rule 21's statement that dismissal is not appropriate for misjoinder does not apply, however, when an indispensable party is absent from the case and cannot be joined. *See* pp. 382–385, *infra*.

F.   JURISDICTIONAL ISSUES

Joinder under Rule 20 must satisfy not only the requirements of the rule itself but also the requirements of subject matter jurisdiction. Under the supplemental jurisdiction statute, enacted in 1990, 28 U.S.C. § 1367(a), when a case is based on federal question jurisdiction, a court has discretion to exercise supplemental jurisdiction over all properly joined plaintiffs or defendants, including all related pendent state-law claims. On the other hand, when jurisdiction is based solely on diversity jurisdiction, 28 U.S.C. § 1367(b) governs. Section 1367(b) states:

> In any civil action of which the district courts have original jurisdiction founded solely on section 1332 of this title [diversity of citizenship], the district courts shall not have supplemental jurisdiction under subsection (a) over claims by plaintiffs against persons made parties under Rule 14, 19, 20 or 24 of the Federal Rules of Civil Procedure, or over claims by persons proposed to be joined as plaintiffs under Rule 19 of such rules, or seeking to intervene as plaintiffs under Rule 24 of such rules, when exercising supplemental jurisdiction over such claims would be inconsistent with the jurisdictional requirements of section 1332.

In prohibiting supplemental jurisdiction over "claims by persons proposed to be joined as plaintiffs," section 1367(b) cites Rule 19 but not Rule 20. As a result, prior to *Exxon Mobil Corp. v. Allapattah Servs., Inc.,* 545 U.S. 546 (2005) (*see* p. 212, *supra*) considerable confusion existed among the courts regarding when, if at all, supplemental jurisdiction may be invoked in a case in which multiple plaintiffs (joined under Rule 20) filed a suit against a single defendant but only some plaintiffs satisfied the amount-in-controversy requirement. In *Allapattah,* the Court applied supplemental jurisdiction in this context (involving a child whose personal injury claim against a single defendant met the jurisdictional amount but whose family members' emotional distress and economic damages claims did not).

§ 14.2   Compulsory Joinder of Parties

A.   OVERVIEW

Generally, the choice of which defendants to sue belongs to the plaintiff. In some circumstances, however, joinder of either additional plaintiffs or additional defendants (or both) is required to ensure fairness to the defendant, to nonparties who might be affected by the case, or to the judicial system. Rule 19 of the Federal Rules of Civil Procedure governs compulsory joinder.

To determine whether to order compulsory joinder, courts apply a three-step inquiry. First, a court must determine whether a party should be joined if feasible under Rule 19(a). This inquiry is often phrased by the courts as whether the joinder of the party is "necessary," although Rule 19 does not use that term. Second, if the party is necessary, a court must then decide whether joinder is feasible. For example, joinder would not be feasible if there is no personal jurisdiction over the absent party. Third, if a court finds that joinder of the absentee is not feasible, the court must then decide whether the party is "indispensable" under Rule 19(b). If the absentee is found to be indispensable, then the case cannot go forward and must be dismissed. Unlike Rule 20, which is liberally construed, courts are frequently reluctant to mandate joinder under Rule

19 or to dismiss the action because joinder is not feasible.

The absence of "necessary" and "indispensable" parties is usually raised by an existing party in the case, but the issue may also be raised by the court *sua sponte*. The purpose of Rule 19 is to protect absent individuals—as well as those before the court—from inconsistent judicial determinations or impairment of their interests. Compulsory joinder also saves judicial resources by preventing multiple trials of similar issues.

The issue of whether a party should or must be joined is a procedural one, and thus is governed by Federal Rule 19 even in diversity cases.

B. DETERMINATION OF WHETHER THE ABSENT PARTY IS NECESSARY

The threshold Rule 19 issue is whether an absent party is necessary and thus should be joined if feasible. If the party is not necessary, then the court does not even reach the question whether the case must be dismissed if the party cannot be joined. As discussed below, Rule 19(a) provides several circumstances in which a nonparty is necessary.

(1) Rule 19(a)(1) ("Complete Relief" Clause)

Rule 19(a)(1) requires joinder (if feasible) when "in the person's absence complete relief cannot be accorded among those already parties. . . ." The focus under the "complete relief" clause of Rule 19(a)(1) is on prejudice to parties, not to the nonparty whose joinder is at issue. As the Advisory Committee Notes point out, "[c]lause (1) stresses the desirability of joining those persons in whose absence the court would be obliged to grant partial or 'hollow' rather than complete relief to the parties before the court."

Under Rule 19(a)(1), only meaningful relief must be available, not necessarily every kind of relief that is theoretically possible. The issue arises, for example, when only two of several obligors under a contract are joined as defendants. If all of the obligors are jointly and severally liable under applicable law, then the absent obligor is not essential to provide complete relief to the plaintiff. Similarly, as the Supreme Court held in *Temple v. Synthes Corp.*, 498 U.S. 5 (1990), joint tortfeasors are not necessary parties, and thus an absent joint tortfeasor need not be joined under Rule 19.

(2) Rule 19(a)(2)(i) ("Impair or Impede" Clause)

Rule 19(a)(2)(i) requires joinder if feasible when the absent person "claims an interest relating to the subject matter of the action," and resolution of the case in the person's absence may "impair or impede the person's ability to protect that interest...."

The "impair or impede" clause of Rule 19(a)(2)(i) focuses on whether the rights of the *absent* person would be harmed without joinder, in contrast to Rule 19(a)(1)'s focus on prejudice to parties. The phrase "claims an interest" is somewhat confusing, because the absent party normally will not have claimed anything. The phrase is usually interpreted to mean "has an interest" in the subject matter of the case. The interest must be sufficiently significant so that the absentee needs the protection of party status.

Whether a nonparty's interests would be impeded absent joinder generally involves a case-specific inquiry. Most courts nonetheless agree on some basic parameters. On the one hand, a mere *stare decisis* effect of an action on an absent person is not enough to trigger Rule 19(a)(2)(i). On the other hand, if issue preclusion or collateral estoppel could be used against the absent person based on rulings in the case, then the absent person's interests would clearly be impaired or impeded by an adverse ruling. Between these two extremes, it is difficult to articulate precise principles.

The "impair or impede" clause serves the same purpose as intervention under Rule 24 (*see* pp. 398–407, *infra*), namely, to avoid impairment of the absentee's interests. Intervention, however, is a mechanism used by the absentee to enter the case, whereas compulsory joinder will usually be invoked by the defendant (or the court). The right to intervene is meaningless, of course, if the absentee has no knowledge of the litigation.

(3) Rule 19(a)(2)(ii) ("Multiple Liability" Clause)

Rule 19(a)(2)(ii) requires joinder when the absent person has an interest in the subject matter and resolution of the case in the person's absence would "leave any of the persons already parties subject to a substantial risk of incurring double, multiple, or otherwise inconsistent obligations by reason of the claimed interest." The inquiry under Rule 19(a)(2)(ii) is whether adjudication without the absent person would expose *existing* parties—almost always the defendant—to the risk of multiple or inconsistent obligations. For example, a defendant might incur double obligations when a receiver claiming the proceeds to a life insurance policy sues in state court and an alternate beneficiary makes a claim in federal court.

C. FEASIBILITY OF JOINDER

If a party is deemed necessary under any of the three clauses discussed above, the court must then determine whether joinder is feasible. Under Rule 19(a), joinder is feasible only when the requirements of personal jurisdiction, subject matter jurisdiction, and venue can be satisfied. In addition, joinder is not feasible if the non-party would be entitled to assert immunity from suit. Whether lack of independent subject matter jurisdiction prevents joinder depends upon whether supplemental jurisdiction can be utilized. As noted in connection with Rule 20 (*see* pp. 375–377, *supra*), the supplemental jurisdiction statute (28 U.S.C. § 1367) can be invoked in cases involving federal question jurisdiction. In diversity suits, however, joinder of parties under Rule 19 must satisfy the requirements of diversity. The confusion among the courts that had existed under Rule 20 prior to *Exxon Mobil Corp. v.*

Allapattah Servs., Inc., 545 U.S. 546 (2005) (*see* p. 212, *supra*) does not exist for Rule 19, which specifically precludes supplemental jurisdiction over "claims by persons proposed to be joined as plaintiffs *under Rule 19* ..." (emphasis added). Nonetheless, several courts have criticized section 1367(b)'s distinction between Rule 20 permissive joinder and Rule 19 compulsory joinder.

D.   RESOLUTION WHEN PERSON SHOULD BE JOINED BUT JOINDER IS NOT FEASIBLE

Under Rule 19(b), if a person who should be joined to the suit cannot be joined, then a court must decide "whether in equity and good conscience the action should proceed among the parties before it, or should be dismissed, the absent person being thus regarded as indispensable." Rule 19(b) identifies four factors that a court should consider in making this determination.

First, a court should examine "to what extent a judgment rendered in the person's absence might be prejudicial to the person or those already parties...." As the Advisory Committee Notes explain:

The first factor brings in a consideration of what a judgment would mean to the absentee. Would the absentee be adversely affected in a practical sense, and if so, would the prejudice be immediate and serious, or remote and minor? The possible collateral consequences of the judgment upon the parties already joined are also to be appraised.

Would any party be exposed to a fresh action by the absentee, and if so, how serious is the threat?

For example, an absent party would clearly be prejudiced if the action had collateral estoppel or *res judicata* implications for that party. Likewise, a defendant in a case in which other potential defendants cannot be joined could, in certain circumstances, satisfy this standard by arguing that it would have to bear the entire cost of liability in the case.

Second, Rule 19(b) instructs courts to consider "the extent to which, by protective provisions in the judgment, by shaping of relief, or other measures, the prejudice can be lessened or avoided...." Examples of such protective provisions and measures include a defensive interpleader action by the purportedly prejudiced defendant (*see* pp. 393–398, *infra*); intervention by the purportedly prejudiced non-party (pp. 398–407, *infra*); allowing a plaintiff to pursue only monetary damages when declaratory relief would prejudice a nonparty who cannot be joined; and permitting a counterclaim under Rule 12(b) and shaping the decree to preserve the rights of parties to a contract who are not before the court. Also, the Advisory Committee Notes point out that the defendant may be able to avoid prejudice by bringing the absent party into the case, for instance through a "defensive interpleader."

Third, Rule 19(b) instructs courts to examine "whether a judgment rendered in the person's absence will be adequate...." The inquiry here is simply whether *meaningful* relief to the existing parties would be available, even if some forms of relief are not available. This factor overlaps to some extent with the second factor.

In many instances, if the relief claimed could be recovered from the existing defendant, the fact that other defendants could be held liable as well does not undermine the adequacy of a judgment solely against the existing defendant. For example, if a corporate employer is sued for the tortious conduct of plaintiff's supervisor and is capable of providing the remedies sought by the plaintiff, the inability to join the plaintiff's supervisor ordinarily would not require dismissal.

Fourth, Rule 19(b) instructs courts to weigh "whether the plaintiff will have an adequate remedy if the action is dismissed for nonjoinder." As the Advisory Committee Notes put it, "the court should consider whether there is any assurance that the plaintiff, if dismissed, could sue effectively in another forum where better joinder would be possible." For example, if a case is dismissed from federal court (because the necessary party would defeat diversity jurisdiction) but the plaintiff could sue all of the essential parties in state court, that fact would weigh in favor of dismissing the case.

The issue of whether to dismiss the action or go forward is ultimately committed to the trial court's discretion. The four factors cited in Rule 19(b) are not exhaustive or ranked in importance. The issue involves a fact-specific weighing of the fairness to all affected persons of dismissal versus continuing with the case. Courts are usually reluctant to dismiss a case under Rule 19(b) unless the prejudice from going forward would be considerable.

E.   PROCEDURAL ISSUES

The issue of failure to join a necessary or indispensable party may be asserted in a responsive pleading or by motion for judgment on the pleadings or at trial. That provision includes both failure to join a necessary party and dismissal for failure to join an indispensable party. According to Fed. R.Civ.P. 12(h)(2), the responsive defense of "failure to join a party indispensable under Rule 19" may be raised at any time, including trial. Indeed, failure to join an indispensable party is deemed so critical to fundamental fairness that it can be raised even after trial or on appeal, and may be raised by the appellate court *sua sponte*. Of course, when the defense is raised late in the proceedings, a court will examine whether the plaintiff would be unfairly prejudiced and whether the delay was in good faith or instead was the result of strategic considerations.

§ 14.3   Impleader

A.   OVERVIEW

Rule 14 of the Federal Rules of Civil Procedure allows "a defending party" (a defendant or a plaintiff who is subject to a counterclaim) to file a complaint at any time after commencement of suit against "a person not a party to the action who is or may be liable to the third-party plaintiff for all or part of the plaintiff's claim...." Prior to 1946, Rule 14 allowed this sort of third-party practice—commonly known as impleader—if the third-party defendant was potentially liable directly to plaintiff. Under the 1946 amendment, however, impleader is allowed only if the third-party defendant is liable to the third-party plaintiff (in the event of the third-party plaintiff's liability to the plaintiff). The rationale for the change is that a defendant should not be able to force a plaintiff to sue an additional party that the plaintiff has chosen not to sue, simply because that additional party may also be liable to the plaintiff.

Impleader promotes judicial efficiency by allowing third-party claims to be tried together with the main claims, and it prevents inconsistent adjudications that could arise if such claims were adjudicated separately. To illustrate, were it not for impleader, then B—in a suit brought by A—would have to defend the suit without the presence of C, even though C would be legally liable to B if B were held liable to A. B would then have to bring a separate suit against C. Not only would the two suits be inefficient, but there would be a risk of inconsistent adjudications (for example, in the suit by B against C, C might prevail by showing that A's claim is meritless, even though A already succeeded in its case against B).

Although impleader in federal court is governed by Rule 14, a court in a diversity case may need to examine state substantive law to ascertain whether the nonparty could in fact be liable to defendant in whole or in part if defendant were found liable to the plaintiff.

B. CIRCUMSTANCES IN WHICH IMPLEADER IS ALLOWED

Impleader is allowed only when the claim at issue is contingent upon or derivative of the main claim. In other words, impleader is allowed only if the third-party defendant would be liable to the defendant (the third-party plaintiff) in whole or in part if the defendant were found liable to the plaintiff. Unlike permissive joinder under Rule 20, it is not sufficient that the claim is part of the "same transaction or occurrence" and involves a common legal or factual question.

Contingent or derivative liability can arise in several situations. One common situation is indemnification, which applies when one party agrees (or is held by law) to hold someone else harmless for certain liabilities. For instance, if a builder agrees to indemnify the manufacturer of equipment for any injuries caused by the use of the equipment by the builder's employees, and a worker injured by such equipment sues the manufacturer, the manufacturer can implead the builder, assuming that the impleader is timely and no other procedural impediments exist. Likewise, an insured who is sued for tortious conduct may seek indemnification from an insurance company that has agreed to insure against such claims in whole or in part.

A second type of contingent liability is contribution. Most states have statutes providing a right of contribution among persons who are jointly or severally liable in tort for the same personal injury or property damage. Thus, a defendant sued for a tort can implead other persons subject to joint or several liability.

A third common type of contingent or derivative liability is subrogation, in which one person stands in the shoes of another for purposes of pursuing a claim. For instance, if an insured party sues his insurance company to recover for injuries suffered in an auto accident, the insurance company can implead the driver whose alleged negligence caused the accident.

Courts generally hold that, as long as the claim is contingent or dependent upon the main claim, the liability of the third-party defendant to the third-party plaintiff need not be based on the same theory as the liability of the defendant to the plaintiff. Thus, the defendant may be liable to the plaintiff in tort, but may have a contractual claim against the third-party defendant.

Impleader is entirely permissive. Even if a non-party may be liable to a defendant for all or part of a plaintiff's claim, the defendant is not required to implead the non-party. A defendant may decide, for example, that it would rather sue the nonparty in another forum in a separate case, rather than to bring that entity into the existing suit.

C. WHEN LEAVE OF COURT IS REQUIRED FOR IMPLEADER

Under Rule 14, leave of court to serve a third-party defendant is not required if such complaint is filed within ten days after the defendant serves its original answer. Thereafter, leave of court is necessary. In ruling on requests to allow impleader, courts look at, among other things, the efficiencies achieved by the third-party claim, the reasons for delay in filing the third-party claim, and the likely prejudice to existing parties and to the potential third party. In general, courts are willing to allow third-party claims that satisfy the elements of Rule 14 unless such claims are raised so late (such as on the eve of trial) that the existing or potential parties would suffer severe prejudice.

D. ASSERTION OF DEFENSES

A third-party defendant can assert all defenses that it has against the original defendant, such as lack of personal jurisdiction, estoppel, and waiver. Likewise, the third-party defendant can generally assert defenses that the original defendant has against the plaintiff. For instance, if the plaintiff's claim has been released or is barred by the statute of limitations, the third-party defendant may assert those defenses, even if the third-party plaintiff decides not to do so. The third-party defendant cannot, however, assert defenses that are personal to the original defendant, such as arguing that the court lacks personal jurisdiction over the original defendant, that the original defendant was improperly served, or that the case was filed in an improper venue.

E. PLEADING REQUIREMENTS

Subject to the requirement for seeking leave in certain circumstances, a third-party action is brought essentially like an original complaint, with the same requirements for service of process. The third-party defendant must answer the complaint in accordance with the Federal Rules of Civil Procedure.

F. OTHER THIRD–PARTY PRACTICE

Rule 14 authorizes or requires additional claims or defenses once a third-party claim is filed. Thus, a third-party defendant is required under Rule 14 to assert any defenses to the third-party claim that exist under Fed.R.Civ.P. 12. The third-party defendant is also required, as provided in Fed.R.Civ.P. 13, to assert any counterclaims that it has against the third-party plaintiff and any cross-claims against other third-party defendants. Rule 14 also allows—but does not require—the third-party defendant to "assert any claim against the plaintiff arising out of the transaction or occurrence that is the subject matter of the plaintiff's claim against the third-party plaintiff." In addition, the plaintiff is allowed to "assert any claim against the third-party defendant arising out of the transaction or occurrence that is within the subject matter of the plaintiff's claim against the third-party plaintiff,'' and the third-party defendant must then assert any defenses available under Rule 12.

Rule 14(a) also allows third-party defendants to implead additional parties (*i.e.*, fourth-party defendants) if the requirements of Rule 14 are satisfied.

Rule 14(b) allows a plaintiff to implead a new party when a counterclaim is asserted against it, and a nonparty may be liable in whole or part to the plaintiff for any recovery on that counterclaim.

G. MOVING TO STRIKE THIRD–PARTY CLAIMS

Under Rule 14(a), any party may move to strike a third-party claim or to have it severed or tried separately. Courts have considerable discretion in deciding whether to allow severance or separate trials. Courts will usually deny separate trials where the matters share common legal or factual issues unless a joint trial would result in jury confusion, substantial delay, or other demonstrable prejudice.

H. JURISDICTIONAL REQUIREMENTS

If the main claim is properly based on federal jurisdiction, the filing of a third-party complaint will not defeat jurisdiction with respect to the main claim. Thus, where there is complete diversity in the main case, diversity is not defeated because a third party is a resident of the same state as the plaintiff or defendant. Nonetheless, while third-party claims cannot destroy jurisdiction over the main claim, a jurisdictional basis must exist to assert the third-party claim.

In cases in which the main claim is based on federal question jurisdiction, jurisdiction over the third-party claim may be based on supplemental jurisdiction (28 U.S.C. § 1367(a)). The issue is more complicated, however, in diversity cases. Under 28 U.S.C. § 1367(b), a court may not exercise supplemental jurisdiction "over claims *by plaintiffs* against persons made parties under Rule 14 . . . ." (emphasis added). *See* p. 376, *supra*.

Under this language, if a defendant impleads a third party in a diversity case, section 1367(b) would appear to allow supplemental jurisdiction over such a claim. By contrast, a plaintiff who attempts to assert a claim against the impleaded party cannot rely on supplemental jurisdiction. Similarly, if a defendant asserts a counterclaim against a plaintiff, and plaintiff attempts to implead a third party under Rule 14, section 1367(b) would appear to prohibit the invocation of supplemental jurisdiction.

It should be noted, however, that the last clause of Section 1367(b) limits the reach of the exceptions to supplemental jurisdiction, stating that those exceptions apply "when exercising supplemental jurisdiction over such claims would be inconsistent with the jurisdictional requirements of section 1332."

One court has noted that, "without its last phrase, subsection (b) would... except from supplemental jurisdiction a claim asserted by the plaintiff against the third-party defendant when that claim is a compulsory counterclaim to a claim by the third-party defendant against the plaintiff." *Gibson v. Chrysler Corp.*, 261 F.3d 927, 938 (9th Cir. 2001). As the court noted, "it would be both unfair and inefficient to forbid the plaintiff's compulsory counterclaim to that claim." *Id.*

§ 14.4   Interpleader

A.   OVERVIEW

Interpleader is an equitable device that allows an individual who confronts multiple—and potentially conflicting—claims regarding a particular fund or *res* to resolve those claims in a single proceeding. This proceeding enables the "stakeholder" to avoid multiple liability, inconsistent judgments, and multiple lawsuits in different courts. In many ways it is similar to a limited fund class action.

There are two types of interpleader in federal practice: "rule interpleader" (Fed. R. Civ. P. 22) and "statutory interpleader" (28 U.S.C. § 1335). Although the two forms of interpleader are similar, they differ in a number of respects, including their procedural and jurisdictional requirements. Both types of interpleader are entirely voluntary; the stakeholder is not required to invoke the device but may instead choose to litigate the claims separately.

Because of its remedial nature, interpleader (both rule and statutory) is liberally allowed by courts.

B. RULE INTERPLEADER

Rule 22 provides, in pertinent part, that "[p]ersons having claims against the plaintiff may be joined as defendants and required to interplead when their claims are such that the plaintiff is or may be exposed to double or multiple liability. . . . A defendant exposed to similar liability may obtain such interpleader by way of cross-claim or counterclaim." Thus, rule interpleader may be invoked by a plaintiff as well as by a defendant.

There are two broad requirements for rule interpleader: (1) the stakeholder's *bona fide* concern about multiple claims against a fund or piece of property; and (2) at least two adverse claimants.

(1) Stakeholder's Concern Over Multiple Claims

To invoke interpleader, the stakeholder must have a genuine concern that multiple claims will be asserted against a fund or piece of property. Numerous cases have made clear, however, that while the fear must be genuine and reasonable, the risk of multiple liability need not be imminent or certain to occur. A threat of having multiple claims asserted will suffice. *State Farm Fire & Cas. Co. v. Tashire*, 386 U.S. 523 (1967).

Moreover, the stakeholder is not required to demonstrate the relative merits of competing claims or show that any individual's claim is meritorious. The stakeholder need only have a good faith concern regarding duplicative liability and multiple court proceedings. Indeed, the stakeholder is permitted to contend that *no* claim against the fund or property is warranted.

(2) At Least Two Adverse Claimants

This requirement simply means that at least two claimants must be competing for the limited fund or piece of property, and that the fund or property cannot be awarded simultaneously to multiple potential claimants. The potential claimants need not be hostile to each other, and need not even know of each other's existence.

(3) Jurisdiction, Venue, and Other Procedural Requirements for Rule Interpleader

Under Rule 22, there must be either complete diversity or federal question jurisdiction. For diversity, the stakeholder must be diverse from all claimants, and the amount in controversy must exceed $75,000. Venue is proper where all claimants reside, where the particular claims arise, or where a substantial part of the property at issue is situated. 28 U.S.C. § 1391. Rule interpleader is subject to service of process requirements and territorial limitations of Fed.R.Civ.P. 4. Rule 22 does not require the stakeholder to deposit the fund at issue with the court or to post a bond.

(4) Two Stages of an Interpleader

An interpleader is a two-stage process. In stage one, the court determines whether the interpleader device is properly invoked. If it is, the court may simply discharge the stakeholder, assuming the stakeholder concedes that one of the claimants is entitled to the fund or piece of property. Of course, if the stakeholder claims that *no* claimant is entitled to the fund or property, then the stakeholder must remain in the case to litigate that contention. In the second stage, the court or jury adjudicates the merits and decides which, if any, of the claimants is entitled to the fund or *res*.

C. STATUTORY INTERPLEADER

(1) Overview

Statutory interpleader was enacted in 1917. Like rule interpleader, statutory interpleader requires the stakeholder to have legitimate concerns over multiple claims with respect to money or property and requires that there be at least two adverse claimants. Thus, 28 U.S.C. § 1335 applies when "[t]wo or more adverse claimants ... are claiming or may claim to be entitled to ... money or property" in the custody or possession of the stakeholder.

(2) Jurisdictional and Other Procedural Requirements for Statutory Interpleader

The jurisdictional requirements for statutory interpleader are substantially easier to satisfy than for rule interpleader, and many stakeholders thus find statutory interpleader more attractive. There are special diversity requirements in 28 U.S.C. § 1335: Diversity must only exist between two or more of the adverse claimants, not between the stakeholder and *all* claimants as required by Rule 22 and 28 U.S.C. § 1332; and the amount in controversy need only be $500, as opposed to the $75,000 requirement of Rule 22 and 28 U.S.C. § 1332. Unlike rule interpleader, which is subject to Fed. R.Civ.P. 4's service of process requirements, 28 U.S.C. § 2361 allows nationwide service of process for statutory interpleader.

Under 28 U.S.C. § 1397, venue lies in the district where any claimant resides. Although this venue requirement is generally more liberal than that for rule interpleader, a stakeholder may occasionally prefer rule interpleader (for instance, if rule interpleader allows the stakeholder to sue where he or she resides, because the claim arose there or the property at issue is situated there, but statutory interpleader does not allow suit in that venue, because no claimant resides there).

Unlike rule interpleader, 28 U.S.C. § 1335 requires the stakeholder to deposit the money or property with the court or post a bond in an amount that the court deems proper. For this reason, some stakeholders may prefer rule interpleader.

One device available to a court in a statutory interpleader case is the power under 28 U.S.C. § 2361 to enjoin other court proceedings involving the same property. Injunctions restraining other courts from proceeding are not normally allowed, so this is a significant device. There is, for example, no specific class action counterpart to 28 U.S.C. § 2361 that allows a court presiding over a class action to enjoin other judicial proceedings.

§ 14.5 Intervention

A. OVERVIEW

Unlike the various other aggregation devices discussed above, which are controlled by parties to the suit, Federal Rule of Civil Procedure 24 allows a *nonparty* in certain circumstances to intervene in an action to protect its interests. By intervening, the non-party becomes a party to the case. There are two kinds of intervention under Rule 24: intervention as of right and permissive intervention. There are strict requirements for intervention as of right. By contrast, the standards for permissive intervention are more flexible, although the court may limit permissive intervention to certain issues or phases in the case.

B. GENERAL REQUIREMENTS FOR INTERVENTION AS OF RIGHT

Under Rule 24(a), a party who files a timely application for intervention is entitled to intervene as of right "when a statute of the United States confers an unconditional right to intervene...." Examples of such statutes that allow certain private parties to intervene are the Fair Housing Act, 42 U.S.C. § 3612(*o*)(2), and the Securities Exchange

Act of 1934, 15 U.S.C. § 78p(b). Other federal statutes permit intervention as of right by the United
States or a state in certain circumstances, such as
when the constitutionality of a federal or state
statute is at issue.

In the absence of a statute, Rule 24 also authorizes a party to intervene as of right if four requirements are met: (1) the motion to intervene is "timely"; (2) "the applicant claims an interest relating to
the property or transaction which is the subject of
the action"; (3) "the applicant is so situated that
the disposition of the action may as a practical
matter impair or impede the applicant's ability to
protect that interest"; and (4) the applicant's interest is not "adequately represented by existing parties." Failure to satisfy any of these criteria is fatal.
Some courts add a fifth requirement—that the intervenor satisfy the criteria for standing under Article III of the U.S. Constitution.

When the requirements for intervention as of
right are satisfied, the court must allow intervention. It is not clear under the case law whether a
court has authority to impose conditions or limitations on intervention as of right, such as allowing
participation with respect to only certain issues or
proceedings, and courts are usually reluctant to
impose any such conditions.

(1) Timeliness of a Motion to Intervene

Rule 24 imposes no specific time limit for intervening in a case. In rare circumstances, intervention may be appropriate even during (or after) trial

or on appeal. In assessing whether an application for intervention is timely, courts consider numerous factors. These include the length of time that the party waited before intervening after becoming aware of the matter; the prejudice that the proposed intervenor would suffer if intervention were denied; the prejudice that existing parties would suffer if intervention were granted; and other case-specific circumstances bearing on the timeliness of intervention.

(2) The Applicant's Interest in the Subject Matter

This requirement is more flexible than that contained prior to the 1966 amendment to Rule 24. The prior version required that the proposed intervenor be legally "bound" by the result in the case. Read literally, that requirement arguably restricted intervention to situations in which the proposed intervenor would be bound by *res judicata*. As the Advisory Committee Notes indicate, the revised rule makes clear "that an applicant is entitled to intervene in an action when his position is comparable to that of a person under Rule 19(a)(2)(i) [governing compulsory joinder, *see* pp. 379–380, *supra*] ... , unless his interest is already adequately represented in the action by existing parties." As the Advisory Committee Notes point out, "[t]he Rule 19(a)(2)(i) criterion imports practical considerations, and the deletion of the 'bound' language similarly frees the rule from undue preoccupation with strict considerations of *res judicata*." Nonetheless, even under the current rule, the applicant must have a direct, substantial, and legally protectable interest in the case. A mere abstract interest in the outcome of the case is not enough.

Some examples of this highly fact-specific inquiry are instructive. Courts have allowed a labor union to intervene as of right in an antitrust suit to oppose a consent decree that would shut down the plant where union employees worked. Courts have also allowed a public utility to intervene in a regulatory action that threatened to shut down its facilities. In addition, courts have also allowed property owners to intervene when their land would be affected by a proposed project at issue. They have also allowed employees to intervene in a Labor Department suit against their employer for violation of the Fair Labor Standards Act. Likewise, courts have allowed intervention by the real party in interest in a case, such as an insurer.

On the other hand, some (but not all) courts have refused to allow a person to intervene in litigation merely because the proposed intervenor would be impacted by the *stare decisis* effect of the suit. Similarly, persons who alleged that a complaint contained false allegations regarding them were not allowed to intervene as of right to seek sanctions against the plaintiffs' attorney. And courts have denied intervention as of right to a non-party claiming that the production of records by a party could be incriminating to the proposed intervenor.

(3) Practical Impairment

The inquiry here is whether, absent intervention, the suit will foreclose the ability of the proposed intervenor to protect its interests. Courts look at, among other things, whether there are other proceedings and fora in which the proposed intervenor can protect its interests, and whether the proposed intervenor can make its position heard simply by filing an *amicus* brief.

(4) Inadequacy of Existing Representation

This element is generally not difficult to satisfy. The applicant meets its burden by showing that the existing representation *may* be inadequate. If the proposed intervenor would offer arguments and theories that the existing parties would not, then this standard is typically satisfied. On the other hand, this criterion is not satisfied if it is clear that an existing party has the same interests as the proposed intervenor, and would likely make the same legal arguments that the proposed intervenor would make.

Showing inadequacy of representation is more difficult when the existing representative is a governmental entity charged with representing the interests of absentees. In that circumstance, courts usually presume that the representation is adequate. Nonetheless, when the applicant asserts a personal interest, as opposed to one common to the public, a court may find that even a governmental representative is inadequate.

(5) Standing

Courts are split on whether a party seeking to intervene as of right must have standing to sue under Article III of the U.S. Constitution in order to intervene. Some have held that Article III standing is required; others have held that it is not; and still others have concluded that the issue is academic because Rule 24 itself poses requirements more onerous than those necessary to establish Article III standing. Those courts holding that standing is required point out that standing is mandated by the Constitution and cannot be disregarded. Those courts, therefore, hold that an intervenor must establish a concrete, particularized interest that is not conjectural or hypothetical. Courts holding that proof of standing is not required reason that, because the existing litigants were required to satisfy Article III standards, proposed intervenors should not be required to do so as well. Of course, as a practical matter, if a party cannot satisfy Article III standing requirements, that party will have difficulty satisfying Rule 24(a)'s exacting requirements for intervention as of right.

C. PERMISSIVE INTERVENTION

Under Rule 24(b), a nonparty may timely intervene in two circumstances. The first is "when a statute of the United States confers a conditional right to intervene . . . ." Statutes conferring a conditional right to intervene include the Fair Labor Standards Act, 29 U.S.C. § 216(b), and the Equal Education Opportunities Act, 20 U.S.C. § 1717. But even if a statute is applicable, it is up to the discretion of the court to determine if permissive intervention is justified.

The second circumstance in which permissive intervention may be allowed is "when an applicant's claim or defense and the main action have a question of law or fact in common." This circumstance, unlike intervention as of right, does not require the intervenor to have a direct personal interest in the transaction or property at issue. In ruling on applications for permissive intervention, Rule 24(b) requires the court to "consider whether the intervention will unduly delay or prejudice the adjudication of the rights of the original parties." In addition, the court must determine whether the application to intervene is timely.

Because the requirements for permissive intervention are generally more liberal than those for intervention as of right, many courts that refuse to find the requirements for intervention as of right satisfied ultimately grant permissive intervention.

The "common question of law or fact" standard is the same as that applied to permissive joinder under Rule 20 (*see* pp. 371–373, *supra*) and similar to that applied to class actions under Rule 23(a)(2) (*see* pp. 38–44, *supra*). This standard—which requires only a single common legal or factual issue—is not difficult to satisfy.

The timeliness inquiry is similar to that for intervention as of right, although some courts have been more stringent on the issue of timeliness when an applicant seeks only permissive intervention.

Rule 24(b) does not explicitly refer to adequacy of representation as a criterion for permissive intervention, but courts generally scrutinize this factor, just as they do for intervention as of right under Rule 24(a). Permissive intervention is less likely to be granted when the applicant's interests are already being represented by the existing parties, especially when the existing party is the government. In those situations, intervention would unnecessarily complicate the litigation. Similarly, courts will consider whether the applicant has any unique input that may be significant and useful to the development of the issues, or whether such input will be counterproductive.

The question whether permissive intervention would unduly delay the rights of the original parties is an issue for the court's discretion. Prejudice could exist, for example, if the proposed intervenor would inject additional issues or witnesses into the case.

Unlike Rule 24(a), in which intervention is required if the criteria of the rule are satisfied, Rule 24(b) gives to the trial court the ultimate discretion to decide whether to allow permissive intervention, even if the requirements of Rule 24(b) are satisfied. As with intervention as of right, the cases involving permissive intervention are heavily fact-specific and offer little guidance.

Courts will often impose conditions on permissive intervention, such as allowing intervention only for particular purposes or phases of the case. A person that is allowed to intervene only permissibly may also be denied the right to participate fully in discovery or trial proceedings.

D.   PROCEDURES FOR INTERVENTION

To seek intervention, a proposed intervenor must file a motion to intervene "accompanied by a pleading setting forth the claim or defense for which intervention is sought." Rule 24(c). The applicant may not incorporate the prior pleadings of an existing party. The motion to intervene and the pleading must be served on all parties by the method required by Fed.R.Civ.P. 5. The applicant becomes a party only if leave to intervene is granted.

When the intervenor's claims involve the constitutionality of a federal statute and the United States (or its representative) is not a party, the court must notify the Attorney General. Likewise, when an intervenor's claim involves the constitutionality of a state statute, the court must notify the state attorney general. Rule 24(c).

E.   JURISDICTIONAL ISSUES

Intervenors must show an independent basis of subject matter jurisdiction to enter a federal case. Thus, an intervenor must plead a federal question, assert diversity of citizenship, or rely on supplemental jurisdiction. The requirements of supplemental jurisdiction are set out in 28 U.S.C. § 1367, quoted on p. 376, *supra*, which was enacted in 1990. (Prior to 1990, an independent basis for jurisdiction was required for permissive intervention but not for intervention as of right.)

Although the exercise of supplemental jurisdiction over the intervenor is permissible when federal question jurisdiction is involved, supplemental jurisdiction in diversity cases under section 1367(b) is more restrictive. Section 1367(b) does not permit supplemental jurisdiction over claims by non-diverse persons seeking to intervene as plaintiffs or over claims by plaintiffs against non-diverse intervenors.

F. *AMICUS* PARTICIPATION

A person who is not allowed to intervene, either as of right or permissively, may in many cases obtain permission to participate as an *amicus curiae* or "friend of the court." The role of an *amicus*, however, is usually limited to submitting briefs (and occasionally participating in oral argument). An *amicus*, unlike an intervenor, does not have the status of a party in the case.

§ 14.6   Consolidation

A. OVERVIEW

Consolidation dates back to eighteenth-century England, when it was used to avoid multiple suits involving the same subject matter. In the United States, the concept was authorized by federal statute in 1813, and was first embodied in Rule 42 in 1938. It filled an important gap caused by the early limitations on permissive joinder. *See* p. 368, *supra.*

Rule 42(a) provides that, when actions within a particular judicial district involve "a common ques-

tion of law or fact," a court may "order a joint
hearing or trial of any or all the matters in issue in
the actions; it may order all the actions consolidated; and it may make such orders concerning proceedings therein as may tend to avoid unnecessary
costs or delay." Rule 42(b), in turn, allows a court
to order separate trials of any claim or issue "in
furtherance of convenience or to avoid prejudice...."

B. NATURE AND PURPOSES
OF CONSOLIDATION

A consolidation does not merge separate lawsuits;
consolidated suits remain separate, and the parties
in one case do not become parties in the other. The
entry of separate judgments is required. This is true
even when cases are consolidated for trial.

The purpose of consolidation is to further the
convenience of the court and the parties, particularly when the cases involve the same witnesses and
same operative facts. Consolidation also serves to
avoid inconsistent adjudications. Although Rule 42
speaks of consolidation "for a joint hearing or trial," and although Rule 42 is located in the section
of the Federal Rules on "trials," as opposed to the
section on "parties" (where the other aggregation
devices in this chapter are located), it is well settled
that cases can be consolidated under Rule 42 for
pretrial purposes as well, such as discovery.

Consolidation is allowed only for cases "pending
before the court...." Thus, Rule 42 does not au-

thorize a court to order transfer of a case from another court. By contrast, the Judicial Panel on Multidistrict Litigation may, in certain circumstances, order transfer to one district, for pretrial purposes, of cases pending in numerous federal courts. *See* pp. 411–416, *infra*. A federal court may also, in certain circumstances, order transfer of a case to another federal court under 28 U.S.C. § 1404. *See* pp. 416–419, *infra*.

C. CONSIDERATIONS IN EVALUATING WHETHER TO CONSOLIDATE

In deciding whether to consolidate cases, courts look primarily at whether there is an identity of issues. Rule 42(a), like Rule 20(a) and 24(b) (and, in the view of most courts, Rule 23(a)(2)), requires only a single common question of law or fact. Courts are, however, more likely to exercise their discretion to consolidate if there is substantial overlap of issues.

Courts also look to whether there is an identity of parties. While the parties do not have to be identical, if there are too many differences between the parties to the cases, courts are less likely to order consolidation.

Unlike certain other aggregation rules, such as permissive joinder, there is no requirement that the cases being consolidated involve the same transaction or occurrence. Thus, the standards for obtaining consolidation are easier to satisfy than those for joinder.

A major issue with respect to consolidation is whether that procedure will result in jury confusion. For example, the Second Circuit has held that consolidation of numerous individual tort cases was inappropriate because of a strong risk that the jurors could not isolate in their minds the facts and circumstances of each case. *Malcolm v. Nat'l Gypsum Co.*, 995 F.2d 346 (2d Cir. 1993). In some instances, however, concerns about jury confusion can be dealt with through special interrogatories and phased trials. And, if the number of consolidated cases is small, the risk of jury confusion is much less of a concern.

The decision whether to consolidate under Rule 42 is left to the sound discretion of the court. That discretion is not unfettered, however, and a trial court will be reversed if it creates a procedure that denies parties fundamental fairness.

D.   SEPARATE TRIALS

Rule 42(b) grants courts broad discretion to order separate trials on individual claims or issues and to bifurcate trials into liability and damages phases. The Advisory Committee Notes point out that "separation of issues for trial is not to be routinely ordered" but should "be encouraged where experience has demonstrated its worth." As Rule 42(b) itself makes clear, however, separate trials and bifurcated proceedings must comport with the Seventh Amendment. See pp. 242–246, *supra*.

CHAPTER 15

OTHER AGGREGATION AND COORDINATION DEVICES IN FEDERAL PRACTICE

This chapter discusses several federal court aggregation and coordination devices that are not contained in the Federal Rules of Civil Procedure. These are (1) transfer under the multidistrict litigation statute, 28 U.S.C. § 1407; (2) transfer under 28 U.S.C. § 1404; (3) the Multiparty, Multiforum Trial Jurisdiction Act of 2002; (4) informal coordination among federal courts; and (5) bankruptcy as an aggregation device. Like the devices discussed in earlier chapters, all of these devices are designed to increase judicial efficiency in resolving complex claims.

In addition to these devices, federal and state courts have occasionally developed informal procedures to coordinate related cases. This chapter addresses those procedures as well.

§ 15.1 Multidistrict Litigation

A. OVERVIEW

The multidistrict litigation statute, 28 U.S.C. § 1407, was enacted in 1968. It provides, in relevant part, that "[w]hen civil actions involving one or more common question of fact are pending in different [federal] districts, such actions may be transferred to any district for coordinated or consolidated pretrial proceedings." Such transfers are made by a panel, established under section 1407, known as the Judicial Panel on Multidistrict Litigation (the "MDL Panel"). The purpose of section 1407 is to achieve judicial efficiency in *pretrial* proceedings. (As discussed below, section 1407 requires that each case be sent back to its original district court for trial.)

Since the statute's enactment, the MDL Panel has transferred more than 100,000 cases for coordinated proceedings. Such cases have included antitrust, securities, mass tort, employment, patent, and product liability suits.

The MDL Panel consists of seven federal circuit and district court judges designated by the Chief Justice of the United States.

B. INITIATION OF PROCEEDINGS UNDER SECTION 1407

Under section 1407, a transfer may be initiated *sua sponte* by the Panel or by motion of "a party in any action in which transfer ... may be appropriate." 28 U.S.C. § 1407(c)(i), (ii). Upon the initiation of transfer proceedings, the MDL Panel is required to notify all parties in all cases in which transfers are sought, and to conduct a hearing to determine whether coordinated pretrial hearings are warranted.

C. STANDARDS FOR TRANSFER

To order pretrial coordination or consolidation, the MDL Panel must determine that one or more common factual questions exist in the various separate cases and that transfer will promote "the convenience of the parties and witnesses and will promote the just and efficient conduct of [the] actions." 28 U.S.C. § 1407(a). The Panel need not find that common issues will predominate over individual issues, but only that common issues exist and that transfer will facilitate judicial efficiency. The Panel can order transfer even if all, or substantially all, of the parties object.

As the *Manual for Complex Litigation (4th)* points out, transfer is suitable when the common issues are numerous, complex, and not susceptible to informal coordination. Transfer is usually not suitable when relatively few cases are pending, when the issues are simple, or when informal coordination among courts would suffice (such as when the actions are all in close proximity to each other).

D. SELECTION OF THE TRANSFEREE COURT

In selecting the transferee court, the MDL Panel considers a wide variety of factors. These include the location of the various cases; location of the parties, witnesses and pertinent evidence; and experience of the various judges being considered. The Panel is not bound by the recommendations of the parties and need not limit its choice to a judge who currently has one or more of the cases at issue.

E. EFFECT OF A TRANSFER ORDER

When the MDL Panel enters a transfer order (and the order is filed with the transferee court), the transferor court loses jurisdiction over the case. Prior to that time, however, the transferor court remains free, notwithstanding a pending motion to transfer, to enter any orders that the court deems appropriate, including orders remanding cases to state court for lack of jurisdiction. When a case is transferred, all orders entered by the transferor court remain in place unless the transferee court modifies them.

Upon transfer, the transferee court has authority to administer all pretrial aspects of the case, including discovery and motions, such as summary judgment motions. The power to administer all pretrial aspects of the case is extremely important, since most multidistrict-litigation cases settle prior to trial and thus are never transferred back to the transferor court. The transferee court also has the power to rule on jurisdictional issues, such as motions to remand for lack of federal question or diversity jurisdiction. In rulings involving state law, the transferee court is bound by the law that would have governed if the case were still in the transferor court. In rulings involving federal law, courts frequently hold that the law of the transferee court's circuit applies, but some courts apply the law of the transferor's circuit.

F. TRANSFEREE COURT'S TRIAL OF A CASE

In 1998, the Supreme Court ruled, contrary to the then-prevailing practice, that under section 1407 a transferee court is prohibited from assigning a case to itself for trial. *Lexecon Inc. v. Milberg Weiss Bershad Hynes & Lerach*, 523 U.S. 26 (1998). Rather, a transferee court, at the conclusion of pretrial proceedings, must remand the case to the transferor court for trial. Legislation has been proposed in Congress that would have the effect of overruling *Lexecon*.

Of course, upon remand, a party may ask the transferor court to transfer the case to the transferee court for trial under 28 U.S.C. § 1404(a) (discussed at pp. 416–419, *infra*), which authorizes a district court to transfer a case in the interests of justice and for the parties' and witnesses' convenience. There is no assurance, however, that a transferor court will grant such a request. Moreover, section 1404(a) can be utilized only if the transferee court is one where the action could originally have been brought. *See* p. 417, *infra*. Other possible ways of securing trial by the transferee court notwithstanding *Lexecon* are described in the *Manual for Complex Litigation(4th)*.

G.   REVIEW OF MDL PANEL RULINGS

There is no appeal or review of an MDL Panel decision denying a motion to transfer. Other orders of the MDL Panel are reviewable only by extraordinary writ pursuant to 28 U.S.C. § 1651. The MDL statute prescribes which federal court of appeals shall hear a particular type of extraordinary writ. For instance, petitions for extraordinary writ to review transfer orders shall be filed in the federal circuit having jurisdiction over the transferee court. 28 U.S.C. § 1407(e).

§ 15.2   Transfers Under 28 U.S.C. § 1404

A.   OVERVIEW

Section 1404(a) provides that "[f]or the convenience of parties and witnesses, and in the interest of justice, a district court may transfer any civil action to any other district or division where it might have been brought." Section 1404 may be invoked by the parties or by the court *sua sponte,* although courts rarely transfer cases under section 1404 on their own motion. Unlike 28 U.S.C. § 1407, section 1404 does not necessarily implicate multi-party situations: Section 1404(a) can be used to transfer a single case from one district to another. Nonetheless, because it can also be used to aggregate similar cases before a single court, section 1404(a) is discussed briefly here.

B. REQUIREMENTS FOR TRANSFER

Section 1404(a) contains a few basic requirements. One important requirement is that a case may only be transferred to a district or division "where it might have been brought." This requirement is applied strictly. In *Hoffman v. Blaski*, 363 U.S. 335 (1960), the Supreme Court held that a court cannot transfer a case, on the motion of a defendant, to a district in which the plaintiff did not have a right to sue. This was true in *Hoffman* even though the defendant, in seeking the transfer, was willing to waive lack of personal jurisdiction and venue over it in the transferee forum. As the Court noted, "the power of a District Court under § 1404(a) to transfer an action to another district is made depend not upon the wish or waiver of the defendant but, rather, upon whether the transferee district was one in which the action 'might have been brought' by the plaintiff." *Id.* at 343–44.

C. FOR THE CONVENIENCE OF THE PARTIES AND WITNESSES

Transfer under section 1404(a) will not be allowed unless it promotes the convenience of the parties and witnesses. This inquiry looks at such factors as the location of the parties, witnesses, attorneys for the parties, and critical evidence, such as pertinent documents.

D. INTEREST OF JUSTICE

The "interests of justice" factor "include[s] such concerns as ensuring speedy trials, trying related litigation together, and having a judge who is familiar with the applicable law try the case...." *Heller Fin., Inc. v. Midwhey Powder Co.*, 883 F.2d 1286, 1293 (7th Cir. 1989). The goals underlying this factor are fairness and efficiency.

E. USE OF SECTION 1404(a) AS AN AGGREGATION DEVICE

A transfer under section 1404(a) is for all purposes, including trial. This contrasts with section 1407, discussed on pp. 411–416, *supra*, which is for pretrial purposes only. Nonetheless, the *Hoffmann* restriction makes it difficult for a court to use section 1404(a) to aggregate cases involving similar issues and parties. Unless a particular case could have originally been brought in the transferee court, a transfer to that court is improper.

Moreover, even if all related cases *could* be brought in a particular court, section 1404(a) requires that each judge having such a case agree to a transfer. This is in sharp contrast with section 1407, in which the decision for all applicable federal cases is made by the Judicial Panel on Multidistrict Litigation.

Like section 1407, section 1404(a) may be used only for transfers between federal courts. It may not be used to transfer cases between state courts or between state and federal courts.

Despite its limitations, section 1404(a) has occasionally been used as a device to aggregate similar cases, such as the transfer of factually and legally similar asbestos cases to a single district in which each of the cases could have been brought. *See, e.g., In re Joint Eastern and Southern Districts Asbestos Litig.*, 769 F.Supp. 85 (E. & S.D.N.Y. 1991).

§ 15.3   Multiparty, Multiforum Trial Jurisdiction Act of 2002

The Multiparty, Multiforum Trial Jurisdiction Act of 2002 provides for federal jurisdiction in a narrow category of mass accident cases, such as airplane and train crash cases, in which traditional diversity rules would have required the cases to be heard in state court. It gives federal district courts "original jurisdiction of any civil action involving minimal diversity between adverse parties that arises from a single accident, where at least 75 natural persons have died in the accident at a discrete location" if one of three circumstances exist: (1) "a defendant resides in a State and a substantial part of the accident took place in another State or other location" (even if the defendant is also a resident where the accident occurred); (2) "any two defendants reside in different States" (even if the defendants also reside in the same State); or (3) "substantial parts of the accident took place in different States." 28 U.S.C. § 1369(a). "Minimal diversity" is defined as existing "if any party is a citizen of a State and any adverse party is a citizen of another State, a citizen or subject of a foreign state, or a foreign state...." 28 U.S.C. § 1369(c). The Act also permits removal from state court of cases that could have been brought originally in federal court under section 1369. *See* 28 U.S.C. § 1441(e). When a district court presides over an action as a result of the Act, it is required to "promptly notify the judicial panel on multidistrict litigation of the pendency of the action." 28 U.S.C. § 1369(e). This information will enable the MDL panel, when appropriate, to consolidate the cases for pretrial purposes before a single judge.

The Act limits jurisdiction of the federal district courts, however, by requiring them to "abstain from hearing any civil action" covered by the Act when "the substantial majority of all plaintiffs are citizens of a single state of which the primary defendants are also citizens" and "the claims asserted will be governed primarily by the laws of that State." 28 U.S.C. § 1369(b).

The Act does not define certain key terms, such as "substantial part of the accident," "primary defendants," and "governed primarily" by the laws of a particular state.

§ 15.4 Coordination Among Federal Courts

As the *Manual for Complex Litigation (4th)* notes, even in the absence of transfer under section 1407 or 1404(a), federal courts can achieve efficiencies through coordination. Coordination devices include (i) assigning all of the cases to a specially-designated judge pursuant to 28 U.S.C. §§ 292–294 (relating to assignment of judges to other courts); (ii) establishing an agreement among the judges assigned to the various cases that one case will be the lead case (with the other cases possibly being stayed); (iii) conducting joint court hearings; (iv) coordinating the appointment of experts, special masters, and lead counsel; and (v) coordinating discovery.

§ 15.5   Bankruptcy as an Aggregation Device

A detailed discussion of bankruptcy as an aggregation device would involve complicated issues under the bankruptcy code and is beyond the scope of this text. It should be noted, however, that a party in bankruptcy may, in some circumstances, provide a vehicle for aggregating multi-party cases. For instance, if a company that declares bankruptcy is one of several defendants in various mass tort cases, that company's litigation will generally end up being consolidated before a federal bankruptcy court, even if the cases were originally in a number of state courts. In some circumstances, as discussed below, other defendants may be able to have their cases transferred to the bankruptcy court as well.

Under 11 U.S.C. §§ 105 and 362, the filing of a bankruptcy petition stays all lawsuits against the bankrupt or debtor, both in federal and state court, and permits the debtor seeking bankruptcy protection to get an injunction against any state or federal proceedings that could impact the debtor's estate. The cessation of lawsuits is one of the major immediate benefits of seeking bankruptcy protection. Through the stay and injunction provisions of the Bankruptcy Code, the status quo of an insolvent debtor can be preserved temporarily to protect the debtor's assets.

After the entry of the stay, another aim of a bankruptcy proceeding is the consolidation of all claims against a debtor into one forum in order to ensure an orderly and fair distribution to creditors. Generally, parties who are litigating against the debtor are creditors. There are a number of statutory devices available to help consolidate pending lawsuits into a bankruptcy proceeding (or at least into the same federal district in which the bankruptcy proceeding is taking place). For example, pursuant to 28 U.S.C. § 157(b)(5), personal injury claims and wrongful death actions against bankrupt debtors may be consolidated in the district where bankruptcy protection is sought or the district in which the claims arose. As the *Manual for Complex Litigation (4th)* notes in discussing mass tort cases, "[t]he automatic stay, combined with the bankruptcy court's exclusive control of the debtor's assets, effectively centralizes that defendant's state and federal mass tort cases into a single federal court." § 22.5. Bankruptcy is thus a powerful aggregation device, particularly because it permits aggregation of both federal and state cases.

Although consolidating all of the legal claims against a bankruptcy debtor into one forum is not usually controversial, there has been significant controversy—particularly in the mass torts area— with respect to one aspect of bankruptcy court jurisdiction. Under 28 U.S.C. § 1334(b), "the district courts shall have original but not exclusive jurisdiction of all civil proceedings arising under title 11 [the Bankruptcy Code] or arising in or *related to* cases under title 11" (emphasis added). "Related to" jurisdiction does *not* require that the related matter be against the debtor claiming bankruptcy. All that is required is a sufficient link between the case and the bankruptcy proceeding. The purpose of section 1334(b) is "to grant comprehensive jurisdiction to the bankruptcy courts so that they might deal efficiently and expeditiously with all matters connected with the bankruptcy estate." *Celotex Corp. v. Edwards*, 514 U.S. 300, 308 (1995).

The Supreme Court has not definitively ruled on what constitutes "related to" jurisdiction, and the federal circuit courts are divided in their approaches. In some circuits, "related to" jurisdiction is quite expansive—permitting parties to use a bankruptcy proceeding as an aggregation device for lawsuits that are only indirectly related to a bankruptcy. "Related to" jurisdiction was utilized in two controversial mass tort cases to consolidate claims against nondebtor corporations: *In re Dow Corning Corp.*, 86 F.3d 482 (6th Cir. 1996), and *A.H. Robins Co. v. Piccinin*, 788 F.2d 994 (4th Cir. 1986).

In *A.H. Robins*, the debtor, A.H. Robins, sought bankruptcy protection in the Eastern District of Virginia as a result of massive litigation caused by defects in its Dalkon Shield intrauterine device. By seeking bankruptcy protection, A.H. Robins was protected by the automatic stay, but many plaintiffs sought to sever A.H. Robins as a defendant in current litigation to pursue the remaining codefendants. Asserting an interest in a common insurance policy, A.H. Robins sought to enjoin these other suits and consolidate them in the Eastern District of Virginia. The district court agreed with A.H. Robins and consolidated all Dalkon Shield cases in the Eastern District of Virginia. The Fourth Circuit upheld this decision of the district court, interpreting "related to" jurisdiction in an expansive way.

A similarly expansive approach was adopted in the *Dow Corning* case. That case involved Dow Corning, the debtor, and the other major silicone breast implant manufacturers. These manufacturers were defendants in thousands of federal district court lawsuits filed throughout the country that were consolidated and transferred to the Northern District of Alabama by the MDL Panel. The district court in Alabama soon thereafter certified a nonmandatory class for settlement purposes that established a $4.25 billion settlement fund. Although 440,000 women chose to remain in the settlement class, many thousands of women opted out. Because of the expected litigation costs of these many opt outs, Dow Corning filed a Chapter 11 petition in the Eastern District of Michigan.

With its Chapter 11 petition, Dow Corning obtained an automatic stay of all pending litigation against it, and sought a transfer pursuant to 28 U.S.C. § 157(b)(5) of all the opt-out tort claims to the federal district in which its bankruptcy proceeding was pending. This transfer included opt-out suits that had been initiated in state court but removed to federal court pursuant to 28 U.S.C. § 1452(a). Dow Corning indicated that it would seek, as part of a bankruptcy reorganization plan, a consolidated jury trial on the issue of whether silicone breast implants caused the diseases claimed by the plaintiffs. Such a transfer and consolidation of litigation pending all over the country would obviously bring substantial savings in litigation costs to Dow Corning. Dow Corning's codefendants also sought to transfer all of the cases in which they were named as codefendants to the Eastern District of Michigan for participation in the consolidated trial requested by Dow Corning.

The district court granted Dow Corning's request but denied the requests of the other codefendants, ruling that there was no subject-matter jurisdiction over the claims of the codefendants because they were not "related to" Dow Corning's bankruptcy proceeding as established by 28 U.S.C. § 1334(b). The Sixth Circuit reversed, ruling that there was "related to" jurisdiction over the claims against the non-debtor defendants. The court reasoned that the threat of suits for contribution and indemnification (as well as the existence of joint insurance policies) was enough to establish a conceivable impact on the debtor's estate sufficient to invoke "related to" jurisdiction. The court remanded the case to the district court, however, to ascertain whether the district court should abstain from hearing the cases of the nondebtor defendants under various abstention provisions of the Bankruptcy Code.

Some courts, however, have applied a narrow approach to "related to" jurisdiction. For instance, in *Arnold v. Garlock, Inc.*, 278 F.3d 426 (5th Cir. 2001), the court distinguished *Dow Corning* from the asbestos claims before it on the ground that in *Dow Corning,* "each of the co-defendants was closely involved in using the same material, originating with the debtor, to make the same, singular product, sold to the same market and incurring substantially similar injuries." *Id.* at 440. By contrast, the asbestos defendants in *Arnold* "use[d] asbestos for brake friction products, insulation, gaskets, and other uses[.]" *Id.* The court likewise distinguished *A.H. Robins* as involving a "unique" product. *Id.*

§ 15.6   Federal/State Coordination

A.   OVERVIEW

Both the multidistrict litigation statute (28 U.S.C. § 1407) and transfer under 28 U.S.C. § 1404(a) apply only to coordinate *federal* cases, not federal and state cases. Consolidation under Rule 42 is even more restrictive: It is limited to cases pending before the *same* federal court. In short, apart from bankruptcy, there is no existing legal mechanism for ordering consolidation of related federal and state cases.

This is not an insubstantial gap: Many of the leading multiparty cases over the last several decades have involved separate lawsuits pending in both federal and state courts. There are several reasons why this has been the case.

First, many plaintiffs' lawyers will deliberately select state court over federal court whenever possible. *See* p. 194, *supra*. Second, depending on the residence of the parties, the nature of the pleadings, and the particular federal court's attitude toward removal, some state cases will be successfully removed to federal court, while others will be remanded to state court (or not removed in the first place). Finally, some plaintiffs' attorneys (contrary to their colleagues) may choose to file suit in federal court (for instance, because they have chosen to assert federal-law claims as well as state-law claims).

As detailed in the *Manual for Complex Litigation (4th),* federal and state judges with related cases sometimes coordinate transactionally-related cases on an informal basis, particularly when the judges are within the same state. Matters for coordination may include discovery, motions practice, coordinated appointment of lead counsel, and scheduling of trials and other proceedings. Indeed, the MDL Panel sometimes transfers related federal cases to a federal court in which similar state cases are pending precisely to achieve such voluntary coordination. As the *Manual* points out, coordination is least difficult when common counsel are involved and when the cases are centered in one state (or relatively few states). Coordination is much harder when the cases are geographically dispersed throughout the country.

B. REFORM EFFORTS ADDRESSING COORDINATION OF FEDERAL AND STATE CLAIMS

Various proposals have been made to address the issue of coordinating federal and state claims. Perhaps the most elaborate and widely-publicized one was made by the American Law Institute (ALI) Complex Litigation Project in 1994. A major feature of that proposal was to allow removal from state to federal court of a case not qualifying for diversity jurisdiction when (1) the case arises from the same transaction or occurrence (or series of transactions or occurrences) as a case in federal court and (2) the cases share a common factual or legal question. A proposed Complex Litigation Panel (modeled after the Judicial Panel on Multidistrict Litigation) would decide whether to allow removal, and also whether the removed case should be consolidated with the case or cases already pending in federal court. Under a proposed choice-of-law provision, the court presiding over the cases would in many instances be allowed to apply a single, uniform law to the cases, even if they arose from multiple states.

The Complex Litigation Panel would have exclusive jurisdiction to remove such transactionally related cases under the ALI proposal, and the parties themselves would not be permitted to remove such cases unilaterally. Removal could be initiated upon motion by any party to a state proceeding or upon certification by a state judge before whom one of the actions was pending. The panel would then decide whether removal was appropriate. In addition, the proposal would in some circumstances allow cases in federal court to be transferred to state court for coordination with similar cases.

The ALI proposal generated substantial controversy—including federalism concerns—and did not make any headway in Congress. Nonetheless, the proposal is thoughtful and creative and is worthy of serious discussion and debate.

*

INDEX

References are to Pages

---

†